MAJOR-GENERAL MAX HOFFMANN

WAR DIARIES
AND OTHER PAPERS

VOLUME ONE

TRANSLATED FROM THE GERMAN BY
ERIC SUTTON

The Naval & Military Press Ltd

Reproduced by kind permission of the Central Library,
Royal Military Academy, Sandhurst

Published by
The Naval & Military Press Ltd
Unit 10, Ridgewood Industrial Park,
Uckfield, East Sussex,
TN22 5QE England
Tel: +44 (0) 1825 749494
Fax: +44 (0) 1825 765701
www.naval-military-press.com
© The Naval & Military Press Ltd 2004

In reprinting in facsimile from the original, any imperfections are inevitably reproduced and the quality may fall short of modern type and cartographic standards.

Printed and bound by Antony Rowe Ltd, Eastbourne

GENERAL HOFFMANN

CONTENTS OF FIRST VOLUME

	PAGE
PREFATORY NOTE	7
INTRODUCTION: GENERAL HOFFMANN, BY KARL FRIEDRICH NOVAK	9
CHIEF DATES IN GENERAL HOFFMANN'S LIFE	33
WAR DIARIES, 1914-1919	35
THOUGHTS ON 1914	257
INDEX	267
MAP OF EASTERN FRONTIER	

PREFATORY NOTE

THE following account of historical facts and events is based on detailed information obtained from General Hoffmann during a close friendship with the Author that lasted over many years; and it has been extensively confirmed and enlarged from other sources. Details of his military career have been contributed by a number of his brother-officers.

Hoffmann's account of the development of the battle of Tannenberg is confirmed by his manuscript diary of those days: it was long thought to be lost, but was discovered under a mass of papers after his death. There, too, are recorded in his own handwriting the original dispositions of the troops, and the orders that were drawn up and issued as a result of his decision to attack the Army of the Narev on the night of August 20th-21st. It is there plainly established that Colonel-General von Prittwitz's much-canvassed telephone conversation with Colonel-General von Moltke regarding a retreat behind the Vistula must have taken place on the 20th August, not the 21st. Without the latter's concurrence the orders quoted in Hoffmann's notebook could not have been issued. The Prittwitz Army Command must have approved them, and after such a rearrangement of his forces—especially only a few hours before they were to begin a sixty-kilometre advance east of the Vistula—on 21st August the General could not possibly have talked of retreating behind that river.

The exact wording of the orders for the disposition of the I. Army Corps in the night of 20th-21st August—

PREFATORY NOTE

the 3rd Reserve Division had in the meantime been ordered to Deutsch-Eylau—reads as follows in Hoffmann's notes:

"Gosslershaussen—Lindenau, with advance posts at Strasburg.
Bischofswerder—Freistadt.
Amm.-Col. and transport Luskovitz; Schmettau's garrison troops, Marienwerder."

This establishes the time and scope of the much-disputed order.

In this connection it appears from further notes of Hoffmann that the I. Army Corps had already received orders to push forward troops with a minimum of equipment, etc., to the line Neumark—Weissenburg Railway Station, which they were to hold.

At the same time the 1st Cavalry Division was sent to Gerdauen, and received directions to keep contact with Lötzen and Königsberg, while the XVII. Army Corps was already on 21st August ordered to proceed to the east of Schippenbeil. The 6th Landwehr Brigade was to march through Rastenburg, Korschen, Bischofstein, and join hands with the I. Reserve Corps.

All these dispositions prove the intention of the Prittwitz Army Command to secure a decision by an attack to the right of the Vistula.

KARL FRIEDRICH NOVAK.

INTRODUCTION

GENERAL HOFFMANN was always a simple and consistent figure in his daily life, in his successful career and in his magnificent services to the State, from the moment when the tall, lanky, almost narrow-chested young schoolboy received his Cadet's commission from the King of Prussia until that sad hour when untimely death fell upon the giant in his fifty-fifth year. What everyone felt in him from his earliest days—what, indeed, he made everyone feel who had anything to do with him—was his presence of mind. Not merely in the sense that he was always unperturbed in the face of things, people and difficulties which so often came upon him unexpectedly. It was more than this: he had a truly forceful spirit that gave him an inexhaustible, exulting and triumphing strength. Many people, especially in the Great War, thought his successes were due to constant, or indeed invariable, good luck. In point of fact this rare gift of fate had never failed him. When, in the year 1906, as a tall, strapping, rather wild young captain, while on a Staff tour with his Section, he solved some hypothetical tactical problem, the Colonel who was criticizing his performance cried out:

" Really, Hoffmann, you didn't deserve such luck! "

Hoffmann—he was always called " der Lange," for none of his brother-officers ever called him by his rank or name—laughed that boyish laugh of his, that he never lost until the day of his death, with due respect to his Commanding Officer, but he added slyly, and with gay gratification:

INTRODUCTION

" Certainly, sir, but—in the long run . . ."

Of course there was more in it than mere luck and ability. Intellect and luck made that great career. But beneath it all was a solid foundation of genius.

He was, in many ways, very unlike his youthful brother-officers of the 4th Thuringian Infantry in Torgau, or his associates at Neisse and, later on, at Lyck. He was almost the worst athlete, horseman, swordsman of them all. The only physical aptitude in which he excelled them was in his terrifying appetite. His capacity for sausages was unlimited: he sat drinking in the Officers' Club, alone for the last part of the time, until seven o'clock in the morning, when he took charge of his company on parade. On his return, and before breakfast, he would wash down his sausages with a couple of bottles of Moselle. He played a first-rate game of *hombre*, but was inordinately lazy at his studies, though his military knowledge was soon considerable, for he learned by listening; all his life long his quick insight grasped the essential point, which an absolutely obedient memory enabled him to hold fast. Such a man, whose amiability was flavoured with a gift of repartee, or rather whose lightning-quick superiority of judgment was tempered by a disarming humour and graceful turn of thought, was naturally given preference before the others to prepare himself for the *Kriegsakademie*. Whereupon he instructed his orderly to stand a light every evening on the table in his window in such a way that the passers-by in the street below might gaze with admiration at the industry of the future strategist. The strategist himself, however, spent his evenings in the Officers' Club, and carefully extinguished

INTRODUCTION

the light when he really came back to the house in the morning. None the less, he passed the Akademie examination with distinction. He was sent to Russia for six months to study. To begin with, he applied himself to a thorough study of the Russian language. When, after his return, he was appointed to the " Russian Section " on the Great General Staff his Staff career was thereby already decided.

His daily life still wore an air of indolent eccentricity. His purse was none too well lined, and his inclination towards lavish ways was even then pronounced, though, as a First Lieutenant or a Captain, he prudently observed: " A man must live economically, but he must also understand how to part with a twenty-mark piece gracefully upon occasion." However, he lived a far from careful life, with sundry cheerful boon companions, so much so that his Colonel one day shook his head and said, with especial reference to him:

" My corps of officers seems to consist mainly of the rich sons of poor fathers."

Count York von Wartenburg, the head of the "Russian Section," had been his first patron, and had asked for his services. When Lieutenant-General von Lindenau succeeded the Count, who had been a failure in the China War, Hoffmann then found an avowed protector on the Great General Staff. The new Chief, himself an uncommonly agreeable and cultivated man, bestowed his favour on the young Hessian, who combined the best characteristics of the irreproachable Prussian officer with a lighter, not altogether North German social aptitude, and sound knowledge, with an imperturbable capacity for putting it into practice. It was characteristic of Hoffmann's unconcern, so seldom disturbed by the most untoward incidents, that on one occasion when he had been ordered to accompany his patron and chief on a journey to Warsaw he left the passports at home; he was quite unabashed, and allowed the General, looking very thunderous, to depart alone, merely shouting after him that he would, according to orders, report himself in Warsaw on the following morning, although there was no other train that night; and on the following day, when the General had only just arrived, he did, in fact, walk into the room. For, since " a man must understand how to part with a twenty-mark piece gracefully upon occasion," he had taken a special train to Warsaw. He did more: he even charged up the cost of the train to the General Staff account. At this point, however, old Field-Marshal Count Schlieffen sent for him. A thunderstorm burst over the head of the officer who had forgotten his papers when travelling on duty. But once more his military ability was allowed to outweigh his thoughtlessness. Count Schlieffen, as an exceptional measure, passed Captain Hoffmann's claim for expenses—which, incidentally, the latter had in the meantime managed to raise from his father-in-law, in case of necessity.

In 1904 he sent Hoffmann to the Russo-Japanese War. The Captain was to report to the General Staff his impressions from Japanese Headquarters.

He travelled through the world with open eyes —a grown-up boy in spite of the dignity of his position. Indeed one of his best qualities was that he always remained a grown-up boy, whether he was using his study-lamp as an alibi or, later, when the doctor forbade him to drink wine, and Hoffmann acquiesced with resignation, and then privately called for Moselle at his club. He looked upon

INTRODUCTION

great cities of the East—their strident colours, their strange happenings and burning problems—with a keen, penetrating gaze, that was always clear and never deceived by dazzling contours. In the Field Headquarters of the 1st Japanese Army he lived a hard, unpleasant, God-forsaken and wearisome existence, for his naturally inquiring mind was oppressed by the monotony of the blind and lifeless isolation in the comfortless melancholy of the Yentai coal-mines. He conscientiously reported what seemed noteworthy to his soldier's eyes. Finally, he saw the fighting on the Yalu, went through the battles on the Shaho and outside Mukden, and walked through the streets of the conquered city of Port Arthur. But when the fighting in the field was over, his thoughts often strayed gloomily away, beyond the marching columns and the artillery fireworks, in the lassitude of homesickness, towards a deeper contemplation of the scene. Suddenly the war stood before him as a dreadful thing, age-long and senseless—men tearing each other asunder:

" It seems so futile when one sees thousands of men, who were thriving and well the day before, now lying maimed, mangled, and dead upon the field — the Russians mostly with the astonished question in their staring faces: ' Why did I die here anyway? What have I to do with this country, this strange land, whose name I have never heard?'"

Always solitary, he believes that for once he understands his own feelings:

" The only bliss in life does really not consist in establishing the most practical method of delivering an infantry attack, and we grow old here waiting. I notice it only in the others, but I think if the others are becoming so horribly old, I must be doing so likewise. . . . Happiness is a gift not granted to many—perhaps I shall only be happy on my death-bed—looking back. So long as I see the ladder before me leading upwards, I am never continuously happy for more than a few seconds together. There are moments of happiness, but then, unfortunately, comes the thought—I must get forward."

In the jottings in his diaries that he sent to his people at home he almost entirely forgets tactics and strategy, and tries — he, a soldier, undistracted by the clash of weapons—to find the meaning of the war, its why and wherefore, and the new frontiers that may result from it, more soberly and more from the historical point of view than the statesmen at the Peace Table now that the enemy were letting fall their weapons. What he then wrote about Russians has been fulfilled. What he said about the Japanese—the wisdom of a policy of moderation—was confirmed almost immediately after he had written it. It then became clear that this boyish young officer, who never seemed to shake off the subaltern, could, with those five wholesome senses of his, grasp a situation and its component elements, analyse them, set them forth and, finally, extract the kernel of truth. It is impossible to say whether it was maturity that so quickly gave him this power, or whether it was simply the clearness of mind which had been one of his christening gifts. At all events, his lightning power of judgment was one of his most outstanding characteristics all through his career.

He liked talking, and he knew that he talked well. He was at once silent when he felt the power of another mind. The giant then sat bent forward and thoughtful. The Far East widened the horizon of the young officer, who came from Torgau, Lyck and Neisse, via the clatter of Berlin, into China's many pasts. He listened silently, when the distant

INTRODUCTION

echo of European industrial unrest reverberated as far as Peking, to the old Mandarin who clapped him on the shoulder at an Embassy dinner and said: " My dear young friend, we had that sort of thing in China two thousand years ago, and we have finished with it. You will have finished with it some time too."

He sat dumb, too, beside the other Mandarin who talked to him about the Boxer troubles, and the meaning of Foreign Missions:

" What would you say if we, too, sent missionaries and, while we were forcing our way into Germany armed to the teeth, wanted to set up our altars in the Kaiser-Wilhelm Memorial Church in Berlin? "

And he nodded approval to the third Mandarin as the latter, with deferential courtesy, excused himself to an aristocratic young gentleman who was talking a great deal about his two-hundred-year-old family:

" Unfortunately we Chinese understand nothing about that. Our older families go back two or three thousand years. . . ."

The young Captain came back to his German home with much varied knowledge and all manner of forebodings. In the Far East he had seen the vast face of conflicting worlds, the perilous abyss of races and of peoples. Germany had not, for a long while, seemed so large, so overwhelmingly powerful when he realized that one may travel for weeks and weeks away from Germany and pass through many strange, different, not less powerful peoples, into far-off mighty continents. In front of the tea-house in Shimonoseki, in which the Japanese and the aged Li Hung Chang signed the surrender of Port Arthur to Russia—the German Ambassador had demanded it, quite unnecessarily thrusting himself forward as spokesman for Germany, France and Russia—in front of the tea-house at Shimonoseki, the Staff Captain said to himself on his departure from Japan:

"I hope we shan't have to pay for this piece of folly."

The Staff Captain had been promoted direct to Lieutenant-Colonel, omitting the intermediate step, when he set out for East Prussia in the World War. Japan now sent Germany an ultimatum demanding Kiaochow. The terms were precisely those of the ultimatum regarding Port Arthur, received at Shimonoseki.

During the war Hoffmann quickly ascended the ladder of outward military exaltation. But it was only vaguely and uncertainly that the people for whose future he was fighting, the great mass of the uninitiated, realized that this Lieutenant-Colonel who started as First General Staff Officer on the Staff of the 1st Army—G.S.O., Ia, in fact—and became Chief of the General Staff to the Commander-in-Chief, Army of the East, was not merely a fine soldier but a very remarkable man.

When the unlucky General Prittwitz, the first Commander-in-Chief in the East, timidly decided to withdraw behind the Vistula, Hoffmann pointed out to him, coolly and soberly, that the retreat could not be carried out without a hard fight with Samsonoff's army; for the Russians were established nearer to the Vistula than the German General's troops. They would get there first, and bar the river passage. It was surely simple to advance upon the enemy and make every possible effort, by means of a surprise attack, to turn an inevitable battle into a possible victory.

INTRODUCTION

General von Prittwitz began by protesting. Then he saw the force of Hoffmann's proposal. He gave up the idea of withdrawing his army behind the river; he was now all for battle and attack. In the great excitement of his momentous decision the General had at once informed G.H.Q. of the irrevocable withdrawal of his troops behind the Vistula. He had not informed them that, in the nervous agitation following upon the development of troop-movements and events, he had immediately reversed his own decision and determined on the attack. Such a commander, who was far too ready to retreat, and had been prepared to give up German soil without a battle, was recalled by the Emperor in disgrace; and with him his Chief of Staff, Count Waldersee. A new Commander hurried to the East, General von Hindenburg, accompanied by the new Chief of Staff, General von Ludendorff. How emphatically fate immediately turned in favour of the German troops in East Prussia, and how disastrously against Samsonoff's army, was generally known only a few days later.

But it was not generally known that the advance which resulted in the battle of Tannenberg had already begun while the special train carrying the two generals was rolling eastwards; that the battle resulting from the First General Staff Officer's plans, and approved by General von Prittwitz, had already been engaged, nor that, at the moment, only two orders had been telegraphed by the two generals on the way: the first being that the 8th Army should be granted a rest of twenty-four hours — for twenty-four hours they were to do completely as they liked—and, secondly, the Headquarters of the Army Command were to be moved forward to a place specified. The twenty-four hours' rest was regarded by the First General Staff

Officer as a grave tactical error, as it might delay the advance. He could not move Headquarters forward to the place appointed, as the troops had long since passed it. The entire Staff had to go back to report to Major-General Ludendorff in Marienburg. But when General von Hindenburg's Chief of Staff there went into the orders that were laid before him he found nothing to alter; the advance preceding the decisive battle was completed.

In subsequent years General Hoffmann never took much credit for the turn of events—at any rate for his share in the battle of Tannenberg. He was vain to some extent of his personal characteristics, and the prestige of his appearance—his Bismarckian skull, with its close-cropped white hair, the bushy eyebrows, bristling so powerfully forth from his forehead, which their possessor was not above training in the way they should grow, his unusually clear-cut features, so often lit up by his fine simple boyish smile, his small delicate hands, and even the creases on his trousers. But in his claims to the merits that were his due he was modest.

He often talked about the issue of the battle of Tannenberg.

"Nobody won the battle," he would say. "It developed entirely by itself. The Russians sent out their wireless 'in clear.' Grünert, the Quartermaster-General, again and again asked me anxiously if we should believe them. Why shouldn't we? At the worst something might happen, but nothing serious, if we were careful. I believed every word of it, on principle. And then the great question whether Rennenkampf would march to Samsonoff's assistance. I'm damned if he will, thought I. I had heard of the scene on the Mukden Railway Station. Samsonoff had then reproached Rennenkampf most bitterly for having left him in the lurch in

INTRODUCTION

the battle of Mukden. The mutual explanations became rather heated, and both gentlemen boxed each other's ears. They had been torn apart, and the Tsar had forbidden them to fight. I made certain that Samsonoff would now be paid out. I don't know whether the scene at Mukden was at the bottom of it, but it did, in fact, not occur to Rennenkampf to march to Samsonoff's assistance."

Hoffmann never reckoned merely with the Army Corps. He always weighed the *imponderabilia*, and tried to consider the enemy who confronted him, apart from the number of troops under his command, from the point of view of his psychology, his connections, his origin and previous history. As regards Tannenberg, General Hoffmann was always anxious to assign the honour much more to Lieutenant-General Ludendorff than to himself. The latter, he thought, deserved the highest credit for planning the thrust at and through Usdau.

He was disappointed when he first read in 1925 a passage from a letter that General von François wrote to him:

" The part played by Ludendorff at Tannenberg was not such, in my opinion, that he can claim any credit for the success. It was on his responsibility that I was ordered to attack, at 10 A.M., on August 26th, the heights of Usdau, with insufficient forces. That was a piece of tactical imprudence that would doubtless have led to complete disaster. The Seeben heights fortunately held up my advance on Usdau for so long that it was only on August 27th at 5 A.M. (by which time the whole Corps had arrived) that the attack on the Usdau heights could begin.

" Further, the order dated August 28th, 12.25, ordered a pursuit in the direction of Lahna. As you know, I did not carry out this order, but pursued the enemy in the direction of Meidenburg. . . . Ludendorff's recollections have no historical value."

As a fact, the Lieutenant-General's attitude at Tannenberg was not that described later in his *Memoirs*. In the course of the battle there was a definite, decisive moment at which General Ludendorff's nerves completely gave way, and he wanted to cancel the orders he had given. At this point old Field-Marshal von Hindenburg, unshakeable in his calm and composure, achieved enduring fame by refusing to allow any over-hasty or muddled alteration of plans that had been carefully considered and adopted, and were now in process of being carried out.

Hoffmann's share in the Tannenberg victory remained obscure. It is almost symbolic that he suggested the name Tannenberg for the battle, originally christened "Frögenau," by General Ludendorff, in allusion to the Tannenberg battles of the old Teutonic knightly orders. In one place only was it known what the First Staff Officer Hoffmann had meant to the Engineering and Technical Services—the Headquarters of the Army of the East.

From that time forward all the important military events on the German Eastern Front are closely bound up with Hoffmann's military work. After the unsuccessful advance on Warsaw, and at the time of the retreat through Poland, he was able to inform General Ludendorff of the exact number of kilometres beyond which the enemy could not continue his counter-attack over the wrecked roads and railways. He then calculated with certainty, and made preparations for, the period of recuperation

INTRODUCTION

in which the retiring troops were able to re-form, carry out their brilliant move against Thorn and, subsequently, the tremendous flank drive on Lodz. But whether he was responsible for all this, and whether, later on, his was the decisive brain behind the battles of the Masurian Lakes, the fighting before Riga, or the Zborov offensive, which destroyed the last remnants of Russia's former military glory, so far as the German public was concerned he worked in entire anonymity. They knew far less of him than the Russians did of their enemy, "General Goffmann." He, however, remained unchanged in the midst of all these successes: since Tannenberg, the glory of which was entirely due to his foresight, though, as he always maintained, he had made no special efforts—since Tannenberg he grasped with a bold but pardonable sense of conviction that no enterprise which he undertook could end otherwise. He trusted in his luck: he basked in the inevitable prospect of success. Difficulties never stayed him, he took them in his giant stride: he saw them but he marched over them. And his luck was such that they really did give way before him.

To the Emperor, who spoke to him anxiously and doubtfully about some imminent enterprise, he once quoted the phrase:

" I had so many troubles in my life, and most of them never happened."

He was born under so lucky a star that fate never gave him the lie, and until the end he remained the undefeated German General. Of course the Commanders-in-Chief let him have his own way; occasionally he did not even consult them. What Marshal Conrad von Hötzendorf said of him—" He is the only man of ideas on the Eastern Front " —was equally well known to his chiefs. They experienced the truth of it every day. He might make gloomy or venomous entries in his diary, but all that was at once forgotten when the moment came for work and fighting. He thrived on work—it was pleasure, it was strength, it was the game his mind loved; and he thrived, too, on his success in circumstances that he had created and made to serve his ends. He could be so malicious and pitiless in his intellectual superiority that in many passages of his diaries the exact phrase has to be suppressed, or can only be hinted at. He could hate without mercy, and despise without pity, when he met with some impersonation of a strategist who could not so much as grasp the main idea of his operations. He had a horror of the army of commonplaces that led so many astray, of personal considerations in the conduct of a campaign, of the hunt for places, Imperial favour and popularity. In the field he spoke his mind fearlessly and unmistakably. After the tremendous successes at Lodz he was convinced that the provision of only two more Army Corps would have put the Russians out of the war. Hoffmann applied to General von Falkenhayn and asked that the two Corps might be sent:

" I begged for them on my knees."

The Chief of the General Staff refused. Hoffmann suspected that the Eastern Front was not to be allowed to be too successful. From that moment, and not merely after Verdun, he persisted in calling General von Falkenhayn " the criminal." He regarded him as responsible for the useless and bloody sacrifices in the West, for the mischief that came of the quarrel with Marshal Conrad—for, though he heartily despised " the Austrians," and was always cursing their troops, on a matter of military judgment he ungrudgingly regarded the Marshal as one of the greatest leaders in the war.

INTRODUCTION

Although not much had hitherto been generally known of Hoffmann, as time went on, in circles where decisions were reached and knowledge counted, his influence became very great owing to his intimate understanding of the whole Eastern question and its ramifications. In practice he was the decisive authority in the East. Chancellors, generals, statesmen, politicians, members of Parliament, commercial magnates — all went to his Headquarters to see him and ask his advice. He was overwhelmed with memoranda and inquiries. Sharp as was his tongue, difficult as he found it to restrain his scathing wit, he was quick to recognize a head with something in it. In attack, in pursuit, and in the actual battle he kept, right to the end, something of the headlong daring of the young officer. But on the question of the U-boat war and Admiral von Tirpitz's adventures he was not for a moment deceived. The experiment was reasonable if there were enough boats to guarantee unconditional success. It was madness if—without any guarantee of success—it merely drove America to join the enemy. With bitter accuracy he reckoned up the number of Germany's enemies: there were so many to think of besides the Russians. The war must be really brought to an end some time: even if one is a soldier one must agree to that. A way to peace must at last be sought and found. Patriots run mad, land-hungry Imperialists with their Belgian, Polish and other aspirations, he repudiated with irony or contempt. He was moderate, cautious over every really complicated problem, practical and perfectly clear, averse from any vain imaginings. As were his statements, so were his demands. When the Emperor William, in the days when the Peace terms for Russia were being discussed at Brest-Litovsk, asked his opinion on the desirability of claiming Polish territory, though he had been ordered by the army chiefs not to speak too freely, he uttered an impressive warning. He said that more Polish territory than was indispensable for securing the frontier would be disastrous for Germany. This conviction, which he courageously defended to his Sovereign, meant a break with Ludendorff, who, apart from the matter in question, insisted that every officer was forbidden to speak to the Emperor without a preliminary interview with himself, even if the Emperor specifically ordered him to do so. General Hoffmann must henceforward learn elsewhere how to obey orders: and the G.Q.M.G. posted him to the command of a Division. But the Emperor vetoed this, and Hoffmann had to stay in Brest-Litovsk.

In Brest-Litovsk, again, he played a part quite different from that assigned him by public opinion. He figured as host to the Peace delegates. He was at once the representative and the interpreter of the views of the "Supreme Army Command." The G.Q.M.G. would not speak to him any more, since he had visited the Emperor, but gave his orders to the Chief of the General Staff on the Eastern Front through his own Staff Officer, until Hoffmann forbade such a proceeding. His position at Brest-Litovsk was difficult, and not merely on account of his open collisions with General Ludendorff. His personal convictions, much more than the views of G.H.Q., coincided with the conclusions of the Secretary of State, von Kühlmann, who represented the policy of the Government; whenever he could see an opportunity he tried to get on with the negotiations for peace. While the Russian Commissary, Trotzky, much more intent upon the proclamation of new Russian gospels of humanity than upon peace itself, claimed an "open window" towards Europe and America, and while the Secretary of State reduced him to a hopeless technical and dialectical impasse, Hoffmann, who was in full accord with the Secretary of State, managed to separate the Ukrainians from the Russians. He disposed them to negotiate, and even induced them to sign the first treaty. Although, as subsequently appeared, the signatories were envoys of a collapsing and powerless Government, none the less the separation of the Ukraine was a great step forward. The self-confidence, the sense of power of an actually defeated enemy, but one who was consciously fighting with new weapons, was shattered by the realization of the possibility of a divided Peace. The General and the Secretary of State had long grown tired of the continual provocations of an adversary who daily repudiated what had been agreed the day before, and daily reintroduced what had been rejected. They had both at last set up a limit beyond which they would not allow him to go.

"You throw me the ball to-morrow," the General suggested to the statesman. "It can't go on like this! Just say: 'The word is now with General Hoffmann.'"

He wanted to take the responsibility of giving Trotzky a quiet warning.

At Trotzky's orders the Commissary Kameneff, after the opening of the meeting of the day in question, astonished the entire conference with a fresh oration, bristling with impertinences, the like of which can never have been so arrogantly delivered by the envoys of a defeated Power. By this time von Kühlmann had also had enough of it. However, he wished to preserve the unmoved superior calm of the diplomatist; he must keep himself free for future negotiations. But he threw the " ball " to the General. Hoffmann remained calmly in his seat, though he was boiling with indignation. He made it clear in carefully chosen words that he considered the Commissary's speech a piece of insolence, and desired to stigmatize it as such. He pointed out that they had " misunderstood the situation. The German armies had advanced far into Russian territory. . . . There is no object in wasting time uselessly. It would be much better to break off entirely than to go on like this."

From this prearranged reprimand, by no means unduly severe, and justified by the continual attempts at insult on the part of the Russian Delegation, legend has created General Hoffmann's historical blow of the fist on the table at Brest-Litovsk. In point of fact there was no such blow. General Hoffmann was accustomed to produce his effects by looks and words rather than by martial demeanour. He was never martial, though he was perhaps impressive—quite a different thing. It is entirely consonant with the idea of truth and history, current among the nations and their teachers, that the General never won any fame from what he actually did during the four years of war. Something that he did not do first brought him a questionable kind of glory: this quite imaginary piece of bombast at Brest-Litovsk.

During the fourth year of war General Hoffmann and the G.Q.M.G. lived in open estrangement. They were not against each other, they worked without each other: the Quartermaster-General, with his vast powers of work, his unshakeable energy in accomplishment, missed the " man of ideas "

INTRODUCTION

who in previous times had not merely drawn up plans of campaign in actual collaboration with the Lieutenant-General but had taken the trouble to work out every situation, every plan, and every possibility up to the very end. At their last meeting in Berlin, at the beginning of the year 1918, the Major-General was disturbed to hear the Quartermaster-General observe that he did not know whether, in the coming great offensive, it would be better carefully to " probe " the Western Front by individual attacks or make a gigantic drive at a given point with concentrated forces.

" Exzellenz," the General had replied to his Commander-in-Chief, " any Second Lieutenant who tried to answer the question in that way would be hopelessly ploughed in his examination."

After that they never spoke at all. The G.Q.M.G. persevered in his probings of the Western Front. Hoffmann held the East with a thin veil of troops until the end. In the meantime, if the battle of the Marne possibly lost the Germans the victory, Quartermaster-General Ludendorff lost Germany the Peace.

When General Hoffmann came home from the war, after a most difficult time, that had daily and hourly subjected him to almost unceasing strain, he found it hard to come to terms with a state of affairs so changed by the Revolution and disaster. He felt himself still too young, too much the man of the moment by reason of his never-failing success, to remain idle. He had to leave the Old Army: it had ceased to hold together. In the New Army there was no place for one who would have been, in other circumstances, the next Chief of the General Staff. He would have nothing to do with the Peace of Versailles. He was one of the few who, having reflected a great deal during the war, never shouted and howled with the rest, but became more reflective than ever, and he changed his view of the origin of many things in the course of history. Now that he could no longer take an active part in affairs, all he could do was to try to give spiritual support to what he approved and contend against what he believed to be disastrous.

Accustomed, as he always had been, to considering and controlling vast situations, he could hardly see the politics of those days. Unprejudiced and unafraid as he was, he found it possible—to the painful surprise of many of his own rank, to whom he had always been suspect ("Intellectual paupers," he would say, "have never liked me!")—to get up suddenly among the audience at a workmen's meeting and confute the speaker by a few facts. His courageous bearing, which all could feel, inspired respect everywhere. But party politics did not attract him. He saw that the World War had created another Europe, which was really only in process of evolution. He abhorred senseless cries for revenge, though at bottom he cherished bitter feelings against France. He realized that France was situated next to Germany, that this could not be altered, that they must both at last come to terms, and that the Continent, and more, would collapse if they could not reach an understanding. If they could, then there would soon arise a great edifice of power, vast and indestructible by reason of common economic interests and exchange of goods, which would for all time put an end to this ruinous antagonism, and made immeasurably strong by two obedient and united instruments of power. Hoffmann was a European of the West. The French blood that flowed in the veins of his mother's ancestors brought him other gifts besides his wit at the dinner-table. He could not see any alliance with the half-savage or stupid barbarous destroyers who, if the Germans and the French quarrelled for much longer, would one day trample pitilessly to earth all that it had taken the two races a thousand years to build up for humanity. He knew the new Russia, and he knew the men who led it even better. He looked on them as the plague. He hated their subterfuges, their lies, their endless and inhuman cruelties, their corruption (to which he would swear), their readiness to destroy everything that man has inherited or created by his labour, their dangerous insolence in wanting to poison the world with new gospels—which were nothing of the kind. Russia was for him the great European nightmare. If the Bolshevist triumph were to continue, then the civilized world would be in continual peril of collapse. Even in August 1918 he had wanted to march to Petersburg. He attached no importance to the re-establishment of a Tsar. Whether there was a bourgeois regime, feudal institutions, a monarchy, or a republic in Russia was a matter of indifference to him, if the new Government could provide justice, and the rule of law, and allow the neighbouring states, Europe, and the world at large to go their way in peace. His proposal was not approved. Admiral von Hintze, to whom the General depicted the future in Russia, would not let him march.

"I know the Russians better than you," said he.

However, it seemed as though the General's knowledge and foresight were superior. Over and over again after the war, in countless casual conversations, in the frank interviews he gave to foreign correspondents—whether he were discussing the Russian attempts to stir up trouble on German soil, the disaffection in the English colonies, in London even, or the convulsions in China—he would conclude his predictions, as punctual as clockwork, with the words: " You'll find Moscow at the bottom of it all." In the Imperial capital the General kept open house for several years after the war. Statesmen, men of learning, foreign generals who wanted to meet the great soldier, Russian spies skilfully disguised, came in and out. His drawing-room often had something of the wild atmosphere of a French revolutionary Convention —of a soil volcanic and hot with passions, when in times of excitement, amid a turmoil of strange people, faces and dialects, some shabby Russian general or marshal of the Court would crash his stick down on the floor with a rather histrionic emphasis and shout:

" Gentlemen, the place reeks of gunpowder ! "

However, the explosion never took place. The General laughed when he, who was always watched and spied upon by Russian agents, was warned of imminent personal danger. In the days of collapse in 1918, surrounded as he was by soldiers' councils and retreating troops, he used to drive or walk unarmed through the area under his command, and no one ventured to molest him. And he smiled when anyone nervously suggested that everything that took place in his drawing-room would be reported. What was never reported were his interviews with diplomats and generals of former enemy nations, who went to see him and never smiled when General Hoffmann spoke of Russia, and foretold developments with their inevitable consequences and results. In truth, up to the last, he hoped that one day yet an army of English, French and Germans would march against the Bolsheviks. He knew the secret history of the Denikin campaign.

He knew and shared the Western mistrust of the horde of Russian emigrants, who were sometimes inclined to accept the means to freedom and then forget their object. He saw that the road on which those warriors meant to march through the Ukraine and the Caucasus to Moscow was not paved with the bourgeois ideals of morality and liberty. He saw the oil trade of the world, the petroleum of Batoum, the naphtha wells, and he reckoned with the motive force of the continued deficits of " Royal Dutch," which were so alarming as to induce interested parties to finance an attempt to re-establish property rights in the naphtha area. Oil in itself was a matter of indifference to him. But he approved of any motive that tended to the extinction of Bolshevism.

It came to nothing. Many listened to Hoffmann in Germany, Holland, and England: Russian aristocrats, who were powerless, Frenchmen and Englishmen, who saw what was to come. Flatterers and fools, who forced themselves upon him, announced the imminent crusade against the Soviets as inevitable in the immediate future. Among them the General himself was the greatest sceptic. He certainly believed it to be inevitable: but only when England's colonies and Asia were ablaze—not till then.

He could no longer have taken command against Moscow. Beset as he had been for years by those who needed help and advice—a wise counsellor in need, and in anxious moments a pillar of strength and steadiness—he had slept but little, stretched for hours on his camp-bed, with half-open eyes and ears; and in those four years of war this giant had, unwittingly, destroyed his mighty frame. To sting his brain out of its lassitude he used to drink tumbler after tumbler of Cognac, and the strongest

Turkish coffee, day and night. If he ever stole out to get a moment's rest, one of his officers was bound to come in with some proposal, or plan for an advance, that he wanted to explain.

"Very well, fetch me the map," says Hoffmann.

The General then worked out the whole thing in outline on the spur of the moment. For a time he showed no signs of breaking: his faith in the mission he still had to fulfil, his hatred of the Bolsheviks, his rational impulse to contribute to the reorganization of Europe—all this kept him strong. In his last years he lived the life of a *grand seigneur*, with a melancholy longing for his long-dead subaltern days. He lunched, went about, and entertained like a great gentleman. Towards the end he realized that a supper—in the times of the general impoverishment, that touched him too—must not cost more than a ten-mark note. He resigned himself to this, but must needs lay an orchid, costing as much again, before the lady who was to share his table. At the end of his days he was the same as at the beginning—witty, amiable, lavish of his intellect and his possessions, irreproachable as a soldier and as a man, trusted by every friend. His word was a rock. He knew what he had accomplished. The last words he wrote, two hours before the death which he knew was near, were eloquent of his anxiety for Germany and Europe. In his last agony he rode once more at the head of marching troops: "Fire, fire . . . !" And then: "Artillery forward!"

That was the end. He died at noon on July 8th, 1927, in Berchtesgaden. On the face of the dead man was Lieutenant Hoffmann's gay and carefree smile.

KARL FRIEDRICH NOVAK.

GENERAL HOFFMANN

January 25th, 1869: born in Hamburg, Hesse-Nassau: son of the County Court Judge, Julius Hoffmann, and his wife, Frederike Charlotte Alwine, descended from the du Buisson family. At his baptism, in the Evangelical Church in Homburg, on February 21st, 1869, he received the names Carl Adolf Maximilian.

From Michaelmas 1879 to Easter 1887 young Max Hoffmann attended the Gymnasium in Nordhausen.

In the spring of 1887, after some delay in passing the leaving examination, Hoffmann entered the 4th Thuringian Infantry Regiment, 72, as a Gentleman Cadet[1] for three years' volunteer service.

From October 1st, 1887, to July 5th, 1888, he studied at the Royal Kriegsschule, in Neisse.

On August 16th, 1888, he received his commission as Second Lieutenant with Imperial " commendation."

From 1895 to 1898 Hoffmann, now a full Lieutenant, studied at the Kriegsakademie, in Berlin.

At the end of 1898 Hoffmann was sent to Russia to study for six months.

From 1899 to 1901 Hoffmann was seconded for service on the " Russian Section " of the Great General Staff.

[1] Musketier und Avantageur.

In 1901 he was promoted Captain, and in March of the same year he was finally transferred to the General Staff.

In 1904 and 1905 Captain Hoffmann was attached as military observer to the Headquarters of the 1st Japanese Army in the Russo-Japanese War.

In 1907 promoted Major.

In 1914 Lieutenant-Colonel Hoffmann joined the command of the 8th German Army in the field, as G.S.O.,I.

In 1916 Colonel Hoffmann, who was simultaneously promoted Major-General, was appointed " Chief of the General Staff to the Commander-in-Chief," Prince Leopold of Bavaria.

From 1919 to 1927 General Hoffmann lived in Berlin.

On July 8th, 1927, Major-General Max Hoffmann died at Berchtesgaden.

[The dates in the General's life, so far as they are ascertainable, are confirmed from Hoffmann's papers, and also by information received from his friend and comrade, Major-General Hans Kundt.]

WAR DIARIES, 1914-1919

The notes to these Diaries, so far as military affairs are concerned, have been contributed by Lieutenant-Colonel Alfred Niemann.

POSEN, *August* 7, 1914.

We have a hard task before us, harder, almost, than any in history. However, I am content, for I confidently hope that we shall be able to deal with it. The Commander-in-Chief is Prittwitz, the Chief of Staff, Count Waldersee, and I am G.S.O.,Ia.[1]

MARIENBURG, GREAT HEADQUARTERS,
August 13, 1914.

Our first idea, at any rate, comes from me. If it comes off, Prittwitz will be a great Commander, if it does not, we shall get into trouble. The responsibility is gigantic, and is more of a strain on the nerves than I suspected. If it is ever known later with how few men we have to hold the Eastern Front, it will be called the greatest piece of impudence in history. I am in complete agreement with the Quartermaster-General, General Grünert: he and I hold together, and until now we have forced our stronger wills on the Chief. Waldersee is rather weak—I hope he will not let us down at the last moment.[2]

[1] The High Command of the 8th Army was formed in Posen. Hoffmann was attached to it as First General Staff Officer—G.S.O.,Ia —whose specific duties consist in the working out of operations.

[2] In *The War of Lost Opportunities* he writes regarding the position at the beginning of the war: " The first considerations that occupied the attention of the Chief of the General Staff and myself regarding the task that awaited us were as follows. The great Russian cavalry raids which had been so much talked about gave us no anxiety: troops on the frontier would deal with them: on the contrary it was desirable that the Russians should, in fact, make such raids, and meet with a failure at the outset. For the rest, we had first of all to reckon with the advance of the armies based on Warsaw and Vilna, the existence of which was already known to us. . . .

" On entering German territory the Russian advance would be split by the obstacle of the Masurian Lakes. The Russians could only go forward with one army to the north and the other to the south of this chain of lakes. Our army had therefore to be prepared to attack one of these two Russian armies, while they were disunited by the Masurian Lakes, and defeat it. Which of the two would offer us the best opportunity could not immediately be foreseen. It might, however, be assumed that the Vilna Army would appear somewhat sooner on the scene than the

The successes in the West are magnificent, and promise well for the future. The capture of Liège was especially important. It had been long prepared for and the place had been thoroughly reconnoitred, so that it was very depressing to learn that the first attack had failed. We were weeks behindhand in the entire campaign,[1] and as everything depends on a speedy victory in the West, our joy over the success was doubly great. I do not doubt that things will go well and that this will soon lead to greater events in the West. The decision will of course be reached there, and, as a result, laurels grow more freely there than here. Still I must not be disappointed. Here we are thrown on our own resources and are independent.

BARTENSTEIN, *August* 21, 1914.

Yesterday was certainly the hardest in all my military experience [2]—retreat before the Russians.

one from Warsaw, which would have to work its way to our frontier through a wooded and boggy area, rather deficient in roads. . . .

"The mobilization and advance of our army was accomplished exactly as had been foreseen. The Army Staff moved to Marienburg on August 8th, and from that day took over the command. . . .

"Up to August 14th it was ascertained from the information available that the enemy was advancing with strong forces to the north and south of the Rominten Forest. . . . The Army Command concluded that, as had been already surmised, the Vilna Army had pushed somewhat more forward than the Warsaw Army, more especially as the airmen's reports still continued to show that the movements of troops could be observed in the roads from the south. The High Command decided to prepare the main body of the army for the attack on the Vilna Army."

In *The Truth about Tannenberg* Hoffmann remarks: "The 8th Army Command did not, as is well known, carry out Schlieffen's great plan of campaign—*i.e.* an immediate attack, with all forces, on the Vilna Army, and then, by a swing to the south-west, an attack on the right flank of the Warsaw Army. The XX. A.C. and the 70th Landwehr Brigade were left on the Southern Front. A suggestion of the Quartermaster-General, General Grünert, that the Landwehr Brigade at least should not be sent up north, met with no response from the Chief of the General Staff, General Count Waldersee.

[1] This refers to the fact that the movement of political events had given the Russians a considerable start in their war preparations for which the existing plans for the German advance had not provided.

[2] On August 20th the battle against the Vilna Army was opened at Gumbinnen. The battle progressed favourably throughout. Both wings

WAR DIARIES 39

Strong forces are advancing from the Narev against our rear and threaten to cut us off from the Vistula. We are to break off the battle so successfully begun, and go back. It is shameful—poor East Prussia! I was against it, but I could not get my way. Grünert and I still saw a hope of victory—a slight one, as one of the Generals Commanding and his Corps had completely broken down—but it was there, and I would have seized it. So we must resign ourselves to defeat, although the I. Corps again made thousands of prisoners, captured many guns, and threw back the Russians.

The 33rd have fired on our own men, the Colonel having been treacherously shot by someone.[1] I am so terribly sad. It is true that our task was very difficult, and could hardly be undertaken with so few troops, but up till yesterday, middle day, I believed we should win a great victory.

MÜHLHAUSEN, EAST PRUSSIA,
August 22, 1914.

Our attack on the Russians at Gumbinnen was more successful than I thought. It is a pity that we could not carry it right through. I was almost convinced that the whole Russian Army could be destroyed. Our 1st Cavalry Division was magnificent.

were victorious. Only in the centre, where the XVII. A.C. was posted, was there anything in the nature of a retreat, and there only in so far as an attack with insufficient artillery support against the previously prepared Russian position had to be broken off owing to heavy losses.

In the afternoon the XX. A.C. announced that the Warsaw Army had reached the frontier on the line Chorzele—Friedrichshof, and that its total strength was estimated at 2-2¼ Army Corps and 2 Light Infantry Brigades. General von Prittwitz then decided to break off the battle and withdraw the 8th Army behind the Vistula. Hoffmann and General Grünert urged without success that the battle should be fought out on August 21st.

[1] The 33rd Infantry Regiment, in the battle of Gumbinnen on the morning of the 20th, stormed the Russian positions on the heights of Ederkehmen from the north and west. In the process, the Colonel commanding the regiment was killed. As the attack was carried out from two sides there was probably a moment when German troops were firing at each other.

It made a series of attacks on the infantry (500 prisoners) and then routed both Russian Guard Cavalry Divisions.

MARIENBURG, *August* 23, 1914.

Great changes in the staff here. G.H.Q. are very indignant that we did not do what Grünert and I had proposed. Prittwitz and Count Waldersee are consequently superseded. The new Commander-in-Chief is General von Hindenburg, formerly in command of the IV. A.C., the new Chief of Staff is Ludendorff, who appeared to-day in all the glory of his honestly earned " Pour le Mérite " ribbon. When General von Wussow fell, he led the latter's storm-column against Liège, and was the only one who held his ground there, so he was really mainly responsible for taking the city.

There has never been such a war as this, and never will be again—waged with such bestial fury. The Russians are burning everything down.

OSTERODE, *August* 30, 1914.

Victory at Tannenberg — a fine revenge for Gumbinnen. To-day I thought would be a day of rest, but there is always something else to do. We have not been able to destroy quite the entire horde, and the rest are advancing on us.[1] Otherwise results are excellent — at least 20,000 prisoners,

[1] On the 30th, when the bottling up of the Warsaw Army was already nearly complete, an air report came in that the reinforced I. Russian Army Corps was marching from Mlava to Neidenburg, and, at the time the message was sent, had already reached a point 8 kilometres from Neidenburg.

The High Command ordered all available troops to march on Neidenburg to meet this menace. But this assistance could only become effective on August 31st. The crisis was overcome by the General-in-Command of the I. Corps, General v. François. He threw such troops as he could get together into the direct line of the enemy advance, without interrupting the encircling process to the north, and detached Mühlmann's force to attack the flank of the Russian column. By this means the Russian thrust was successfully averted.

WAR DIARIES 41

including one Corps Commander, many colours, guns, etc. I could not write, I was busy day and night. Since the beginning of the campaign I have not yet had two successive hours of undisturbed sleep. I am always being consulted and called in. It is complimentary but exhausting. Otherwise I am in excellent form, except that I should like to get a good sleep. Drove yesterday afternoon over the battlefield—all the villages shot to pieces and burnt down, forests on fire, and chaos everywhere. The population are splendid—brave and cheerful.

OSTERODE, August 31, 1914.

The battle was a huge success—greater than we could have supposed. 4-5 Russian Corps destroyed, 50,000-60,000 prisoners, including two Corps Commanders, who have already been brought in here. One entire Russian army is disposed of: now for the other.

AKENSTEIN, September 4, 1914.

We have only gradually been able to realize how great was our success at Tannenberg. 92,000 prisoners have now been sent back—it is one of the greatest victories in history, and won by an inferior force. It is true that we had an ally that I can only talk about after it is all over—we knew all the enemy's plans.[1]

Now we are preparing for something new.[2] Ludendorff is a first-class fellow to work with. He is the right man for this business—ruthless and hard. We get on admirably, and I am proud that some of my ideas have been considered for his new plan of operations.

[1] The Russian wireless was picked up by the German stations, and was successfully deciphered.
[2] Even during the battle of Tannenberg preparations were in hand for a change of front against the Vilna Army.

I hope all will go as well as the other affair; the plans are all settled and in 10 or 12 days I hope we shall have another glorious time behind us.

ROSSEL, *September 9, 1914.*

I have been awarded the Iron Cross for my modest share in the battle of Tannenberg. I had never thought that this finest of all military decorations could be won by sitting at the end of a telephone line. However, I realize now that there must be someone there who keeps his nerve, and by brute determination and the will to victory overcomes difficulties, panics and suchlike nonsense.

INSTERBURG, *September 15, 1914.*

Our second great battle — called after the Masurian Lakes—is at an end.[1] Results are not yet fully ascertainable, but I should estimate about 35,000 prisoners, 180 guns. The Russians lost a great many killed. . . . It was a very fine piece of work, and we are ready for what may come next.

The Austrians are doing badly; they have asked for definite assistance, and we are going with a large part of our army to Silesia to help them: we are probably going to Oppeln in about six days.[2]

Well, well; until now, with our inferior numbers,

---

[1] During the days September 9th-14th the Vilna Army was defeated on the Masurian Lakes. There was no encirclement as at Tannenberg. Rennenkampf extricated himself, but was able to withdraw only the remnants of his army into the forest country to the west of the Niemen, on the line Olita—Kovno—Vileny.

[2] The offensive of the Austro-Hungarian Army in Galicia had completely broken down. The army had to retreat across the San to the farther bank of the Visloka, fighting a number of costly rearguard actions. To the support of our ally, 4 Army Corps and 1 Cavalry Division of the 8th Army were transferred to Upper Silesia, there to form the 9th Army with Woyrsch's Landwehr Corps.

On September 17th General von Hindenburg was given the command of the 9th Army, but at the same time he retained his command over the troops remaining in East Prussia, who, as the 8th Army, were placed under the orders of General v. Schubert.

we have defeated about 15 Russian Army Corps and 8 Cavalry Divisions, and we are not finished yet. " Now for it once again."

BEUTHEN, *September 23, 1914*.

Yesterday was our first row with the Austrians—they aren't out for business as we are. After some forcible explanations on our part they are ready for anything to-day. I am terribly on the stretch to see how the operation will work out. I think it will be all right.

BEUTHEN, *September 26, 1914*.

It looks bad for the Austrians: they have saved money over their army for twenty years, and now they are paying for it.

MIECHOFF, *September 29, 1914*.

In the earlier operations the object was clear—first, the Niemen Army, and then the Narev Army. But on this occasion nothing is clear.[1] We are on the point of a brilliant success: from the moment of our advance the Russian Army ceased to press the Austrians and is now in retreat behind the Vistula. The direction our attack will take cannot yet be foreseen, and depends entirely on the news we get.

KIELCE, *October 2, 1914*.

We shall stay a few days here—how long depends on whether we are victorious or not. I do not believe we shall fail, but we might. In the

[1] On September 26th the 9th Army, accompanied on its right wing by the weak divisions of the Imperial and Royal Army, began a surprise advance against the Vistula, and found only slight enemy resistance; but the roads were almost impassable, and with great efforts they reached the Vistula between Josefov and Ivangorod.

The immediate strategic success was that the Russians hastily demolished their front on the Visloka, and raised the siege of the fortress of Przemysl. The Austro-Hungarian Army was able to march to the San without finding any noteworthy resistance.

first place we must reckon with the Austrians, and we have also left our best Corps and leaders in East Prussia.

I anticipate, however, that all will go well. It may develop into a very pretty piece of work, but there are various drawbacks. If all goes well we shall have thrown the fellows back on to the Vistula; but if it does not come off, then we must take to the defensive. We have already won a great success in so far as the Russians have ceased to press the Austrians and have retired. This, from both a military and political point of view, is a great thing. But in the last resort we can only get some air here in the East if we win a victory, in the sense in which we understand that word.

KIELCE, *October* 6, 1914.

No victory here, unfortunately. The Russians bolted behind the Vistula as we came up. Only about 3000 prisoners, etc. However, the strategic success is enormous, as the whole Russian Army on the Austrian front is in retreat.

KIELCE, *October* 6, 1914.

Our victories continue to grow smaller. The Russians are in such terror of coming to close quarters with us that they stopped the crossing of the Vistula, which they had just begun, and retired behind that river, so that we have been able to capture only comparatively few of them. Tangible result—only 3000-4000 prisoners, 15-20 guns and a large number of machine guns. On the other hand the strategic success is enormous. The Austrians are advancing at our side,[1] and the

[1] The Austro-Hungarian Army was to cross the San and attack the left flank of the Russian Vistula front. The attacking power of the Imperial and Royal Army proved so weak, however, that they did not succeed in forcing the crossing of the San.

Russian main army, which had forced its way deep into Galicia, is in full retreat. They had collected 9 Army Corps, with which they intended to fall upon us, but we were too quick for them, and by the 5th we were on the line of the Vistula, so that they had to fight to cross it. It is really marvellous how our men marched.

KIELCE, October 8, 1914.

Here everything is in excellent order, except for the Austrians! If only the brutes would move! They are letting the success we have given them slip through their fingers.

We are on the line of the Vistula and have the Russians opposite us on our entire front. A direct attack is impossible—the river is too wide (800 metres). The casual fighting has up till now brought us 4800 prisoners and 16-20 guns.

We are planning a very daring coup: let us hope it succeeds; otherwise we must wait.[1]

RADOM, October 12, 1914.

The Russians have launched four armies against us, so they mean business. By tremendous marches, taking risks that will go down to history, we got here before them, drove back their advance-guard and are now opposing their crossing of the Vistula.

---

[1] The Russians duly shifted their centre of gravity towards the north. General von Hindenburg had therefore to extend his front, by lateral and turning movements, northwards to Kalvarija. The XVII. A.C., reinforced by 4 Divisions, he sent against the Russian salient to the south of Warsaw. On October 12th, after victorious fighting, the Corps stood firmly established south of Warsaw, where it successfully repelled the Russian counter-attacks. In order to release further units for the support of the XVII. A.C. the front of the Austrian Army was extended to Ivangorod. The XVII. A.C. was withdrawn to a position between Rava and Lovicz, where it made connection with the lately brought-up Landwehr Corps under Woyrsch. South of the Pilica an attacking force, composed of the XX., XXI. and the Guard Reserve Corps, was to fall on the Russian flank when they moved against the XVII. Corps. At the decisive moment, on October 27th, the Austrian Army gave way. The position on the Vistula became consequently untenable.

Heavy fighting the last three days, many attempts to force a passage on a large scale—weak as we are. It was indeed the hardest time of the campaign in my experience: the strain goes on day and night—endless panics and alarms. And to-day a false report from an airman nearly destroyed us. Ludendorff and I stand by and support each other, and the Chief says: " God be with us, I can do no more! " I hope we may be out of the wood by to-morrow. One Corps is still heavily engaged and we cannot support it until to-morrow. If it has to retreat it will not be a very serious misfortune; we shall just have to straighten things out again. Then we shall stand on the Vistula and wait until the Austrians at last do something. Of course they attend to their own affairs first of all. The Russians have had to give up the siege of Przemysl—one of our successes.

RADOM, *October* 18, 1914.

Here we are in the midst of heavy fighting, and more to come: and what will be the end of it, God knows. We have done all that human wills and powers could do. We are not afraid, but it is possible that we may have to withdraw in the face of great superiority. We cannot place the smallest reliance on the Austrians, otherwise everything would be so simple. At any rate we have achieved much more than could be hoped. It was the best piece of work in our campaign hitherto. The Russian plan is upset, but 15 Army Corps against 6 is a little too much. I still count on victory; Ludendorff does so no longer. Nothing can go wrong. If we have to retreat, the Russians can follow us only for three days—after that they will be short of food. I have meantime had the Russian railways this side of the Vistula converted into roads. Without railways they cannot feed their troops.

RADOM, *October* 21, 1914.

Ludendorff has become frightfully nervous, and the chief burden lies on me. The main Russian forces are opposite us. I had hoped that perhaps we could still take Warsaw by an energetic thrust before the Russians got here, but, in spite of some incredible marches, we were too late. As, therefore, the Russians threatened to encircle us from the north, we have withdrawn our troops from before Warsaw. Our men carried out the retreat last night so admirably that the Russians did not notice it at all, but bombarded our deserted positions for hours yesterday morning with concentrated heavy artillery fire. On the right our faithful allies, the Austrians, moved up yesterday to reinforce us. To-morrow they are to attack. . . .

I should have thought it better to settle first either with France or Russia. If we had been given only 2 or 3 more Corps here I could have guaranteed a decision. As it is, we have to struggle on against this great superiority in numbers. If all our hopes fail, and we have to retreat, we have destroyed the entire railway and bridge system of the kingdom of Poland so completely that it will be weeks before the Russians can get forward. . . .

I am full of admirable schemes. There is already a shortage of food and coal in Warsaw—so we were informed by the men of a Russian company who shot their captain the day before yesterday and came over to us.

KONSKIE, *October* 24, 1914.

It seems mysterious to us that progress in the West is not quicker. If they had given us those fresh Corps I intended to have finished up our business here quick enough. They must have made some incredible mistakes. The worst of matters here is that Hindenburg simply cannot understand why we do not win another victory like that in East Prussia.

CZENSTOCHAU, *October 29, 1914.*

We were on the high road to a victory, greater than any until now, when the Austrians in our rear let themselves be defeated. . . . We have no fear of the Russians, even when, as at present, they outnumber us by three to one. Of course we shall not be able to avoid giving up a bit of German territory, so as to be able to strike a blow somewhere.

Apart from everything else I shall thank my Maker when we are out of this God-forsaken country. The roads, the filth and the vermin are beyond all belief. And with it all the land is rich and fertile—vast, picturesque, beautifully situated estates, like Konskie, where we were the last few days.

There will, of course, be tremendous excitement in the district when it is known that we must retreat. Our attempt on Warsaw achieved great success, in so far as we have so thoroughly destroyed the railways for the Russians that for weeks they will not be able to bring supplies and munitions up to the frontier—but this will not be thought enough. Ludendorff and I get on excellently, in spite of a few differences of opinion, over which he finally gives way. Things go forward in the West, but very slowly. They cannot help us and are more anxious than we are. I had to telephone yesterday to tell them not to worry.

CZENSTOCHAU, *November 1, 1914.*

If only the Austrians had done what we told them! The position is now very serious, and we do not yet know how we can hold on. In any case we shall not stay here much longer. I fancy that we—*i.e.* Hindenburg, Ludendorff and I, with a small Staff—shall move to one of the frontier fortresses to reorganize the defence of the East. The idea is in this way to form a sort of small General Headquarters for the East. We get no troops from the West, and must depend on our own resources. Of course we cannot prevent the Russians crossing the frontier. We must send for certain sections of the 8th Army and see what we can do. In all, there are about 20 Russian Army Corps in movement against us from the line Ivangorod—Warsaw. We have beaten all the Russians we have met in open fighting, but we are being outflanked on our right and left . . . the ground was unfavourable.

Ludendorff was in Berlin the day before yesterday, to confer with Falkenhayn and Grünert.[1]

POSEN, *November* 11, 1914.

. . . However, our movements have hitherto been smoothly carried out, and I hope to be able to announce a great success in a few days.

[1] The retreat had been successful. On the line Czenstochau—Sieradz the 9th Army found safety and a breathing space. It was covered by Cavalry Divisions north of Sieradz and on the left was in touch with Landsturm formations on the line Kalisch—Warsaw—Thorn. Behind the cavalry was collected a strong attacking force based on Hohensalza and Thorn, for a proposed thrust in the direction Lodz—Lovicz, and an attack on the Grand Duke Nicolas' exposed left wing. General Ludendorff's attempts to get reinforcements from the West for these operations had been unsuccessful. G.H.Q. merely placed 2 Cavalry Divisions at his disposal. This important re-grouping had therefore to be carried out with the forces of the 8th and 9th Armies. The 9th Army, in the district north of Czenstochau, was relieved by Böhm-Ermolli's army.

On November 1st, Lieutenant-General von Hindenburg was appointed "Commander-in-Chief, East." His command included not merely the 8th and 9th Armies, but the districts of the I., XX., XVII., II., V. and VI. Army Corps, with all their Staffs, troops and fortresses.

On November 10th the re-grouping was complete, and the 9th Army was ready for attack.

Posen, *November 19, 1914.*

The great battle, that we have opened, is now in progress. I hope it may be a great success. By all human calculations we must win, but waiting is nervous work.[1]

Posen, *November 22, 1914.*

Our left wing is defeated. How we can get them out, and put things straight again, I don't yet know—but perhaps something will occur to me. We are on a razor-edge. It might have been a great victory, but the troops failed us; the poor fellows could do no more: their officers are dead and the enemy were too many for them. We have completely defeated 3-4 Corps in the last week— we have brought in about 50,000 prisoners; but now our strength is at an end. There is no ground for anxiety; the German frontier will hold. In particular, West Prussia need have no fear. We are standing firm on three fronts near Warsaw—but we have too few men. My nerves were worn out. Five nights' suspense is too much — one cannot keep it up. Now I feel steady as a rock and can look misfortune in the face.

I am only afraid that the Austrians are done for. I have made it clear to Ludendorff that he must go to see the Emperor at Mezières the day after to-morrow at the latest. We must know why, and for what objective, we are fighting. I can carry on

[1] On November 17th, after victorious fighting, the 9th Army stood before Lodz, and had already pushed forward a Corps through Brzeziny to the south. A force in echelon on the left wing covered the operation against counter-attacks by the Russians from the direction of Novo-georgievsk. Powerful attacks by the Russians from Skiernevicze produced a critical situation for the 9th Army on November 24th and 25th: it was successfully dealt with, but involved an important gain in time for the Russians. The reinforcements now sent by G.H.Q. came in driblets and too late, so that the Russians succeeded in closing the gap between the Vistula and Lodz, withdrawing themselves from our encircling movement, and forming a closed front farther back.

WAR DIARIES 51

for a long time, but in that case there must be a guarantee that there will be a victory in the West. Otherwise they had better give it up and bring the army over here.

Posen, *December 1, 1914.*

The situation has worked out, from the military point of view, better than I could have dared to hope; especially after the idiotic way in which the 9th Army behaved. Morgen, especially, is splendid —his Corps made 36,000 prisoners in the last fortnight alone. So we hope to win a definite victory in the battle of Lodz. However, we cannot end the campaign here as I had at first thought. We should need some help for that. We have impressed on every section of the line engaged that they must do their utmost, but they can do no more. I am horrified at the way the war is being carried on in the West. Falkenhayn is the evil genius of our Fatherland, and, unfortunately, he has the Kaiser in his pocket. Now we must depend on ourselves.

Insterburg, *February 9, 1915.*

All in order here. We are even beating them again. I have only one anxiety, lest the Russians may get away, and we are not attacking hard enough. Up to date there are about 6000 prisoners, 15 guns, etc. I have strong hopes of 50,000. We shall not publish a figure until we get a respectable total. The snow is a nuisance. On our left wing, round Memel, it lies a metre and a half deep, and the attacking columns cannot get forward.[1]

[1] Russian Main Headquarters had planned a great offensive for the spring of 1915, in the north against East and West Prussia, in the south against the passes of the Carpathians.

The Austrian Command wanted to meet this offensive by an attack. For the support of this operation the German Southern Army was formed at Munkacz.

The Commander-in-Chief, East, also decided to anticipate the Russian

March 1, 1915.

The position yesterday was very unpleasant. The Russians had collected, on foot and by rail, about 12 Army Corps, and fell upon our whole line from the south up to this sector. We had to give up Prasznicz again, as a Landwehr Brigade under incompetent leadership gave way at this point. Now we are gradually getting things straight again.[1] If we had completely cleared the Augustovo forest— *i.e.* brought in our many hundred captured guns —then it would all be very simple: we should go back to the railway with our 10th Army and start a new scheme. But we must struggle on for a few days. We cannot leave our booty behind.

LÖTZEN, *March* 3, 1915.

Solf and Metternich here yesterday; to-day we sent them both, with Sven Hedin, who is also here, up to the front line. Mumm is coming to-day. The

offensive by an attack in East Prussia, and for this purpose asked for a reinforcement of 4 Corps lately formed in Germany. Three of these Corps were to constitute the 10th Army, and take up a position on the left wing of the 8th Army immediately south of the Memel, in order to outflank the exposed Russian northern wing. The IV. Corps, reinforced by an Infantry Division of the 8th Army, was to move forward south of the Masurian Lakes, crumple up the weak left wing of the Russian Army, and so effect a double outflanking of the Russian Army.

On February 7th the southern group advanced to attack Johannisburg and the Pissa sector: the 10th Army advanced one day later.

The ensuing battle, which was called the " Winter Battle in Masuren," led to the destruction of the 10th Russian Army, whose southern wing was encircled in the Augustovo forest. Strong counter-attacks of the Russians from Ostrolenka, Novgorod and Lomza continued through the whole of March.

[1] From the middle of February onwards, the Russians began to make another push in the direction of Mlava. General v. Gallwitz, who had been ordered to the southern front of East Prussia, decided to anticipate the Russian attack, and for this purpose was reinforced by divisions taken from the 9th Army front. The push that began on February 22nd led to the recovery of Prasznicz. But the enemy counter-attacked. The divisions had to be withdrawn and, in the face of savage Russian attacks, took refuge southwards behind the frontier position then being constructed. A further German push on March 8th came to a standstill on March 12th to the north of Prasznicz. Here, also, the fighting lasted until the end of March.

Imperial Chancellor is announced—we are having quite a gay time, in fact.

March 6, 1915.

I have just read Kapp's [1] article—it is a delightfully extravagant piece of work—anyone who thinks differently and is not prepared to hand the universe over to the victorious German people is no better than a scoundrel. With the railway system of to-day and modern facilities it is much easier for us than for Napoleon to march to Moscow, etc.

The man is quite right, but he proceeds from a false assumption. We have not yet won the victory and have no prospect of completely defeating all our enemies. In the West we are standing on the defensive, and without 8-10 additional new Army Corps have no chance of attacking anywhere with success. In the Eastern theatre of war we have, by our great victories, gradually reduced the enormous Russian superiority in numbers. We cannot utterly destroy the Russian Army—we could do that only if we were at war with Russia alone. In addition to this the Austrians are defeated. Galicia is hopelessly lost to them, and Przemysl will certainly fall by the end of the month, without any Russian attack—starved out.

I believe we can't be defeated, but equally that we can't so destroy our enemies as to be able to dictate conditions to them: I have said this to the Imperial Chancellor. We are *beati possidentes*; in other words, all our armies are standing on enemy territory. It is, accordingly, for us to ask them what they really want. I have spoken openly against an annexation of Belgium and Antwerp. Liège, perhaps. Antwerp would be an apple of discord

---

[1] *Generallandschaftsdirektor* Dr Kapp stood for an energetic war policy. Later on he made a sharp attack on the Imperial Chancellor, von Bethmann-Hollweg.

for a hundred years, and the additional population would be disagreeable, undisciplined and ultramontane. Colonies are a different matter: we must have the Congo, etc. Here, too, in Russia I am against any considerable extension of territory. About the Baltic Provinces there can be no question—we have never conquered them and never can. Moreover, their population is not German and will have none of us—Balts, Finns, etc. Of the other Russian frontier provinces, with the exception of a few strips, I would take nothing: we have enough with Poland. That is my view. For the rest I find the Chancellor, with whom I had two long conversations, very reasonable. He takes some time to make up his mind, but he does not do so lightly.

. . . Kapp is living in Utopia, and for that reason can only do harm. Someone must have a quiet talk to him.

LÖTZEN, *March 9, 1915.*

Really, the whole of Berlin seems to have gone mad. We are winning the greatest victory known to history, and three days later they all behave as if we had been defeated, because the pursuit comes to a stop after 200 kilometres. We stood, and part of the army still stands, before a strongly fortified Russian line. As we do not want to attack it we are retiring at certain points, to induce the Russians to come out . . . so that we may again attack them in the open. Our whole army stands on Russian soil. It is true that there was hard fighting at certain points, but all fighting is hard.

March 13, 1915.

We had prepared a nice little trap for the Russians to the north of the Augustovo forest, but they did not quite fall into it. They had so solemnly announced that they would chase us out of Grodno that I counted on at least 20,000 prisoners. But there were only 5000. As soon as they noticed we were attacking them to the north of the forest they ran like rabbits.[1] The bitter cold was bad for us and caused us almost more losses than the enemy. We are now waiting to see whether our Russian friends will attack again. We have driven them back through Prasznicz to the south, and are so strong everywhere that we are ready for any eventuality.

From the political point of view as well the position is not unfavourable. It is true that the Italians are blackguards, but they would be stupid not to make capital out of our embarrassments. Why on earth was our policy so idiotic as not to force Italy into the war on our side? Why did we declare war on Italy instead of allowing her to declare it on us? It was only that which gave them their *casus fœderis*. The attack on the Dardanelles is, I think, all in our favour, politically.[2] They are now quarrelling over Constantinople, and the Balkan states are all in a state of irritation. They none of them want either England or Russia at the Dardanelles.

HEADQUARTERS, *April* 3, 1915.

When I have nothing to do I usually walk round my little room and try to think how we can give another twist to the military situation, but nothing occurs to me. We are stuck fast on the whole Front. Perhaps, now that our wire entanglements are

---

[1] The 10th Army had withdrawn its left wing to the Seiny area, so as to be able to make another attack in case the Russians followed them up. It was hoped to repeat the manœuvre of the winter battle. But the Russians shirked the blow.

[2] On March 18th the combined Anglo-French Mediterranean fleet attacked the Dardanelles. The attack failed. It was then decided to make a landing operation on the Gallipoli peninsula. The first attack at this point took place on April 25th.

electrified, we could release some troops at certain points and move them up to our flank, so as to make a further push, in case the enemy gives us a chance—but we have not the strength for an operation of any importance. I am convinced that we shall be able to prevent the Russians ever invading Germany; but that is all we can promise, unless we are given a new army. There is no prospect of that, though I do not see why they need so many new Divisions in the West. I trust they are not going to start another Ypres.

Kluck really has—and has had all his life—marvellous luck. Now he has actually been wounded.

From the military point of view our position is undoubtedly good, in so far as all our armies stand on enemy soil and we have obtained control over valuable properties, such as railways and coalmines. But we are nowhere victorious, in the proper meaning of that word. Neither in the East nor in the West have we brought down the enemy: on the contrary, both the French and the Russians live in the certain hope of victory—thanks to the utterly mendacious news that reaches the armies. For instance, a short time ago Prince Hohenlohe received a letter from a Russian princess, in which she said how ridiculous it was of the Germans to publish these figures of prisoners taken—not a word of it was true—there had never been a Tannenberg nor any defeat of the 10th Army. Still, all our enemies at the Front have gradually been penetrated by the conviction that it will none the less not be so simple to bring us down by force of arms, but they all rely on England's guarantee that Germany will be starved out. Every day Russian airmen throw down proclamations on us: " Surrender, lay down your arms, your wives and children are starving! " In addition to this the Russians regard themselves as having beaten the Austrians, as, indeed, they have. We have again sent three Divisions to the Carpathians, and there is some hope that the line will hold—but no more. It is well known that there is deep depression in Austria.

We have constructed strong positions everywhere, which will enable us — with the Divisions (more than 7) lent to the Austrians and a few reinforcements from the West—to remain on the defensive and hold on.

A second question arises: was this stagnation on both fronts inevitable? This may be flatly denied; and the plain truth is that the responsibility is due to the failure of G.H.Q. The utter breakdown of every sort of initiative on the Marne was incredible, but this was only one of the many blunders. After the retreat it should have been possible to concentrate forces for a unified effort and get hold of the coast—the Belgians should not have been allowed to slip through our fingers after the capture of Antwerp, and we should never have committed the crime of those isolated, senseless attacks on Ypres. History will deliver judgment on us later.

Now, however, there is only one possibility of victory. The centre of gravity of the war must be shifted to the East. We begged and prayed that this might be done in November. We were treated like troublesome poor relations, and then got the bare minimum of help we needed in driblets and not as a whole.

The blunder lay in not allowing Headquarters to remain in Berlin, where it still ought to be—and for that reason France continues quite undeservedly to be regarded as the main seat of war, and the East as secondary. It was perfectly understandable that at the outset, before the Russian hordes got under way (especially before the Siberian troops could arrive), we should have tried to defeat France and possibly the English Expeditionary Force. But after that both sides became of equal importance: and they are still not considered so.

How can this war be brought to an end? The simplest way would be to come to an understanding with one of the parties. The most obvious would be France, as I always said before the war: in alliance with France we could rule the world. But it is impossible. In France there is an epidemic of utter madness. Moreover, Poincaré and Co. have established nothing more nor less than a reign of terror, and the voice of reason is not allowed a hearing. They will be sorry for it later, but at the moment the slightest overture on our part would be published with scorn in Paris as a sign of complete collapse.

Russia: with whom can we negotiate? The Tsar might be willing, but Nicolas would simply have him murdered. There is a disposition to peace in Petersburg, but Nicolas has a marvellously energetic grip of the situation. For example, I am quite convinced that the arrests for espionage in Petersburg are no more than an intrigue against the friends of peace. Besides, what could we offer Russia? Galicia and Constantinople? But that would mean beginning to betray our allies.

Last of all, England: the English hate us and would like to destroy us, but they are gradually realizing that this is not so easy. It is interesting to follow the English newspapers. For some months now there has been no more talk about the Kaiser being arrested and taken to St Helena, nor is it suggested that we are to scrape an existence as charcoal burners and wretched peasants and fishermen. On the contrary, our newspapers are more venomous than the English ones—and rightly, I may add. Sir Edward Grey—God damn him!—has recently stated under what conditions peace can be obtained from him; the main point is the restoration of Belgium, for England cannot allow a German Antwerp—against that she must fight to her last penny. Personally, I have no use for a German Belgium; we do not want an increase of Social Democratic and ultramontane agitators. We cannot defeat England—at least, not yet. I shall live to see it, but not in this war. Therefore, in my opinion, we ought to try to make terms with England. She will negotiate—she is hard hit at many points: heavy losses, especially of officers, domestic troubles (the effects of our U-boats have, incidentally, been much over-estimated), Egypt, the Sudan, India, the Dardanelles, and especially Japan! We could make the following conditions: the return of our Colonies, together with a few additional ones, the Congo in particular, a few Colonies from France, and 25 milliards in money. Until the payment of this sum we should occupy the mining area of French Lorraine; from Russia a few slices of frontier territory, and favourable terms for Austria.

England would then retain Calais and Boulogne, and would have, of course, to keep in close relations with us in order to protect herself against her former Allies.

I should regard this as a possible basis for negotiations. It is, of course, possible that I am mistaken. We may have a piece of luck, such as Turkish successes against Egypt, or a revolt in India, or else an earthquake, that may improve our situation. It may, on the other hand, deteriorate, owing to Italy, Rumania, the total collapse of Austria, or something else.

The Field-Marshal wrote to the Chancellor a few days ago more or less on these lines.

LÖTZEN, *May* 30, 1915.

H.M. is entirely under Falkenhayn's influence and does not love us. The military situation is such that we are gradually reaching a dead end. Of course we are intentionally rather thrust into the background. I already knew that a great many people did not like me. So long as I can remember only half my acquaintances have liked me. The less gifted have no use for me at all. However, I remain unmoved—I must bear it with resignation.

June 16, 1915.

In the military sense there is nothing fresh here. G.H.Q. goes on stripping us, so that we are glad if we can hold on and stick to what we have. Whether it is all necessary of course I cannot judge, but there is certainly some dirty work about it.[1]

---

[1] The position on the Austro-Hungarian Front had taken a very unfavourable turn. The advance to the relief of Przemysl had come to a standstill, and the Russian attacks on the Carpathians were being only feebly repulsed. In order to relieve the pressure on their allies German G.H.Q. decided to attack the Russian Front between the Carpathians and the Vistula and break through.

On May 2nd, General v. Mackensen, with the German 11th and the Austrian 4th Armies, took the Russian positions in the Gorlice-Tarnov sector, and by May 15th had already reached the San.

The Russians withdrew troops from all along their line opposite the Commander-in-Chief, East, to support their tottering left wing.

There were grave differences of opinion on the question as to how the C.-in-C., East, could best support General Mackensen's offensive, which was increasing to ever greater dimensions.

Hoffmann himself writes on the subject in *The War of Lost Opportunities*:

" I held the view that it was essential to bring into action on the left wing of the 10th Army all available forces from the area under the command of the C.-in-C., East, as well as all the troops that could be obtained from G.H.Q.: Kovno should be taken by a sudden attack, and the offensive movement driven through Vilna into the rear of the main Russian force. . . .

" Major v. Bockelberg, the G.S.O.,Ia, of our Staff, who as a result of many years' collaboration with General Ludendorff in the second section of the Great General Staff enjoyed his especial confidence, pleaded for an offensive across the Bobr to both sides of Osoviec. We had a pretty lively difference of opinion. I considered that an offensive across the swampy lowlands of the Bobr, where we should be quite unable to support our infantry attack with the mass of our artillery, was wrong, and that such an attempt would be doomed to failure from the very beginning.

WAR DIARIES 61

LÖTZEN, *June* 18, 1915.

We sit here waiting to see whether G.H.Q. will also take from us the last 2 Divisions, that we have scraped together out of our entire Front, so as to be able to take the offensive again. If they need them in Galicia too we shall have to remain simply on the defensive: whether this is necessary, of course we are not in a position to judge. For the rest the position on the whole Eastern Front is good, and in Mackensen's command, excellent. Heavy fighting in the West; they cannot break through, but the losses are serious.

LÖTZEN, *June* 20, 1915.

Nothing new here. We have not men enough for any important undertaking, and G.H.Q. do not seem inclined to give us any. Whether they cannot, or whether they want to avoid the mischance of our again bringing ourselves to the notice of our worthy fellow-citizens at home by an important victory, I am not, of course, in a position to judge. They are, rightly, sending every available man to the Galician Front, but I am curious to know what they have in mind after the capture of Lemberg. With two Corps we could win another splendid victory.

His chief objection to my plan was that the capture of Kovno would take too much time.

" General Ludendorff decided for my view. . . .

" The preparations for the advance on Kovno and beyond were begun. The Orders, at least as regards the movement of troops within the area of the C.-in-C. on the Eastern Front, were already drafted when, on July 1st, Field-Marshal von Hindenburg and General Ludendorff were summoned by telegraph to report to H.M. the Kaiser at Posen.

" In the afternoon I received a telephone message to hold everything up: another plan was to be adopted. While in Posen H.M. the Kaiser had approved of General v. Falkenhayn's scheme, by which General v. Gallwitz was to break through the line opposite him, and take the offensive against the Narev. By this, in my opinion, the last possibility of carrying out a destructive operation against the Russian Army was lost. However successful the Gallwitz scheme might be, it could only result in the Russians having to leave Warsaw, and give up their salient positions in Poland."

June 29, 1915.

I am rather in a hurry, as I have to get off a longish telegram to Pless, giving our view of the progress of the campaign. It is rather a difficult business, as my opinion differs from that of Ludendorff and Bockelberg. I can do no more than state my own.

June 30, 1915.

Yesterday evening and early this morning I had to fight for my own ideas. Then the four Army Commanders had a meeting here; all agreed with me. Ludendorff now convinced. But G.H.Q. are trying to interfere. We are too weak to do what they want.

July 2, 1915.

Bockelberg, who went off with the Chief, has just telephoned what we are to do—of course not what we wanted. I am sorry; I thought our idea was better and more practicable. Well, well, so it must be; at least they are not taking any troops away from us. I had got so pleased over the other scheme, it would have been such a pretty bit of work. The Chief is coming back at eleven o'clock this evening; he will be furious.

LÖTZEN, *July* 5, 1915.

This evening I was able to make a hurried visit to Tilsit to dine with the Army Commander, General von Below. I regard him as one of the ablest and shrewdest of our commanders. In the evening we sat talking until twelve o'clock, both of us cursing G.H.Q. for interfering with our proposal and ordering us to do something which we all—Ludendorff especially — thought impracticable. G.H.Q. did not think our proposal would do. Ludendorff came back from Posen in a savage temper.

July 6, 1915.

Erni Hohenlohe, who has been so long with us here, is leaving this evening; he has been appointed ambassador in Constantinople. Whether Wangenheim is ill, as is reported, or superseded, I do not know. Less importance is attached to Hohenlohe's intellectual ability than to his connection with the King of Rumania (brother-in-law) and his friendship with the Bulgarians owing to the Coburg Regency.

July 7, 1915.

Meantime we are making the necessary troop movements so as to carry out the desired attack according to orders. Personally, I think the place and the objective wrong, but none the less we are taking every possible step to ensure a success. Moreover we, or rather G.H.Q., have had a piece of luck —the Russians are withdrawing considerable forces from our Front and sending them to Galicia.

July 9, 1915.

I'm sick of Headquarters. The fellow is not satisfied unless he can abuse us every day. Probably he hopes that some time he will get us out of patience and put us in the wrong. Well, we must bear this too.

July 10, 1915.

General Tappen, Head of the Operations Sections, arrived to-day in a special train from G.H.Q. to see whether we were carrying out our instructions properly. He gave another reason, but that was really what he came for. Hindenburg's and Ludendorff's fury can be imagined. I endured it with the utmost self-control, and even put forward my views again. So on the whole Eastern Front a great decisive battle will be opened on the 13th, 14th and 15th. I hope we shall have as much success as Linsingen and Mackensen.[1]

July 11, 1915.

To-morrow at noon we are going down to the Southern Front—viz. the Mlava-Prasznicz sector—and on the following day we are attacking at that point and on the day after in Kurland as well. And Mackensen's great attack starts again on the 14th. I hope the whole thing goes well. We have made such preparations as we could, and got together all available artillery and ammunition. I am fairly confident, but now, as before, of the opinion that it would have been better to concentrate on Kurland, and make an overwhelming attack there, capturing Kovno at the same time.

July 15, 1915.

The attack by Gallwitz's Army Group took the Russians completely by surprise, and in our first rush we took the first line, which comprised three fortified positions. Prasznicz, my child of sorrow, is again in our hands. Early yesterday morning we drove along the only traversable road through Mlava, and by 10 A.M. we had reached Prasznicz, which had been entirely destroyed, and abandoned by its inhabitants. Tremendous enthusiasm, of

---

[1] The 12th Army—the force hitherto under Gallwitz's command—stood ready on July 13th to break through the Russian positions on both sides of Prasznicz. Their forward movement forced the Russian Army Command to order a general retreat from Poland.

In the middle of July the army of the Niemen, on the left wing of the troops under the command of the C.-in-C., East, made a thrust in the direction of Kovno. The Eastern Command renewed its representations to G.H.Q., and requested that all available troops from those under Woyrsch's command, and from the 12th and 8th Armies, might be brought up in support of the 10th Army, so as to make a thrust beyond Kovno against Vilna.

G.H.Q. reinforced the 12th and 8th Armies by a Division each, but rejected the Eastern Command's proposal.

course, on the part of the troops at the sight of Hindenburg. We telegraphed to H.M. as soon as we got there. Good progress on the Niemen Front; and to-morrow, in the south, Mackensen and the newly formed Army of the Bug begin their offensive again.

July 16, 1915.

Gallwitz has broken through a further strongly fortified Russian position, south of Prasznicz, and the Russians are in retreat along the whole Front. Mackensen's advance, if successful, will be his decisive stroke. He is reopening his attack early to-day on the whole Front with a trifle of 40 Divisions: surely that must do the trick.

We are, of course, very much annoyed with G.H.Q. over the question of publicity. In the West every capture of 150 metres of trenches is a victory. Gallwitz has driven the Russians back on a Front of 120 kilometres, taken 12,000 prisoners, 13 guns, some 30 machine guns, and is fobbed off with two lines. Well, well, let us forget it. The main thing is that all goes well. If Mackensen wins a victory in the grand style, and that he cannot fail to do with his resources in troops and heavy artillery, it is to be hoped that Russia may collapse. [Here follows a brief but, at the date of publication, unreproducible criticism of his General-in-Command.—*Note by Editor.*]

LÖTZEN, *July* 18, 1915.

Things have gone well to-day too. The Russians have evacuated the whole position in front of the 9th Army, and have retired to the famous Blonje position before Warsaw. All is going well with Gallwitz, too, and to the north of the Niemen we have now taken more than 30,000 prisoners over the entire Front. This gives us food for thought.

The great question is whether we can succeed in crossing the Narev and getting at Warsaw from behind. And that depends on whether Mackensen is successful, as, in that case, the Russians will need their reinforcements down there, and cannot send them against us. Anyhow, we are in the thick of the greatest battle that history has ever known.

July 19, 1915.

All is in order here. Apparently the Russians are actually playing 1812 all over again, and are retiring along the entire Front. They are burning their own villages by the hundred, removing the inhabitants, etc. It is an appalling piece of lunacy, which will do milliards' worth of damage to the country, and is quite useless from a military point of view.

Gallwitz has reached the fortified positions on the Narev (Pultusk, Rozan, Ostrolenka), and is preparing an attack on them. His total of prisoners has mounted to about 30,000, so that since the 13th we have taken about 40,000.

July 20, 1915.

This time we are out for the big thing. If all goes well, we shall get Warsaw. In recognition of our good behaviour we have actually been promised two more Divisions.

July 22, 1915.

To-day Gallwitz launches his attack against the Narev. As we had anticipated, it moves very slowly, while in the area where we wanted to carry out the operation—in the neighbourhood of Kovno, and north of the Niemen—our attacks with the weak forces at our disposal have, of course, been marvellously successful. Well, we shall get across the Narev, and then Warsaw must fall this time.

July 23, 1915.

All is going well here. The great bridge-head position at Pultusk has just been stormed, and we are making good progress north of the Niemen, where the Russians are in full flight. The question of Warsaw is becoming acute, because to-morrow we are attacking the last position in front of that city.

On the West the position seems, unfortunately, a deadlock. We seem to have got a proper black eye at Arras. I heard to-day that our men would not have stood their ground if the French had attacked—*i.e.* with their infantry—but the French infantry in that part of the line can no longer be induced to attack. So the situation was saved.

H.M. is with Woyrsch to-day. Perhaps he, too, is to become a Field-Marshal. I wonder if he may chance to be a Field-Marshal who really does something himself. I doubt it.

July 24, 1915.

Notable successes yesterday and to-day. The Niemen Army has completely defeated and shattered[1] the Russian 5th Army, and Gallwitz has forced the passage of the Narev in strength. In the Wolff telegram little notice of course is taken of the victory of the Niemen Army in particular, as this was our idea and in conflict with the view of G.H.Q.

Well, we must bear it as well as we can—the main point is that we completely smashed our friends opposite.

[1] In June the Niemen Army had reached the line of the Dubissa at a point south of Schaulen, and the line of the Wenta and the Windau as far as the heights of Hasenpot. At the beginning of July they received the order to envelop and attack the enemy who had established themselves in the neighbourhood of Schaulen.
The Russians were completely taken by surprise and, after heavy fighting, the entire Russian 5th Army was flung back in the direction of Ponjewicz. On July 29th, Ponjewicz, and on August 1st Mitau, were taken.

July 25, 1915.

Of course we could not expect things to go on so smoothly as they have until now. The Russians facing Gallwitz have collected every man they could lay their hands on, and are putting up a desperate defence. It is quite natural, and we foresaw it—every frontal offensive comes to a stand some time and then goes no farther. And, unfortunately, that is what has happened to Mackensen. I hope G.H.Q. has now sense enough to bring an army up from Galicia and put it into the line where we wanted it at the beginning.

On Below's Front (the Niemen Army) we continue to do well. Unfortunately we are not strong enough there for the effect to be felt on the entire Front. I am curious to know how to-day's attack by the 9th Army, aimed direct at Warsaw, has developed.

July 29, 1915.

Not a word of truth in the news from Warsaw. We had tried to break through the Warsaw position, but had to give up the idea: it was too strong and we were too weak. However, Woyrsch has succeeded in crossing the Vistula, north of Ivangorod. For the time being, of course, this has had no great consequences, but it must make the Russians very anxious. The news from Mackensen to-day is also good. I hope I may be disappointed and that he is still advancing victoriously: I was afraid that he might get no farther. So much the better if I am wrong. It does not matter who wins the victories. To-morrow we shall start again also. Gallwitz, as well as Scholtz, had outrun their ammunition owing to the bad roads. To-day it has caught them up, and I hope we shall get forward. We must knock these fellows out while we are about it. The

American note is a piece of impudence, I hope we shall be able to get our revenge for it later on. H.M. may see from the American attitude what sort of thanks he gets for his affability to the Pork King and the Steel Magnates.

July 31, 1915.

Mackensen did very well yesterday, and Woyrsch's crossing of the Vistula is a very pretty piece of work; but it all takes a very long time and costs many lives: nor can we move any quicker here. The position is quite simple: we can get a quicker result only by turning the Russian flank. It is not such a glorious affair as the papers describe it, especially as there are no indications in Warsaw of any preparations for retirement. However, we are moving forward, and that is the main thing. And the situation in the West is quite satisfactory. The last attack on the Loretto heights cost the French so many lives that they cannot rely on their men for another great offensive. Their man-power is giving out. It has been calculated that, by February at the latest, the French will have lost so many men that from that date they will not be able to keep the effective strength of their armies up to the same point as formerly. Joffre has to reckon with this, so everything hangs on the English and the Neutrals. As regards the munitions question in the Dardanelles, opinions differ. Many take a pessimistic view, but there was a recent report that the Turks were much better off for munitions than had been thought.

August 3, 1915.

I might date this " The Eve of the Capture of Warsaw." It really looks as if the Russians intend to evacuate the place.[1] On Gallwitz's left wing the situation has improved, now that we have again replaced one of the Corps Commanders. I have been exchanging telegrams all the morning with G.H.Q. It seems to be gradually dawning on them that we were right after all. It is still not too late. We cannot, of course, get back the 25,000 killed and wounded that we lost so needlessly, but if they give us the necessary heavy artillery, and then allow us a free hand, we could have Kovno[2] in 10-14 days. In that way we should have a secure base for our whole left wing, and the possibility of an offensive against the unsupported Russian left flank.

August 4, 1915.

The 9th Army is fighting in the Warsaw line of forts. The Russians are evacuating the town. It is undoubtedly a great triumph for the Falkenhayn plan, but it is not a crushing defeat of the Russians. This could only have been brought about by a concentrated flank attack — *i.e.* with our 10th Army. Apparently G.H.Q. are gradually beginning to realize this. At least they are no longer vetoing the attack on Kovno, which is to begin on the 8th.

We are still a long way from peace; the Tsar will not have it. In the first place he is firmly convinced that we, Germany, attacked him, and, secondly, he is too honourable to withdraw from his treaty with France and England. Unless it comes to a Revolution—and of that there is at present little prospect—the war will go on.

[1] At the beginning of August the Russians in front of the 9th Army evacuated the outer works of Warsaw and the town itself. Warsaw was occupied by the 9th Army on August 5th.
[2] On August 17th General Litzmann crossed the Niemen and took the eastern forts of the Kovno fortress and Kovno itself. The Russians began a hurried retreat to Vilna.

WAR DIARIES 71

It would now be easiest to overthrow France. All those who know the conditions assure us that could we break through at one point France would collapse. But I rather feel that we should first think of the Balkans. We are now really well off for munitions; but apart from this the Turks are not, I fancy, entirely trustworthy. Our people think that the Dardanelles is so important for us that when that campaign is over we shall be forced to clear up the situation in the Balkans—probably we shall deal with Serbia next. However, all this is still a long way off.

August 5, 1915.

In consideration of the fact that Warsaw, for which we have been fighting since last autumn, fell to-day, G.H.Q. were prepared to give us their special attention.[1] They cancelled our orders for the future disposition of the troops of the 9th Army and placed it under their direct control. Apart from the (deliberate) choice of the occasion for such a change, we also considered the proposed disposition was a blunder. We forced the Field-Marshal to the point of threatening resignation—he refused, until Ludendorff threatened to resign. Such was our day of triumph!

August 6, 1915.

As a result of Hindenburg's threat of course we had two slimy telegrams from G.H.Q. to the effect that no one had meant to hurt his feelings, that a Division from the West would be sent to us, etc.

Falkenhayn is so powerful with H.M. that no other opinion has any weight. The great victory that could have been won has not been won, and

[1] On August 5th Woyrsch's Force and his 9th Army were removed from the control of the C.-in-C., East, and, as the Army Group of Prinz Leopold von Bayern, placed under the direct orders of G.H.Q.

now it cannot be won. The Russians are getting troops together from all parts of their Front and moving them into the line against the Niemen Army. I don't really think that anything can go wrong, but we have not won the great victory that was easily possible. We must wait and see whether we have any further luck over Kovno. The worst of it is that Falkenhayn's frontal operation goes so slowly. And time presses: we must deal with Serbia somehow, so as to bring the Bulgarians to a decision and thus control the Dardanelles—the greatest problem of the war.

August 7, 1915.

All goes well here: the envelopment of Novo-georgievsk is almost completed; Gallwitz has apparently soundly defeated the enemy, and the bombardment and the attack on Kovno are to begin to-morrow. The Niemen Army makes me a little anxious, as the Russians are moving large forces in that direction. If only we had been able to handle the 9th Army as we wished I need not have felt any anxiety, for, in that case, an Army Corps would have been sent off yesterday to the north of Kovno. Well, we must hope for the best.

August 9, 1915.

Generally speaking, all goes well here. Novo-georgievsk is cut off; Gallwitz is making good progress. I count on the capture of Lomza to-morrow, and we are moving steadily towards Kovno. The quarrel between Falkenhayn and Hindenburg is developing. The Field-Marshal is at last telling him the truth. Nothing at all will come of it, and we shall all have to suffer for it, but he could not go on ignoring all these insults—petty and otherwise.

WAR DIARIES

August 11, 1915.

All goes well. The situation is developing as we foretold—*i.e.* we are forcing the Russians back frontally—but, thanks to G.H.Q., there will be no crushing defeat. Of course we must not underestimate what we have achieved—the capture of the Vistula and Narev line, and the conquest of half Poland—but Russia is not smashed.

August 13, 1915.

Tirpitz is here to-day. If you listen to him you think he is right. According to him, the world is much more evil, weak and aimless than people have been accustomed to think. When one gets a close view of influential people—their bad relations with each other, their conflicting ambitions — all the slander and the hatred, one must always bear in mind that it is certainly much worse on the other side, among the French, English and Russians, or one might well be nervous. Of course he puts it on a bit—so as to make as good an impression as possible himself.

The race for power and personal position seems to destroy all men's characters. I believe that the only creature who can keep his honour is a man living on his own estate; he has no need to intrigue and struggle—for it is no good intriguing for fine weather.

August 14, 1915.

The frontal fighting in Gallwitz's sector is proceeding and we get no reinforcements for the left wing. We must see what we can do for ourselves. Interminable explanatory telegrams go daily backwards and forwards between Pless and here: in form very courteous, in content pretty forcible. I think it all rather pointless, but Hindenburg and Ludendorff insist on it for the historical records, which are a matter of more or less indifference to me.

For the first time in my life I have, during the whole war, seen "History" at close quarters, and I know that its actual process is very different from what is presented to posterity; in the final issue a few meannesses and misrepresentations make little or no difference.

August 15, 1915.

I am much more concerned by the fact that I hoped we should storm one of the Kovno forts to-day, and we have not succeeded. Otherwise our position here is excellent. If we could only put 3-4 Army Corps into the line on the left wing between the 10th and the Niemen Army then we might succeed in destroying the Russians. Unfortunately we have not got them and G.H.Q. will not let us have them.

August 16, 1915.

However, things are going better than G.H.Q. deserve. There will, indeed, be no smashing Russian defeat, but I believe the Russians will suffer pretty severely.

It is to be hoped that G.H.Q. will then make up their minds as soon as possible and send an army against Serbia, so as to clear up the Dardanelles situation at last. We cannot hope to wear the Russians down in the course of the winter unless we keep the Dardanelles firmly closed. We can only attack the English in conjunction with the Turks—via the Suez Canal.

August 18, 1915.

There is, of course, great rejoicing here—it will soon be all up with Novogeorgievsk. At any rate we have intercepted a message from the wireless officer, in which he said good-bye to his wife, in view of his approaching departure to a German war prison. H.M. has sent a gracious telegram to Hindenburg: " Pour le Mérites " for Eichhorn and Litzmann. If Novogeorgievsk falls, 3 Divisions will be released, which we can put into the line north of Kovno. Then we can proceed against Vilna without reference to G.H.Q. Otherwise the position is, in general, good. It is to be hoped that G.H.Q. will be sensible and make up their minds to go through with the scheme.

August 19, 1915.

Novogeorgievsk is still holding out. I had, in fact, reckoned on its being taken to-day. How right we were about Kovno is proved by the fact that the Russians have abandoned their positions on the whole front of the 10th Army and are in retreat behind the Niemen. With only 1-2 new Corps —but we have not got them. We can only bring in the troops that have been besieging Novogeorgievsk, but they must take the place first.

August 20, 1915.

Yesterday evening the fall of Novogeorgievsk could be seen to be imminent. As a result of this a telegram came in at eight o'clock from Pless, to the effect that H.M. would proceed there to-day. No mention of Hindenburg. Ludendorff and I were quite clear that this would never do. If the Kaiser visited troops under Hindenburg's command Hindenburg must be there, unless H.M. expressly forbade it. So a special train was at once put together and at 11 P.M. Hindenburg, Ludendorff, and Bockelberg as well, rumbled off to

Novogeorgievsk. I, of course, had to stay here. I am very curious to know what kind of faces H.M. and Falkenhayn made when they saw Hindenburg and Ludendorff.

The prisoners taken at Novogeorgievsk (85,000) are more than I had expected, and all goes well elsewhere. If only Gallwitz's persistent frontal attacks did not mean such heavy losses! Our conscience is clear—we set ourselves against any frontal advance.

August 21, 1915.

The others have come back from Novogeorgievsk. Meeting courteous but cool. Falkenhayn said to Ludendorff: " Now, are you at last convinced that my operation was right? " Answer: " On the contrary! " H.M. made a few non-committal remarks. Then decorations were distributed—to the wrong people, of course — troops reviewed, speeches delivered, and so home. And so it goes on. The futility of our (so-called) Great Headquarters is beyond description.

August 25, 1915.

From the tactical point of view we are going on well, and so is Mackensen farther south. The Russians don't seem in the least anxious to hold Brest-Litovsk, their last great fortress. Of course these are all notable successes, but we have not smashed them; and we could have done.

We are more and more annoyed with G.H.Q. As a memento, apparently, of the anniversary of Hindenburg's appointment in the East they have deliberately taken Poland from us and put it under a Governor-General at Warsaw (Beseler) directly responsible to H.M. So the Field-Marshal has asked to be allowed to alter his title of " C.-in-C.,

East," as this designation had been for some little time painfully ironical.

I hope Great (?) Headquarters will not be too late in deciding on the campaign against Serbia, the object of which is to hold out a hand to the Bulgarians.

August 28, 1915.

Nothing special to report here. On our right wing the Russians continue their retreat; on the left there is still heavy fighting in the direction of Vilna, but I hope we shall pull it off. We must do without Riga—unless the Russians abandon it to us. We are too weak up there. We are, of course, now sending reinforcements from Gallwitz up to the Kovno area, but it all takes time.

Another long series of instructions from G.H.Q. to-day. Good God, what an idea these people have of war! Of course we don't do anything they tell us, so there is no harm done.

August 30, 1915.

The answer to our telegram about " C.-in-C., East," was, as might have been expected, conciliatory. Since H.M. had been on the Eastern Front, the title was, of course, incorrect. But it had not been altered so as not to give the impression that Hindenburg's position was in any way diminished. There was even less cause to alter it at present, since the Eastern campaign would very soon have reached a defensive stage and the entire line would then be again handed over to Hindenburg, etc. Well, we have annoyed them, and that's the main thing.

As regards politics, the Rumanians appear to be strongly inclined to the Quadruple Alliance. It is high time that the Austrians made their offensive in Eastern Galicia. The Russians are cut off there owing to their retreat, so that an envelopment would be possible. If those fellows conducted the campaign with reasonable sense they might win a great success—free the rest of Galicia and drive some of the Russians on to Rumania. The latter would be especially desirable, as in that case the Rumanians would have to show their colours. The Serbian scheme, too, seems to be taking palpable shape. The attacking troops are to be the so-called Alpine Corps, hitherto stationed in Tyrol.

August 31, 1915.

The one thing that makes me anxious is the futility of G.H.Q. They are like a pack of Social Democrats—they can't make a decision and stick to it. The Turks are howling, the Bulgarians are ready, and the fellows — or rather the fellow — cannot make up his mind to send off these three Corps to Serbia. They have got them waiting ready behind the Front. Whether they are afraid the French in the West may make another great effort to break through, and they may need Reserves for that, of course I don't know. That would be the only excuse, but no real reason.

September 1, 1915.

As regards the situation in general, G.H.Q. seem to have come to a decision; whether a right one, it is too early to say. In any case we shall have to suffer for it, as the centre of gravity is to be shifted elsewhere. We shall probably be presented with what troops are left, and told to hold up what are left of the Russians. Well, we can do it. Falkenhayn probably hopes that something will go wrong somewhere and we shall let ourselves in for a minor reverse. He needn't worry! . . .

WAR DIARIES

September 2, 1915.

In the meantime we have at last got our way on one point against G.H.Q. They really wanted to hold up everything and carry off all the troops they could get. We simply could not allow it: we are still in the middle of an attack and—just as much as the 9th Army—must stick to it. After a lengthy dispute they gave in.

Vilna is a difficult business. The Russians are attacking there with greatly superior forces. Our men have held on up till now, and if they can hold till to-morrow then all will be well.[1]

September 3, 1915.

Here all goes well. At Grodno we have taken the fortifications this side of the Niemen and the city itself on the opposite bank—the latter by surprise. The Russians are now defending themselves desperately and trying to drive us back over the Niemen. All goes well in the Vilna direction: the Russians have had such enormous losses in their attacks that they have given them up and dug themselves in. Meantime the two Divisions we sent have arrived there, and all danger is over. But it will be four or five days before we can make the projected attack. It is tedious waiting, but the Russians have learned something, and so destroyed the railways

[1] It was not until the middle of August that G.H.Q. sanctioned the offensive towards Vilna. For this purpose the 10th Army was reinforced by the siege-troops from Novogeorgievsk, and by certain Divisions transferred from the 8th and 12th Armies. The reinforcements appeared so late that the decisive attack could not take place until September 9th.

The Niemen Army received orders to advance on Dünaburg. The Russians had to surrender Vilna, but the German advance then came to a standstill. The Russian retreat from Poland had already so far settled down into an orderly movement that the Russians could easily move Divisions to any threatened point.

The Niemen Army came to a stop, also, before it reached Dünaburg.

The counter-attacks of the Russians were everywhere repulsed with bitter fighting.

everywhere in their retreat that we have not yet finished repairing them.

September 9, 1915.

Bulgaria: so far as I know, the agreement with Turkey has been signed. 4-5 Austrian and 2 German Army Corps are now being transferred to deal with Serbia. I fancy the Serbians will be inclined to ask themselves whether they would not sooner make peace, and resign Macedonia to Bulgaria, taking Northern Albania instead; otherwise they will have to face a combined attack by Bulgaria and ourselves. I don't believe that Rumania will come in yet—I think the successes of Italy have frightened her off a little. But whether this is actually the scheme, and whether it will be actually carried out in this way, I don't know. Mackensen is to have the command of the expedition. Now that all available honours, titles and orders have been showered in so short a time on this one devoted head, after the capture of Belgrade there is nothing left for him but to be rechristened "Prinz Eugen." Large forces from the Eastern Front are being transferred to the West—let us hope it will lead to a success. We, too, shall have to give up a good many troops, but not until after the conclusion of the Vilna operation, which began early to-day, and of which I have great hopes.

The Tsar's decision to assume the Chief Command himself, and to supersede Nicolas, seems to me very significant. It is a *coup d'état* on the best model. Even if the Tsar does not want peace because he is convinced that we attacked him and made war inevitable, the removal of the Grand Duke, who kept the situation together with such iron energy, can only be to our advantage. I view the matter as the first step towards peace.

September 10, 1915.

The extract from *The Times* article has aroused general approval. It is exactly what we explained to G.H.Q. two months ago. Unfortunately there is no means of inducing General von Falkenhayn or H.M. to read the article. Hindenburg will send it to Lyncker, who will, of course, silently suppress it. It is poor comfort to reflect that we are guiltless of this folly. Yesterday I was told by Dürr (Adjutant-General of the Grand Duke of Baden, who did not leave until early this morning) that he had been officially informed that Bulgaria had come to an agreement with Turkey as well as with us and Austria. The treaties were signed three days ago. Mackensen has got the command against Serbia. I am sorry we did not get it. There is then to be an attack at one point in the West. I suspect that it will be conducted by Falkenhayn under his own orders and those of the Crown Prince, so as to put himself in an agreeable light in the latter's eyes.

September 13, 1915.

Yesterday I was in a bad humour. To-day things are better, although the Vilna business still fails to come off. They ought to be moving forward, but they seem to be hanging about doing nothing. The worst of such a situation is that one does not know where the cause lies. Probably there is some failure somewhere that the culprit will not confess and does not report. And so the whole line is held up. In the meantime the Russians have time to move up reinforcements by railway. However, it won't be another Brzeziny. Let us be content with a modest success — no more adventures. . . . I do not know when the campaign against Serbia is to begin; I assume at the end of the month. I hope our people will come to a friendly agreement with the Serbians and that Serbia will make peace, receiving the whole of Albania and the coast now claimed by the Italians, and giving Macedonia to Bulgaria. Then a serious word or two will be all that is needed to deal with Rumania. The Austrians can use the forces thus set free against the Italians and take Venice from those blackguards. Here am I disposing of kingdoms!

On the 16th, H.M. is coming to Kovno for a few hours. The Field-Marshal and Ludendorff must of course be there to meet him. Ludendorff wants me to go with him. He means it kindly, but it would give me no pleasure. These people do not like us, and what is the use of going there merely to be treated offensively (as happened, for example, in Novogeorgievsk, so Bockelberg told me)? However, I shall have to eat the sour apple, I suppose.

September 14, 1915.

Nothing special to record—the operation against Vilna is still in progress. It must be ended in three days if it is to succeed. I have just had a row with the G.O.C. 10th Army, who is inclined to be too venturesome, and one with Ludendorff, who wants to make a frontal attack. I want to strike a middle course, content myself with 50,000-60,000 prisoners, and take no serious risks. What they now decide between the two of them is all one to me. I have said my say to both of them, and wash my hands with proverbial innocence. Tactics gradually get on one's nerves rather, particularly when one always has the worry of them, without being able to make the decision.

September 15, 1915.

Our operation against Vilna is proceeding. To-day things look a little better, as the 1st Cavalry

Division succeeded in destroying a railway some considerable distance in the rear of the Russians, but we have lost at least one day through the hesitation of the 10th Army. However they are now going to carry on according to my ideas.[1]

September 17, 1915.

... In the Royal train. H.M. had meantime reached Kovno. Dinner of ceremony. H.M. between Eichhorn and Ludendorff, and opposite Hindenburg. I next to Ludendorff, then Admiral von Müller, and opposite me Reischach, Treutler and also Valentini. Conversation not specially interesting. Treutler thought the Rumanian question quite simple. If the Austrians did not commit too many follies, he believed that he could keep the Rumanians out of it until our offensive against Serbia gets moving. As the Austrian railways are working so abominably, this will not be until October.

September 18, 1915.

All well here. Our offensive in the direction of Vilna prospers. The Russians are in retreat on their whole front as far as Galicia. . . . I was just now interrupted to be told we have got Vilna. Now G.H.Q. themselves must realize how right our view was.

As the Austrians have partly failed against Serbia, and we have to send more troops to that Front, our offensive in the West is held up for the present. I am glad of it, because that means we shall not have to give up any troops in the near future. Now

---

[1] The 1st Cavalry Division, far outstripping the infantry divisions, had reached the important railway Vilna—Molodeczno. They were heavily attacked by the Russians but decided to hold their ground until their own infantry came up. But the infantry advanced so slowly along the bad roads that the Division had finally to evacuate Smorgon with heavy losses.

we shall get at least as far as Minsk, and I can now see Riga in the distance.

Since yesterday we have had a Papal Prelate on a visit here. Apparently a German Jesuit. An unusually able fellow, a thorough diplomat, a friend of Erzberger. The object of his visit is to see what former possessions of the Catholic Church in Poland had been taken from them by the Russians, so that a claim might be made for their restitution. The Pope is, for that reason, rather disposed to be in favour of German annexation of Russian territory. On the other hand, the Pope is against the partition of Belgium. I liked what he had to say about Austria. The Pope thinks that after the war Germany must infallibly make a military convention with Austria. . . . There must be an exchange of officers. Great hopes are placed on Princess Zita, the wife of the Heir to the Throne. She is said to be clever and energetic; he is rather . . . , but "enough sense for a ruling sovereign." The most important thing was to break the power of the aristocracy in Vienna. Did we know any means of doing so? I said I knew of none, except strychnine.

September 20, 1915.

Nothing new here. Our Vilna offensive has still not produced the result I had hoped—*i.e.* a round figure of prisoners and guns. It is certainly a great strategical success, as the Russians are on the run along their whole line—quite like old times: they seem unimpressed by the fact that their Little Father the Tsar has taken over the supreme command, and has clearly stated that he now proposes to win the war. The citizen at home wants a victory, but he must have it expressed in figures, and so long as we have not got 50,000 prisoners it won't do.

September 24, 1915.

Heavy fighting last night. The Russians are attacking desperately where they are being outflanked. Alas, we are always just an Army Corps short. The operation succeeded all right: we have got Vilna, the Russians are retreating along the entire Front, but we have not got the 50,000 prisoners I had hoped for. Our men are exhausted, added to which the railways are useless. Complete chaos, no telephone lines—a very difficult situation. In a few days we shall have reached the line that we were fighting for, and then we shall stop.

September 26, 1915.

Our offensive is slowly coming to a standstill. The Russians are defending themselves desperately. Moreover, we have to give up some troops. I wish we could have reached the Molodeczno defile; it would have shortened the line and by occupying it we should have some troops over. Then we could dig ourselves in, and the fighting in the East would be over.

September 27, 1915.

Heavy fighting over in the West.[1] On the 3rd Army Front our first line is lost: the second holds. Heavy losses: the French losses are, of course, heavier, but they are making the most desperate attempts to break right through. H.Q. has been on the Western Front for the last three days. It is difficult from here to realize what is going on, but I feel pretty sure that the new line will hold. Any troops we can spare are of course being sent towards the railheads, but it will be nearly three weeks before they can reach the West—we are 200 kilometres

[1] At the end of September the powerful Entente attacks started at Loos and in Champagne.

off the railway. It is at least fortunate that the Guard and the X. Army Corps had already been sent back from Galicia to the West.

We are now coming to a halt at last, and constructing a strong position which can then be held with as few troops as possible.¹

September 28, 1915.

Yesterday went well for us in the West. It is to be hoped that the main storm is over. No troops from here can reach them in less than three days.

We have to-day withdrawn our left wing to the position intended for it. And with that the serious part of the operation is over. It will now take a fortnight or three weeks to get everything straight and then the war of positions will begin. It has been rather a disappointing affair. I had counted on 40,000-50,000 prisoners, but we actually made only about 30,000. I now know quite well why we did not do better. The infantry no longer attacks. The troops are without officers, especially without proper company commanders, and they are gradually deteriorating. The only comfort is that the other side is, of course, in the same case. We want a good long rest for our tired Divisions, then all will be well. We shall now have to put off the Riga affair.

September 30, 1915.

Heavy fighting in the night on the Western Front. But there is now a general conviction that the line will hold. To-morrow the I. Army Corps we sent from here will arrive at the most dangerous point. Three others will follow immediately and then three Divisions. It was very careless of G.H.Q. to send that Corps off to Serbia before the Corps had arrived from here to replace it.

¹ The Line Beresina—Kovno—Lake Narocz—Lake Drysviaty—Lake Novo-Alexandrovsk—Düna.

October 3, 1915.

In the West the affair seems to be over. Our losses are not so high as I had feared. The missing, excluding those taken prisoners, do not, as the French announce, amount to 23,000, but only 11,000. The total losses are only about 50,000, while those of the French and English must be enormous. So Falkenhayn has a little breathing space, which he employs in insulting us assiduously. Ludendorff will not stand it, so that on both sides there is much drafting of offensive telegrams.

It is important that the Serbian expedition should succeed quickly, so that we can get the way clear to Constantinople. If only we could send a few batteries of heavy howitzers, so as to prevent the English ships from landing provisions and water, the Gallipoli business would soon be over. When the Russians then saw that there was no means of exporting their wheat, or importing war material, there would be a gradual collapse in that country. And the English would be nervous about the Suez Canal.

In the West we must wait. French man-power is coming to an end. In the course of the winter France must reach the point when no more recruits will be forthcoming; in other words, it will no longer be possible to replace current losses. If, in addition, they become convinced that we can hold on, and mean to, they will gradually weaken. But this will take time and we must be patient.

October 4, 1915.

The danger in the West is apparently averted. There would have been none but for an idiotic piece of carelessness on the part of G.H.Q. A Brigade-Commander lately transferred to this

Front came through here the other day and told us an incredible story. The 3rd Army had foreseen the attacks in Champagne, and when, in spite of this, their last Reserves were taken from them, the Army Staff protested. Falkenhayn refused to listen, and the Chief of Staff (the Bavarian General von Höhn) asked to be relieved of his post, as he could no longer be responsible for the situation. He was relieved; a creature of Falkenhayn's took his place, and the French nearly got through. It is really unbelievable. Now they have got adequate Reserves which have been taken from us. As a result we are having a rough time, for the Russians have noticed the withdrawal of troops from our Front and are attacking in force. Well, we have had rough times before and got over them, and we shall do so again.

October 5, 1915.

All goes well in the West. At Souchez, as well as at Rouvroy, in Champagne, we have retaken the lost heights that served us as artillery observation posts. And the French and English seem to have had enough of their losses for the present.

Yesterday and early this morning there were no Russian attacks. Whether they are fed up, or are beginning to move off, we can't yet say. In any case we have now time to give our men a rest and dig ourselves in. In three or four days I expect everything will be straight here and we shall be able to face matters calmly. On the Serbian frontier our people are behaving very foolishly, in my opinion. Instead of getting on with it they are still hesitating over the first move. The main point was that the Serbians and the Bulgarians should fire the first shots. I don't really think that the Bulgarians could now draw back, but I would not trust these damned Balkan people an inch.

October 6, 1915.

Yesterday I had a long interview with the Under-Secretary of State, Wahnschaffe. The Imperial Chancellor sent him. There is no prospect whatever of peace: nor, in his opinion, can there be any in the immediate future, at least as long as we claim what the Jingo elements want—the whole of Belgium, French Lorraine, the whole of Poland, Kurland and Lithuania. I took the opportunity of expressing my view that a discussion of Peace terms could have any object only when one of the parties showed signs of wishing to negotiate. If Russia approached us separately we should have to treat with her, perhaps giving her back Warsaw. Warsaw is a distinctly troublesome point. We can't give it to Austria; it would be awkward for us; and Poland as an independent buffer State would be equally awkward. If England approached us separately we should have to give her concessions in Belgium. I am only afraid that neither of them will make any advance. In those circumstances—the worst possible for us—it will end in a war of exhaustion. In that case we must stick to what we have got and go on sticking to it. Our talk was really only a repetition of what we both knew, but again confirmed my view that the civilians, in general, do not know what they are talking about.

October 8, 1915.

Nothing special here: more trouble with G.H.Q. Ludendorff had sent an offensive telegram and to-day of course got an even more offensive reply. There is little point in the quarrel, as we are getting the worst of it.

We have visitors as usual every day here—Dernburg yesterday, and to-day Prince Henry is here again. Dernburg is certainly the most ill-mannered brute I have ever met in high places. He asked me what my exact position was here. I had a good mind to answer that I was on a visit, just as he was, but I stopped myself, for he certainly would not have understood. And the fact that I, like him, conducted the interview with my hands in my trouser-pockets did not make us any more disposed to be friendly. However, he had some interesting things to say about America.

Things were more quiet in the West yesterday and to-day. This afternoon they are proposing to attack Tahure, where the French broke through the day before yesterday. I hope they will succeed.

The King of Greece has plucked up courage to send Herr Venizelos packing. I shall be interested to see how long he is for this world. I believe the English Government pays good prices. If Greece remains absolutely neutral it would be a great advantage, for the enemy cannot march inland from Salonika with the mobile Greek army in their rear, not knowing what it may do.

October 10, 1915.

We are constructing our entrenched positions and quarrelling with G.H.Q. In the last dispute they were actually right. Ludendorff is getting nervy and loses his temper unnecessarily. On the 3rd Army Front the French are occupying our second line at Tahure and we can't get them out. However I don't think the position is critical. They have had so many reinforcements from us here in the interval that they must surely be able to hold on now.

To-day, for a change, we have had three Turkish Princes to visit us. It is rather a good move on the part of our Government; they have brought the three Princes next in succession to the Turkish Throne to Germany and are educating them here. All three of them make a very pleasant impression. Incidentally, I delivered a discourse to them.

In Serbia, Bulgaria and Greece everything seems satisfactory. The Serbs are defending themselves bravely and putting up a good fight. The Bulgarians are to launch their attack to-morrow. Whether the King of Greece can hold out remains to be seen. At any rate he is staking his head in our interest.

October 12, 1915.

Eisenhart [1] came back to-day from Berlin, where he had been for a conference, and brought with him much interesting news, some of which I may quote. The embezzlements in which Suchomlinoff was involved reached a total of 600 million roubles. The party mainly implicated was, however, the Grand Duke Nicolai Nicolaievich—hence his removal from the post of Commander-in-Chief. One must admit that the fellow does things on the grand scale. I can only suppose that the money was needed for distribution in many and various quarters in return for subsequent support of his claims to the Tsardom.

The most competent authority gives the following reasons for our withdrawal in the matter of the U-boat question: "We were on the verge of war with America. They could do us little damage by force of arms, but they could injure us financially and by political influence in the Balkan states. England would have pumped 20 milliards out of them, not merely 500 millions, as at present. America would have allowed the enrolment of recruits for the English Army, and all the Balkan

[1] General von Eisenhart-Rothe was Q.M.G. at Headquarters, East.

states would have been against us. Bulgaria had stated openly that if America was against us, then we could not win, and she would not play. For these reasons we had to give in." There is really nothing to be said on the other side, and our Foreign Office seems really to have handled the Balkans better than they used to do. . . .

It has been established that there is about twenty times as much German money invested abroad as there is foreign money in Germany. In England alone there is about 20 milliards of German money. This is a state of affairs that was scarcely realized before the war, especially in view of possible reprisals. There have been many complaints in the papers about the unjust decisions of the French War Tribunals. The French Government have offered that the documents should be examined by Neutrals. . . . Further, the French Government offered to exchange all documents affecting German prisoners of war against the documents of German War Tribunals affecting French and Belgian subjects. After careful examination our Government had to refuse the proposal: which speaks volumes.

October 17, 1915.

The Russians continue to attack at Dvinsk.[1] I do not feel at all anxious. The French show signs of being satisfied with their apparent achievements in the West. Yesterday also there was no attack. So that we have got past one of the worst crises of the campaign. It is to be hoped that G.H.Q. will now have the sense to return to Berlin or Potsdam. H.M. should then have a C.-in-C., East, and a C.-in-C., West. He can always move to the point where anything is going on.

[1] Russian name for Dünaburg.

October 18, 1915.

Ludendorff did not bring back much interesting news. Zimmermann was very pleased with his Balkan policy, and well he may be. Rumania has promised to remain neutral and to refuse any passage to the Russians. Greece, too, is still behaving irreproachably. In this connection, however, we can never be sure whether Venizelos may not again get the upper hand.

Yesterday was a critical day for us in the area south of Dünaburg. Very strong Russian attacks, but they were all beaten off.

Things are moving in Serbia. But the Serbs are stout fellows and are holding out magnificently. We have let it be known that if they soon make up their minds to give up the game, Serbia will be allowed to remain intact; otherwise it will be partitioned. At present they still seem to be relying on the Quadruple Alliance.

October 19, 1915.

To-morrow we are moving to Kovno. Exactly a year ago we changed our quarters from Radom to Konskie. It was the beginning of our retreat from Poland. Our position is now much better, but it was then far more interesting. At that time everything was still before us, we looked forward to mighty battles and mighty victories—now we are merely waiting for what may happen. It is a negative situation: we do nothing, we just prevent the other party doing anything to us.

October 31, 1915.

One of the most interesting of my experiences in Berlin was my visit to Zimmermann. He was very cheerful and optimistic. He hoped that Serbia would collapse very shortly and that Italy would then follow suit (perhaps at the end of December). The others have not expressed any very audible desires for peace. There was indeed one private inquiry from an influential personage in France (Paul Cambon) as to whether we should not soon be making overtures for peace; which was of course met with a flat denial. Zimmermann was, however, of the opinion that this was a good sign. In Russia the dislike of England was quickly increasing, and Isvolski, too, had entirely turned against England.

November 1, 1915.

We are making good progress in Serbia, and we may soon expect the end. On our Front the Russians are attacking persistently at Dünaburg and there is rather serious fighting there, though nothing that need make us nervous.

Yesterday B—— gave me some news from the West: very edifying. I believe the people there hate Falkenhayn more than we do.

November 2, 1915.

We are all in a state of disturbance and upset. Although there are no great tactical movements on hand, there is much to do. Ludendorff is getting bored and keeps everyone on the run from morning till night. This restlessness—work for work's sake—is extremely uncomfortable for everybody round here.

Yesterday there was the devil of a business in front of Dünaburg: the Russians attacked like men demented, and broke through one of our Divisions. Fortunately, we had another Division near by that we were able to throw into the line, so that all is straight again to-day. I think Morgen is breaking up. Whether it is nerves or his unpopularity I don't know. I shall go to Lauenstein early tomorrow morning and find out what is really the matter.

In Serbia the Bulgarians seem to be making a mess of things. They appear to be afraid that the French and English, who have lately landed, may take them in the rear, and are sending strong forces to form a southern Front, instead of going all out against the Serbians, and knocking them out before the Allies can come up. Not one of the operations is going forward as had been planned.

November 6, 1915.

Still heavy fighting in front of Dünaburg. The Russians are absolutely determined to break through and are squandering men and munitions. We have held on up till now and shall certainly go on doing so. In the West, also, all is well. We are prepared for the possibility that the French may make a last attempt. Now that we have plenty of Reserves in hand it could only be to our advantage. Good progress in Serbia. The Bulgarians have taken Nish. Consequently I do not attach much importance to the fall of the Zaimis Cabinet. It is clear that Venizelos is doing all he knows to get back to the helm.

November 13, 1915.

In Serbia a Bulgarian Division seems to have got into difficulties. A part of the Serbian forces is trying to break through to the south. Whether there has been some error in leadership it is impossible to say, but it would be regrettable if the break-through succeeded. From the news up to date it seems that 4 weak Serbian Divisions are involved, otherwise everything is going well in the West and in Serbia. I am very curious to know what plans our G.H.Q. is now making. In Serbia more than two of our Corps have been withdrawn as, owing to the concentric advance, there is no room for them. We have not the least idea of their destination—perhaps Salonika, via Sofia.

November 18, 1915.

G. had really nothing particular to tell us. He gave us a description of the disgusting state of affairs in Austria. Things are very likely worse there than we had hitherto supposed, and the worst of all is the old Emperor . . . with his old Habsburg hatred of the Hohenzollerns. Prices have doubled just as they have with us. The Government does nothing, because the highest aristocracy—in particular the Archduke Frederick—are doing very well out of it all.

November 19, 1915.

I have said fifty times before that we are fighting for our existence; that it is a hard fight and will grow harder; and that we shall never be in a position simply to impose our Peace conditions on the other side. However, I must keep on saying it.

The incompetence of the authorities and of G.H.Q. is greater on the other side than with us; and that is saying a good deal.

November 22, 1915.

The position here is unchanged, and will remain so for a time. The Russians seem to be very busy training new troops so as to attack us in the spring with their formations up to full strength. We shall do the same, so as to give them a suitable reception. There is no indication of an end anywhere. The hope that Serbia would weaken and make a separate Peace seems unlikely to be fulfilled. King Peter will probably act like Albert of Belgium. He has got a guarantee from England that his kingdom will be restored : he is satisfied with it, and reigns for the time being *in partibus infidelium.* According to all one hears, the war will last at least one year longer, and it is good to prepare one's mind for it, if only that one may not become impatient.

November 27, 1915.

The only interesting item is that negotiations between Austria and Montenegro are actually in progress; Nikita does not seem inclined to fall upon his kinsman Peter's rear and increase his territory at Serbia's expense.

November 28, 1915.

It is unfortunately true that we have not, and never have had, a definite political aim. The misfortune is that the Chancellor is actually a clever man, but he cannot bring himself to any decision; worst of all is Falkenhayn's ascendancy over H.M., so that the latter only hears what Falkenhayn thinks fit to tell him, and has a false idea, or no idea at all, of the real position.

December 2, 1915.

I am very curious to see the results of the Reichstag debates. Anxious as I am that our incompetent Administration, and in particular Herr Delbrück, should get a thorough dressing-down, I very much hope, all the same, that this process may not take place at a full sitting, but in committee, so as to avoid making a bad impression abroad. The only disadvantages will be that, in that case, there will be probably no change of ministers, and that idiot will go on ruining the Empire.

December 14, 1915.

We are all anxiously watching Salonika. The Greek is certainly in a painful position. If he throws over the English they will stop his imports, and produce a famine in a fortnight. On the other hand he would like to come in with the Central Powers, because he believes in a German victory. So he tacks laboriously backwards and forwards. Apart from this, the Greeks regard the Bulgarians as the hereditary enemy, which does not make matters easier. In order to avoid any Greek gun going off unintentionally, the Bulgarians have halted on the Greek frontier until the German and Austrian troops arrive. Then, and not till then, will Salonika be attacked, unless the English and the French prefer to clear out beforehand.

December 17, 1915.

The War Minister was here the day before yesterday. I sat next him at table and had a most interesting conversation. In particular he was able to remove certain of my anxieties regarding the possibility of our success. We have ample man-power to carry on the war for one more year. Naturally, we cannot commit any extravagances. I was amused to note that we were in complete agreement regarding the frontiers we should claim here in the East. He is the first man I have met who wants the same from the Russians as I do— namely, a line in front of Kalish, along the Warthe, then south of Vozlavek-Plotzk, south of Mlava, then straight ahead through Rozan to Bialystok, including Lithuania and Kurland. Poland and Warsaw he wants as little as I do.

December 17, 1915.

As a result of my last conversation with G.H.Q. we have again telegraphed to-day to ask for a

Division as reinforcement. I am curious to see whether we get it. They have enough in the West, and 3-4 Divisions have also been sent to the West from Serbia.

December 19, 1915.

Nothing fresh here from a military point of view. According to what the Austrian told me, Constantine of Greece still hopes that he may amicably induce the Entente to sail away from Salonika. I don't think he will manage it. If they do not withdraw voluntarily, the attack can begin at the end of the month. Until then Gallwitz will still be busy with his supplies and railway communications. There will also be a simultaneous Austrian expedition against Montenegro from the West.

The Bulgarians, incidentally, have not been content to remain on the Albanian frontier; they are pushing forward through North Albania to the West. To the great disgust of the Austrians they want to reach the sea, for which one cannot blame them. I shall be eager to see what happens when they come in contact with the Italians. I suspect that the latter will bolt without more ado.

December 21, 1915.

By way of celebrating the New Year, we have had an active row with G.H.Q. They want some heavy artillery from us, and we won't let them have it. Their tone is so insolent that I do no understand how Hindenburg stands it.

There was a slight mishap on the Austrian Front near Czernovitz yesterday,[1] but matters seem to have been put right again now. Here the position

[1] The Russians had made another attack on the extreme south wing of the German Army and the Austrian 7th Army. The latter were involved in heavy fighting in the Bukovina, which lasted into January. The Austrian positions were, for the most part, maintained.

is unchanged. Unimportant patrol fighting and artillery duels, but in general all is quiet. Our new Division is on its way, so that our minds are at rest for the future. According to news from Russia, they are suffering from a serious shortage of guns. It seems that foreign countries will deliver only against payment in gold. Moreover, the only way they can be got into the country is by the Siberian railway. Their position seems gradually deteriorating, while with us it is improving. When I read in the papers about the great new Russian Army of two million men I simply laugh.

January 3, 1916.

Nikita would like to, but he can't. He is threatened with famine if he does not negotiate. Besides, strange as it is, the Serbians and Montenegrins still believe in England's ultimate victory. They know all the bungling . . . that goes on in Austria and they cannot imagine that that country can come through. And yet the Austrians are doing better. Until now they have repulsed all the Russian attacks. The Russians apparently want to make an impression on Rumania.

Nothing fresh here. Young Hindenburg, who is G.S.O.,I, with the VII. Army Corps in the West, was here for a few days on a visit to his father, and told us some interesting news. God, what follies were committed over there in the early days of the war!

January 7, 1916.

Kapp would be a good catch, but I hardly think it likely. Solf has never had the slightest chance for the Chancellorship. I had not until now heard anything of the other things against him. My main objection to him was simply that he was a pessimist and spread the most incredible rumours. As regards Bulgaria, I never believed that they had joined us for our *beaux yeux*. They are quite rightly pursuing their own purely Bulgarian policy. The best of it is that we can promise them at least as much as the English, since we can divide up the whole of Serbia, but if the Bulgarians were to get too near Constantinople there would be objections on the part of Russia.

The money question is naturally a difficulty, since Rumania insists on payment in gold. However . . . even if the outlook for us is not very favourable, it is much worse with the others, and especially with Russia. The war will not end for want of money.

The times when Hindenburg could get his way against Falkenhayn are long past. Time has taken the trumps out of his hand. The times have changed, the times of our Great Deeds are long past, and also the times of Falkenhayn's grosser blunders— viz. Ypres, etc. I do not see how the situation can possibly change under the present Emperor. It is involved in the system. They all hold together and support each other. His Majesty has no notion of the position.

I don't much approve of an understanding between Ludendorff and the Crown Prince. There would have been no object whatever in a visit from Ludendorff, and it would only give the other side ground for suspicion. In the first place, the Crown Prince's entourage take an even more extraordinary view of the state of affairs; further, the Crown Prince is completely under the thumb of the Chief of his General Staff, Knobelsdorff, who is on the worst possible terms with Ludendorff. Besides, what is worse, he has quarrelled with everybody, even from the time he was in charge of a Staff Department.

KOVNO, *January* 10, 1916.

The Austrian attack on Montenegro from the Cattaro direction is making good progress. General Gröner, who is in charge of field railways, was here yesterday and gave us some news of the general situation. The attack on Salonika is to come next. The difficulty is not so much a question of railways and supplies: it is a matter of politics. The railway up to the Greek frontier is ready. On the other hand the Austrians and the Bulgarians cannot agree. The Austrians, of course, began by being quite idiotic again, and actually claimed the Negotin district—*i.e.* the southern bank of the Danube south of the Iron Gates—for themselves, and intended to bestow on the Rumanians only a small strip of Macedonia. Now the Bulgarians are being difficult and claiming more and more. At present, not only the whole Negotin district, but the Morava Valley—*i.e.* the most fertile part of Serbia —has been assigned to them. Now the quarrel is over the Morava railway, which the Austrians will not let out of their hands.

We are trying to mediate, and Falkenhayn has been several times in Belgrade and Budapest about the matter. In my opinion the Bulgarians are right.

January 11, 1916.

Yesterday we had a crowd of guests at dinner. Our representatives on the governments of Lithuania and Kurland have been staying here for the last few days, and a few officials from Berlin have also arrived. It was very interesting to hear everyone's point of view. Yet I am actually none the wiser, for not one of them could contribute anything definite or new.

As to the question of supplies, it is only as regards

oats that the position is serious. Until the harvest we are short by more than 1,000,000 tons, and the communications with Rumania are so defective (railways are deficient and the Danube is not really navigable at the Iron Gates) that we import from there only 600,000 tons at the most in the next four months. We shall then be in for a real shortage, an experience we knew nothing of last year. However, we shall manage somehow. It is amazing how there is only one opinion of Delbrück's incompetence and disgraceful conduct, and yet it does not seem possible to get rid of the fellow.

The Austrian attack on Montenegro is moving slowly but surely forwards. It seems to be gradually dawning on the Montenegrins that they may go the same way as the Serbians.

January 16, 1916.

Even in our prison camps there is not one useless mouth. All the prisoners who are fit for work are working, and from all sides comes the cry: "Make prisoners; we want still more prisoner-battalions." But even with everyone digging and sowing we could not have got through. Apart from this, every possible acre has been cultivated in the German Empire and in the occupied territories. Most unfortunately the harvest of 1915 was the greatest failure that we have had for forty-four years. The yield was about 2,500,000 tons less than was expected. That is bad luck, and we must see how we can struggle through. This unfortunate fact is not very apparent from the newspapers.

January 24, 1916.

I have crawled through all the trenches and told the people in the dug-outs some news for which they were suitably grateful. The mud is terrible.

On the third day of my journey it began to thaw, the trenches were under water and everything was floating. The men were continually pumping the water out of the dug-outs, which are built on piles, but it was no use. And yet in spite of all this I was astonished at the extraordinarily cheerful spirit that I found everywhere. With the softening of the snow the car kept on breaking down, and we had to force our way forward with constant pushing and towing. One day I used six cars and eleven sledges to make my round; but in our billets in the evening they all wanted to be told what things looked like in the great world. I had nothing new to tell them, but the mere sight of a new face is a diversion to men who must move in a narrow daily round.

January 25, 1916.

The position in Greece is this: it would suit us best if they remained neutral; worst, if they joined us. In the latter event the English would instantly occupy all the Greek islands and thus create pledges which we should have to redeem with parts of Belgium and France. They are consequently using every dodge they can to drive Greece in on our side. Our Foreign Office has to do everything they can to prevent them joining us.

January 26, 1916.

Nothing special here. We have received a very interesting report from Russia. The majority of the population are war-weary, but the Tsar, however, is the soul of the war, and is by no means so insignificant as has been assumed. The disarming of Montenegro is proceeding according to plan. For the rest the Russians have apparently given up their attacks on the Bukovina frontier and are now collecting their forces in front of the Southern Army for an attack there. That is a mixed army of Austrians and Germans, and I feel no anxiety about the event.

January 27, 1916.

The situation in Montenegro is now clear. Nikita, in person, has withdrawn to the Entente, Mirko has taken refuge with the Austrian Army, and the army is capitulating. In this way nothing can go wrong. If the Entente wins, Nikita will come back to the throne; if the Central Powers win, Mirko will be King of a greater Montenegro.

January 29, 1916.

We thought something was going to happen, but we were mistaken. However, there was no quarrel —just nothing at all. No one knows why Exzellenz von Falkenhayn took the trouble to go to Lida and ordered Ludendorff to meet him there. He wanted information about the position, the morale and health of his army — and that was all. Either G.H.Q. has no important plans for the future, or, if so, they hardly think enough of them to tell us what they are. Ludendorff mentioned my idea of an offensive across the Düna, but this was rejected for the present. Otherwise all was amiable and pleasant.

January 30, 1916.

Nothing new on the East Front. The Russians seem to be collecting all the troops and heavy artillery that they can manage to move in front of the Southern Army (Linsingen), so as to try to make another decisive attack in that part. There are now 5-6 German and Austrian Divisions in reserve down there, and in all human calculation they cannot possibly be driven back. From the other Fronts we hear little or nothing. We have just got another gas regiment, and I find myself wondering how we can provide it with an opportunity to carry out its agreeable duties.

February 2, 1916.

I have been labouring all the morning over a mighty work which the Chief is to submit to G.H.Q. I should like to win another victory. For weeks past I have been trying to convince people that we can win a great success at Riga if G.H.Q. will give us the necessary troops. It is of course clear that there is no tactical necessity for an attack in that part. Moreover, it will probably not decide the war in our favour, but after all it will bring us in 100,000 prisoners and carry our left wing forward to the Peipus Lake. If, however, G.H.Q. is collecting all available forces for a blow in the West—the decisive point—or if they think they will bring Rumania in on our side by an attack in Galicia (which I doubt), then they will strike at one of those two points, and we shall get nothing. But if a decisive action in the West is impossible, etc., and if they want to go on waiting about doing nothing, and wasting time and men in useless small enterprises, then in the late spring, when the fodder shortage makes itself felt in Germany, the moment will come when the people will want another victory. I can provide it—if we can have another 7 or 8 Divisions. Whether the proposal succeeds—that is, whether Falkenhayn will sanction it—I don't know: at all events I have set my military conscience at rest by calling attention to the opportunity.

February 3, 1916.

Our Foreign Office is delighted with Rumania. The import of corn, as well as other questions, is satisfactorily settled. These alarmist rumours were nonsense. On the other hand there are further difficulties with the Americans. They really are shameless. Our people think that we must give way because the money-market could not stand a rupture with America. Partly in consequence of this, and partly as a reply to the *Baralong*, the U-boat war and the Zeppelin attacks are to be energetically pressed against England in March. I do not know why they were ever stopped. Probably some notion of H.M.'s. The latest news in high politics is that Tirpitz and Falkenhayn have met. Who will come to grief as a result of it is a pleasing speculation. The reference in the Speech from the Throne in the *Landstag* to a reorganization of the Prussian franchise is explained as an attempt on the part of the Imperial Chancellor to conciliate the parties of the Left so as to protect himself against the Tirpitz-Falkenhayn alliance.

February 4, 1916.

My discourse of yesterday in the presence of old Kessel and Kröcher was a complete success. I simply detailed all the occasions on which we made sensible proposals to G.H.Q. and were turned down. The Field-Marshal himself was unmistakably struck. . . . At the end I tried to interest the two of them, each of whom has a large and influential following, in my Düna offensive. In the meantime my scheme has gone up to Falkenhayn. For the moment he can't, of course, do anything for us, being actually engaged in an offensive against Verdun. I hope they may apply their minds to the matter a bit later—in May, perhaps —and gradually get used to the idea. In any case I feel at ease in my conscience.

February 6, 1916.

Incidentally, Keller, who has been to see his sick wife, brought the news that Falkenhayn is to be Chancellor. In my view this means that he is firmly convinced that all is going well, otherwise he would have let the others bear the odium.

February 11, 1916.

Knobelsdorff, at present Chief of Staff with the Crown Prince, will probably succeed Falkenhayn. I would prefer Ludendorff. However, it is better for us that he should stay here. Owing to considerations of age I could not succeed him (Eisenhart is older than I am), and I should then probably have to look out for another job, as I should not be able to work with a new chief. My position here with Ludendorff has been a far too independent one for that.

February 14, 1916.

Generally speaking, Staff officers may not be promoted out of turn. Falkenhayn has broken through this tradition in the case of three of his people—Pappen, Gröner and Seekt—mainly from a desire to emphasize how much more important and splendid were their services to the Fatherland than ours. At least it seems that Eichhorn, who asked that his Chief of Staff, Hell, might be promoted General out of his turn, gave some such explanation. Prince Oskar's wound was certainly a piece of carelessness. Eichhorn was visiting the positions of one of the Divisions of the XL. Corps. They were imprudent enough to walk along the fire trenches in a compact body. The Russians, of course, opened on them with artillery fire. As a result Lieutenant-Colonel Mengelbier, Chief of Staff of the XL. Corps, was unfortunately killed, and Hell and Prince Oskar slightly wounded. I saw them both on the following day. Mengelbier I knew very well — we were at the same time Divisional General Staff officers with the I. Corps —he was with the 37th Division. The Prince got a graze on the ear and a bruise on the hip, and Hell three scratches on the head.

I had a long interesting letter from Thiel. He favours an offensive against Livonia. He is working on Swedish propaganda. I shall write to him that if he can only get us a few Divisions and some heavy artillery he can have all Livonia.

February 15, 1916.

In the West it is apparently still raining, and nothing can happen as long as the bad weather goes on. They need dry weather for the new gas-artillery.[1]

February 16, 1916.

I have recently spoken to hundreds of men on the Fronts of three armies. I have sat with them in their dug-outs—alone, without their officers— and everywhere I have heard nothing but praise for the commissariat. I always say that Hindenburg has sent me to see how they are getting on and whether they are in need of anything: they all become confidential, but I have never heard a single complaint. Some did say they would like some leave, but that was all—not a word about ill-treatment either. Of course there is solid drill these days, and the men are better and more thoroughly trained than in the times of pressure; but it was high time too. There have also been deserters—Alsatians to a man. We had a number of unreliable Alsatian and Lorraine troops over

[1] The attack on Verdun had to be continuously postponed on account of bad weather. It began on February 21st.

here. But all that is months ago. It is quite untrue that there were any deserters in the Dünaburg area.

February 17, 1916.

The Imperial Chancellor has again defeated the conservative attack on him. He went to G.H.Q. and returned with the assurance of H.M.'s fullest confidence. That was what made him so truculent. The suspension of the Economy Committee of the House of Deputies was unquestionably his right, and in itself correct: but the subsequent published statement was a piece of folly — it was merely flogging a dead horse.

February 28, 1916.

I have read a very interesting discussion of the U-boat war by von Tirpitz. He guarantees that England will be forced to make peace in six months if everything is torpedoed without regard to America and the Neutrals. If that is so, then he can go ahead, but we shall have to reckon with America as well.

March 2, 1916.

Things are at a standstill at Verdun owing to the powerful French counter-attack and the delay in getting up our artillery. G.H.Q. is confident; they are waiting for Verdun to fall. That would undoubtedly be a great success—calculated to destroy the ineradicable French belief in victory. I hope our people may prove to be right.

March 4, 1916.

There seems to be a high political crisis over the question of America. Zimmermann is of the opinion that we have had enough U-boats to carry the thing through, and on that account he is unwilling to depart from the position set forth in the last Note—and on that hypothesis he is, in my opinion, right. It seems that losses at Verdun have not hitherto been great—indeed, from some points of view, actually small — and the influential people are full of hope for a successful issue.

March 6, 1916.

Deliveries from Rumania are at present punctual and good. We owe it to the energy of our Inspector-General of Field Railways, General Gröner, that the carrying capacity of the Hungarian railways and the Danube transport has been doubled, and that in the month of February double the January amount of maize, barley, etc., was imported from Rumania—*i.e.* about 170,000 tons. Whether we can still increase the amount, which would be very desirable, I do not know. Rumania would gladly send us more in spite of the English purchases. They have two years' harvest to dispose of, and could export about 5,000,000 truck-loads, while the English order was only for 80,000 trucks.

It is certainly true that our Army Reports on Verdun were not very inspired. The G.H.Q. view is that hopes should not be raised too high, and the papers should be prevented from publishing too much nonsense. In spite of this the papers insist on talking about a break-through, etc. What we feel is that if we actually succeed in taking Verdun, but don't break the line, the English and French Press will turn our victory into a failure, as there was no " break-through." Hence this careful and restrained phraseology.

March 11, 1916.

Our G.H.Q. seems to have been rather to blame over Fort Vaux.[1] It seems that it was never in our

[1] The attack on Fort Vaux on March 6th was pushed right up to the fortifications, but at the last moment was brought to a standstill by French flanking-fire from Danloup and the Vaux ravine. The hasty report of the capture of the fort proved incorrect.

hands—at least so the French persist in maintaining. Whether the troops were mistaken and, having occupied some other fortified position, reported in good faith that they had captured Fort Vaux, or whether G.H.Q. was too optimistic and anticipated the event, is not quite clear. In any case, it is an unfortunate affair. The only advantage is that, if we were never inside it, we could not have been driven out of it, and cannot have had heavy losses. G.H.Q. continues cheerful and confident. No further news.

March 12, 1916.

I am doubtful about these rumours of peace by September. There is, I do not doubt, a desire and intention to come to terms with the French, but I don't see how anyone can speak of it to-day, and fix a date.

As to the officers in Wiesbaden, I take rather a different point of view. The Bulgarians behave so discourteously to our officers in Bulgaria that it does our Bulgarian comrades in Wiesbaden a great deal of good to be shown their proper place. As regards the Austrians, no one can expect a German officer who has to fight in their company to love them. One of these days, the next time a man from the War Ministry is here, I will make inquiries on the subject.

The Kaiser is, of course, in the West. The Imperial Chancellor is still at G.H.Q. and seems to have got his way over the U-boat question. He wants the U-boat campaign carried on as it was in the year 1915—*i.e.* that the enemy ships should be hailed and their crews given the chance of getting off in the boats; neutral ships to be sunk only if carrying contraband. Tirpitz would sink every ship approaching the English coast, without challenge or warning. The latter course, if he had enough U-boats, would of course force England to make peace in a few months. As he has not, he must inevitably involve us in war with all the Neutrals, and that would be too much even for me. So I hope they will be reasonable.

March 14, 1916.

It seems that the Russians have been planning an attack against us, and I am wondering whether we should bring up our Reserves by railway or not. As the Chief is away, the decision rests with me alone. On the one hand, I don't want to show too much anxiety, if I move the troops too soon; on the other, I am responsible for seeing that they arrive at the right time. I have all in readiness, but I shall certainly take no steps to-day. We have got so unused to the idea of responsible decisions that I am almost a little excited. What suggests a Russian attack is the fact that the French will, of course, urge that something should be done. The Italians also began a fresh attack on the Isonzo Front—of course with no success. The Chancellor has apparently won a complete victory over the U-boat question: Tirpitz departs. I cannot weep over him. If he had built more U-boats and fast cruisers, and fewer battleships for Naval Reviews, we should have been in a better position to-day.

March 16, 1916.

The report about Vaux was an error—we never got into the place and, consequently, were never turned out of it. As G.H.Q. had announced the storming of the fort with so much jubilation they would not contradict themselves, and lied about it. I should have thought it better and more practical to admit the mistake without more ado. The result is that everyone thinks our losses in the affair were enormous.

March 17, 1916.

There is a violent conflict of opinion over the question of the U-boat campaign. Tirpitz seems to have used every possible means to get his way, and incidentally to have made terms with the Bavarian, Hertling. He is to be Imperial Chancellor, and in return the King of Bavaria is to support Tirpitz. Whether all this is true remains to be seen, but these are the stories going about Berlin. It seems that Falkenhayn has allied himself rather closely with Tirpitz, and as a result of the Chancellor's victory, and sundry other matters, his position with H.M. is somewhat shaken.

March 19, 1916.

The Russians have attacked very strongly at more than one point, and until now have been beaten off everywhere with heavy losses.[1] In front of the XXI. Corps alone 9270 Russians dead, lying in front of their own lines, were counted from our positions. We have not yet needed to bring up any of our Reserves, and our own losses are amazingly slight—about 560 men, up till now. So we await developments with equanimity.

[1] The German attack at Verdun produced attacks on the other Entente Fronts, designed to relieve the strain.
   The Russians began to attack in March. The main attack came off between the Visnieff and Narocz lakes, and in the neighbourhood of Postavy. The object of it apparently was to envelop and drive in with flanks of the German XXI. Army Corps and so make an opening for a break-through on a larger scale towards Vilna and Kovno. Other attacks, by way of diversions, took place in the Vidzy area (south of Dünaburg), at Dünaburg and Jakobstadt. After heavy drum fire, mass attacks by the Russian infantry were launched on March 15th, March 18th-21st, and on March 26th there was danger for a time between the two lakes and near Postavy, but this was happily averted.

WAR DIARIES

The news from the West sounds good. There is progress at Verdun, though it is slow. We have no details, but I was informed to-day that the army in the West is in magnificent form.

We happen to have a naval officer at Headquarters who is here on duty. He gave us some very interesting information about the U-boat campaign, and gave me the numbers of the boats now on service, and those that have been lost; and I am only confirmed in my opinion that the Chancellor is right and Tirpitz wrong. However, that does not prevent Tirpitz making propaganda for himself and his U-boat campaign, and getting questions asked in the Reichstag, in a way that almost amounts to high treason.

March 20, 1916.

Tirpitz wants all ships that approach the English coast to be torpedoed without warning, whatever they are, enemy or neutral vessels. That would unquestionably be the best method of bringing England down, and the Foreign Office agrees, but we have not enough boats to manage it. Moreover, as a result, we should unquestionably have to declare war on all Neutrals—America, Holland, Denmark and Rumania. Added to which, the Turks and the Bulgarians would probably break away. This would be too much for us, and we must consequently impose limitations on the U-boat campaign such as we announce in our Note to America. However regrettable the matter may be —presupposing that we have, in fact, too few boats I believe that the standpoint of the Foreign Office is correct. The essential point is the number of U-boats, and that I do not know.

Yesterday and the night before there was heavy fighting at several points on the XXI. Corps Front.

The Russians, with their usual indifference to losses, kept on hurling masses of men against our positions. I estimate their losses at 50,000-60,000 at least. We have hitherto had to bring up one regiment only from our very strong Reserves.

March 22, 1916.

Yesterday the Russians made another furious attack. Unfortunately one of our Divisions was driven back. Two regiments broke and, of course, suffered severely. As might have been supposed, it was one of the Western Divisions — a Baden Reserve Division. The Russians will, of course, hurl themselves with redoubled force at the point where they have scored a success. We at once sent one of our good Divisions into the gap. Another good Division is arriving by rail to-day—at least, the first part of it. Personally I feel no anxiety whatever about the battle. Still, it is little failures of this kind that particularly get on one's nerves.

March 23, 1916.

The Foreign Office and Bethmann say that we have not enough U-boats to go through with it, that we should foolishly and to no purpose bring the Neutrals about our ears, and that this would be more than we could cope with. One could only decide which side was right if one knew the number and the capacity of the U-boats. According to the information put before me we have not enough. I am, consequently, on Bethmann's side in this matter, and I consider Tirpitz's conduct is a public danger, and the attacks of the parties in the Reichstag are, in my opinion, something like high treason. It is true that Bethmann is not suited to the position of Chancellor. If it is thought best to supersede him, let it be done, but the people should not be allowed to get in such a state of irritation over a question of national defence. They, of course, believe that we had 200 U-boats, and that refusal to go on with the campaign was simply Government imbecility, or, as someone wrote to me yesterday: " International High Finance has won, we are not to be allowed to destroy England." People are really too idiotic—nothing can be done with them. Bethmann will carry on the U-boat campaign on the same lines as before. It was incredibly stupid of our Government to allow the newspapers to start all this business about the " U-boat war of annihilation."

May 4, 1916.

There seems to be a deadlock before Verdun, which is, of course, not pleasant. It is mainly due to the bad planning of the operation and poor leadership.

May 7, 1916.

The Austrian offensive against the Italians seems to have petered out. Fleischmann is beside himself over the incompetence of the leadership on that Front. They were all ready a month ago and waiting only for good weather. Then the Italians attacked at the Col di Lana, and various other points — nothing of any importance — but the Austrian Government got nervous, and actually brought up strong reinforcements to the points in question. As a result of this idiotic marching to and fro, the Divisions involved really suffered as much damage by their exertions in the mountains as if they had been through a bigger campaign than the one they were about to start.

May 10, 1916.

The American reply seems—at least, as reported in the Reuter telegram—a gross piece of impertinence. The fellow would probably treat Mexico with greater courtesy.

May 12, 1916.

From the West we hear of various changes in the commands. Among others, some Chiefs of Staff are to be superseded. Falkenhayn is apparently looking for scapegoats for his own and Tappen's failures.

May 22, 1916.

The situation here is unchanged. I see it stated that as a result of the creation of special authorities for the distribution of food in Germany there is a general belief abroad that Germany will be done for by the autumn at the latest. The Russians think, consequently, they need attack no more, as starvation will settle our business for them. Well, that is all to the good. The Austrian offensive progresses favourably. I think it by no means unlikely that the Italians will squeal so loudly that the Russians will find themselves compelled to start an offensive in Galicia to relieve them. In that case they will probably move some of the troops accumulated on our Front down farther south. Then perhaps we shall be able to get something done, even without G.H.Q.

May 23, 1916.

I have not yet read anything about the change of feeling in America, but I do not place much reliance on it. The most important event of the moment is the excellent progress of the Austrian offensive in Italy. In my opinion, it will inevitably have the effect of making the Russians attack either us or in Galicia. For the latter purpose they will have to move troops down from here. In either event we shall have something to do, and get rid of our boredom.

Whether the choice of Batocki was a good one remains to be seen. He is certainly a clever man, but quite unpractical in many respects. Besides, I have the impression that there are too many heads in the Food Ministry to allow of exact and smooth administration.

May 24, 1916.

I have a distinct feeling that the Russians are moving troops away from our Front, probably to the south against the Austrians, but I cannot yet prove it. Perhaps they will so redistribute their strength that we shall be able to start another show.[1] I hope that in any case the Austrians will not allow themselves to be influenced. The Italian operation is progressing excellently at present. The Italians seem to be simply fading away. Otherwise the capture of such enormous numbers of guns compared with so small a number of prisoners can hardly be explained. The moment Cadorna evacuates the Isonzo, so as to avoid being cut off, that will mean a decisive Italian defeat.

May 26, 1916.

In Italy the offensive has come to a temporary standstill in consequence of the snow, at least on

[1] In dealing with this point in *The War of Lost Opportunities* Hoffmann writes : " The most desirable point of attack for us would have been Riga. But we could not have managed this with our own forces. . . . If G.H.Q. had been in the position to place six more Divisions at our disposal it would have been possible to carry this plan into effect. It offered the prospect not only of destroying the Riga bridge-head, but of developing into a notable blow against the Russian Army. . . ."
General von Falkenhayn refused the request for the transference of the Divisions.

one of the Austrian wings. However, I think this rather fortunate, as it gives time for the rear formations, more especially ammunition and supplies, to come up. On our Front it certainly looks as if our Russian friends contemplated an attack, at one point only, but in great force. Well, I don't mind, we are prepared for everything.

May 27, 1916.

He will arrive on Monday evening.[1] His arrival will be followed by an address of welcome, a dinner, and then he will depart. I don't think the pronouncement that will doubtless follow is likely to prelude any radical changes — *i.e.* any fresh appointments to responsible positions—or at least I venture to hope not. I doubt if the idea for an offensive that was originally put forward by me will go through without objection. It depends on whether the West can help us. It will not be possible to break off the operation at Verdun, nor indeed could we advise it, and whether they have something else in mind I do not at present know. In any case I am all on the stretch. I am up to the eyes in work, as all the arrangements for H.M.'s safety and reception fall on me, apart from the fact that I am working out the speech that the Field-Marshal is to make.

May 29, 1916.

I share Kapp's views about Batocki: I consider his selection was a mistake. Gröner is very able— it is possible he will get the control into his own hands.

Here we are all in a state of feverish activity for this evening. The hope that Falkenhayn would

[1] H.M. the Kaiser was expected in Kovno to visit the district under the command of the C.-in-C., East.

WAR DIARIES

not come with him has failed—he is coming. Only Tappen is staying in the West. After what has happened at Verdun they cannot all travel about the country. I don't anticipate much from the visit. It looks more like an attempt to get a little change and distraction. Besides us, it is proposed to visit all the Army Commanders, and they will all of them have to make speeches. So as to avoid any nonsense, I sent for all four G.S.O.,Ia's, of the armies yesterday, explained to them what will be said here, and got them to tell me what their Commanders wanted to talk about. I'm against any surprises. So far all seems correct. We shall be rather short of food in our villa, as the Royal train alone is bringing sixteen visitors.

May 30, 1916.

A very pleasant visit, which went off excellently, but from a military and political point of view quite futile. There was a great reception at the railway station, then we drove through the prettily decorated streets to our quarters. Speech by the Field-Marshal. Present: H.M., the Field-Marshal, Ludendorff, I, Falkenhayn, General von Lyncker, and Chelius — representing Plessen. Everything possible was said in support of an advance on our Front. Whereupon Falkenhayn replied before H.M. spoke, and explained that, though our idea was certainly good, the operation on the West must be fought out first. If all that H.M. and Falkenhayn said is a correct statement of the present situation then they are right, and we must acquiesce. How far it is so, it is of course impossible to judge. I spoke to the officers of the Operations Section who were there, but unfortunately too briefly to get any insight into the position. However, they assured me that the situation in the West was good. Our losses before Verdun are heavy, but those of the French are much heavier. The English are continually growing stronger, but do not show any inclination to attack. In any case we must have strong Reserves there to cope with an English attack.

June 2, 1916.

Here the position is still unchanged. South of Smorgon the Russians are pushing forward, but they have not yet attacked. The suspense makes one a little nervous—will they or won't they?

There is of course great enthusiasm over the naval battle.[1] According to the German report the English have lost more than 100,000 tons, and we about 20,000. I am of course very excited to see the English report. Probably they will deny everything as usual.

June 3, 1916.

Well, the English admit their heavy losses in the naval battle, with the exception of the *Warspite.* The latter point is so far interesting in that the *Warspite* is one of the larger modern battleships, and they want so to distort the story of the battle as to make it appear that we came into action only with their cruisers, and when their heavy ships appeared we broke off the fight. In this way the confidence of the English people in the superiority of their ships of the line may remain unshaken. I hope our Admiralty may be able to produce definite proof of the loss of this vessel.

If it were feasible, an early attack by our fleet would be an excellent thing, so as to show the world that we were not much damaged.

Yesterday we had news from the Western Front

[1] The battle of the Skager-Rack was fought on May 31st.

that Fort Vaux had been taken.[1] I am anxious to know whether this is all right—*i.e.* whether they have really got it—for my information comes from the Operations Section; the question is merely whether the French have surrendered it to us. This would of course make a great moral impression.

The Italians are wringing their hands and crying for help—they do appear to be in a bad way. Now of course it will be for the Russians to effect a diversion. The simplest way of doing so would be a strong Russian attack on the Rumanian frontier. They would perhaps be prepared for this —only they have all their Reserves, or, comparatively speaking, the main part of them, here on our Front. The difficult question for them now is —shall they entrain part of them again and send them south against the Austrians or shall they attack us? In any case, the question is urgent and must soon be decided.

June 6, 1916.

We had a damper to-day again, after all the recent encouraging military successes. The Austrians have got another thrashing from the Russians in the neighbourhood of Rovno. Linsingen, in whose Army Group the affair happened, has sent a furious report. . . . It seems that the entire Russian Reserves are on our Front, and in Galicia the Austrians have the superiority in numbers. . . . It is a raging scandal. Wails for help, of course, from Teschen to Mézières, and an inquiry from them: " What can you let us have ? " We can't let them have anything with a good conscience, all we can do is to help them out for the time being. And, even so, we shall have to apply to the West

[1] Fort Vaux was stormed on June 2nd; the fighting in and about the fort lasted till June 7th, when the garrison, which had been buried underground, capitulated.

to fill up our gaps. . . . Well, once more we shall have to manage somehow.[1]

June 7, 1916.

It is always the same story: the 4th Austrian Army retires as soon as it is attacked. As it is under the command of an Archduke nothing can be done. The disaster is of course merely local. Meantime the necessary Reserves are on their way to repair the damage.

Kapp has just sent me his Memorandum against the Imperial Chancellor. It contains a great deal that is right, especially as regards the food question, but is so aggressive that one cannot be surprised that the Chancellor has defended himself pretty savagely. The other pamphlet which the Chancellor inveighs against is an anonymous and destructive attack on our entire foreign policy for the last twenty years. It is nominally directed against the Chancellor, but it is indirectly intended for H.M.

June 9, 1916.

The Russians are themselves so astounded at their victory that they came to a halt yesterday, and

[1] The general Entente attack on the Germans was timed to begin on July 6th, in the West on the Somme, and in the East on the Baranowiczi—Smorgon sector. The main Russian attack there was to be supported by subsidiary attacks at Riga, Luck, Tarnopol, and on the Dniester.
 The effect of the situation in Italy was that the intended Russian subsidiary attacks on the Russo-Hungarian were launched prematurely. When, on June 4th, the Russians attacked the 4th Austrian Army at Luck and the 7th Austrian Army in the Bukovina, both gave way without putting up any serious resistance. Luck had been already taken by the Russians on June 7th. On the 13th their advance-guards reached the Stochod, S.E. of Kovel. In the Bukovina, after the capture of Czernovitz, their advance reached the line Dniester—Kolomea—Kimpolung. This success led to the alteration of the Russian plan of operations. In order to exploit their success, the Russians moved strong Reserves to the south, but in spite of that they remained strong enough to attack on their other Fronts. On June 13th a heavy attack was launched against Woyrsch's Army Group at Baranowiczi: and secondary attacks took place at the Narocz Lake, Smorgon, Dünaburg, and the Riga bridge-head.
 G.H.Q. had to make up their minds to withdraw strong forces from the West so as to re-establish the position in the East. This was all the more difficult as the Entente attack on the Somme was then awaited.

have done nothing since. In the interval the troops we sent have had time to come up. I think the situation will soon be put right again.

June 11, 1916.

Hard at work to-day again over the affairs of our honoured allies. We are, of course, sending all the help we possibly can. The amusing thing is that probably no one could be more astonished at the victory than the Russians themselves. As before, they were preparing their main attack against us up here in the north. In the south, on the Austrian Front, it was considered only as a demonstration on a large scale. Unfortunately the Austrians misunderstood the affair. Our own G.H.Q. must bear part of the blame. They should never have withdrawn all the German troops from the Austrian Front. We were needed to keep them steady. The chief disaster is the break-through at Luck: and this, I hope, will be put straight again in a few days. The chief culprit, the Archduke, who was in command, has at last been superseded. His successor is a Hungarian general with an unintelligible name.[1]

June 12, 1916.

The position here is still unchanged and the great Austrian *débâcle* at Luck shows signs of improvement. There are so many German troops there by this time, and others on the way, that there seems no more need for anxiety at that point. This is of importance to us in so far as any further retirement on the part of Linsingen's Army Group would have affected the position of Woyrsch and the 9th Army, and then we should have been in the soup. This danger is now over. . . . What is tragic, or rather

---

[1] General von Tertszczanski.

tragi-comic, is that our G.H.Q. is cheerfully releasing more troops to help the Austrians than we needed for our offensive.

June 14, 1916.

The reinforcements are on their way to the Austrians: part of them are already there, and then we shall gradually have everything in order again. The Rumanians have now loyally announced that they will disarm the Russians that cross the frontier, but I rather think that if the Russians cross the Rumanian border with strong forces Bratianu will content himself with a protest on paper.

June 16, 1916.

G.H.Q. wants a long statement of the Field-Marshal's opinion on the situation, so I had to set to and write it and leave everything else aside. . . . The position here unchanged. As regards the Austrians the counter-measures we have arranged take time and we must accordingly have patience. The Austrian defeat is not, of course, agreeable, but we must not pull all our hair out at once.

June 19, 1916.

As the situation stands at present, the Austrians could not hold Czernovitz, so they had much better give it up instead of losing 100,000 more men over it. For we could not help them there. There are no railways to those parts, or rather only one little single-track line, on which reinforcements could not be brought up quickly.

The whole situation on the Eastern Front is as follows. The Russians have planned a great offensive, probably in conjunction with the French and English—and certainly against us. On the French

Front, Verdun has intervened, where the French Army is gradually being destroyed. Whether the English are still for it, or whether they will not venture after the recent battles at Ypres, still remains to be seen. In any case the Russians had collected their main forces, about 76 Divisions, on our Front. The Austrians, suspecting nothing, had over-confidently withdrawn too many troops from their line and sent them to Italy. Our G.H.Q. made the same mistake, and likewise withdrew the majority of the German troops that were on the Austrian Front and sent them to the West.

Why the Russians did not carry out their plan I do not know. However, it is very flattering to us that, in spite of a three- and fourfold superiority, they did not venture to attack us. What they did do was—urged by Italy, they collected such forces as they could on the Austrian Front and made a purely local attack. . . . The Russian success was so great that they said to themselves: " We don't want to take any risk with those damned Germans: we had much better bring our Reserves down south and make the most of our victory." This is what they must have thought, for they have been marching off from our Front as fast as they could go for the last forty-eight hours.

The Austrian Front is now supported on all sides —the Austrians themselves, by our G.H.Q. and by us. At Luck we succeeded in getting them to hold on and, at certain points, to counter-attack: farther south, especially in the Czernovitz district, nothing could be done, as I have said before, simply owing to the nature of the railways. We can only help them considerably farther back. Naturally, this is a great moral encouragement to our enemies, but it is not without its advantages. The Austrians had become so conceited that there was no speaking to them. So we must wait patiently; it will all come right in the end.

June 20, 1916.

In the Kapp Memorandum the main line of attack is, as before, the U-boat policy. People are stupid about this—we have not got the boats, unfortunately, and without them the desired results cannot follow.

June 21, 1916.

On many points I am in entire agreement with Kapp, but not on the U-boat question. On the latter point the general conclusions are wrong. If, at the beginning of the war, we had had our present number of U-boats, and if, before the English had organized their defensive measures, we had declared an energetic U-boat blockade of England, and had carried it through, then it was feasible. Now, what with mines and net barricades, the arming of thousands of fishing-boats and patrol-vessels, the organization of flotillas with drag-nets, the situation has become much more difficult for the U-boats. No boat can come up in the neighbourhood of the English coast without being at once attacked on all sides. The U-boat campaign must, consequently, be transferred to the high seas, and for that purpose we want many more boats than the trifling number that Kapp and the conservatives assume to be necessary.

We knew that the English Fleet, or at any rate part of it, was at sea. Our entire fleet does not go out to catch a few merchant ships. As a result of bad leadership the English suffered very heavy losses in the first engagement, so that the decision of our Admiral to break off the battle after he had received a report that another English squadron was coming up, which threatened to cut off our retreat, is open to question. The English, in fact, did nothing, and we could perhaps have fallen upon this fresh squadron with all our strength. However, criticism after the event is easy, and there are no precedents for naval battles. It was a German success, and a great success—this is unquestionable, even if it is not quite the victory that it was first made out to be. Only those ships whose names have now been published were lost. Of course there is also a great deal of damage, part of which will take months to repair. However, we have certain information that the number of English ships needing repair is very much greater. There is only one point in the whole sea-fight that I do not understand: what was the entire English fleet doing in that neighbourhood? In any case, they must have been intending some great coup, which beyond question failed.

June 22, 1916.

We are still to send troops to the south, and I had to get them on the move. The Russians seem, in fact, to have given up any idea of an offensive against us, and are sending all the troops they can down south. We are making progress at Luck, but slowly, as our people have to do all the work. We are quite strong enough there now. We must get the position straight at Luck first before we begin to think of Czernovitz. In the West we are waiting in complete confidence for the English attack. Whether the French are going to make a simultaneous offensive at some other point remains to be seen, but I do not think so.

June 29, 1916.

Willi Solf rang me up yesterday. He wants to come here and deliver his speech about our future

Colonial policy. It seems no one wants him, and I am sure we don't want to listen to some pessimistic lucubration. He is still dreaming of an understanding with England, and wants colonies without a big fleet—that is, more or less by England's favour.

June 30, 1916.

Well, I got the Field-Marshal to sanction Solf's visit. He is to appear next Wednesday. Helfferich also had previously proposed himself. What all these people want I don't know—mainly, I suppose, the Field-Marshal's support for their policy.

July 2, 1916.

The Anglo-French offensive has begun. They have been accumulating such masses of artillery and ammunition that our line cannot help being driven in, and we cannot help losing prisoners— we must make up our minds to that.[1]

July 2, 1916.

It seems that the Chancellor has made a fresh attack on Falkenhayn. Whether he will pull it off seems to me, however, still doubtful. H.M. will surely realize that the present difficult military situation is to be ascribed to the mistakes of G.H.Q., but I hardly think he will draw the necessary conclusions and dismiss Falkenhayn. And the Chancellor is certainly not energetic enough to handle so vital a question successfully. If he does so, then Falkenhayn will fall, but Bethmann will sit firmer in the saddle than ever. For the time being, therefore, I think it would be more practical for

[1] On July 1st the Somme battle began with a powerful attempt at break-through.

Kapp to do nothing at present, because no good can result. At the moment we have, unfortunately, no other Chancellor in prospect.

It is all rather exciting. Ludendorff, of course, is very much up in the air. The only person who truly preserves an Olympian calm is the Field-Marshal.

July 4, 1916.

We're in for a devil of a business here—it would be a pleasure to be a soldier if our G.H.Q. and the Austrians were a little better. All the Russian attacks upon us were driven back without effort. Now we are scratching troops together from all possible holes and corners to send down south, where there is danger. I went home at 2 A.M. this morning and have been at the telephone again since 6.30. In the West they are well content—the English are not advancing at all, and the French gains on the Somme are not so important that they need cause any anxiety. Of course there will be heavy fighting on all Fronts in the near future—but personally I am entirely confident of the result.[1]

July 5, 1916.

With us all is in perfect order; on the other hand there is heavy fighting on our right. We are sending them everything we can spare. The idiocy of the thing is that we are not in supreme command. The Austrians were quite willing, but Falkenhayn will not allow it. Ludendorff and I have explained

[1] In the second half of June the German and Austro-Hungarian reinforcements arrived in the Luck salient, on the Dniester and in the Carpathians, and began a counter-attack, which, however, soon came to a standstill in the face of the Russian superiority in numbers.

The hard-won gains in the Luck salient had to be given up. On the Styr, to the south of the Dniester, and in the Carpathians, the Russians gained ground in the middle of July: and a serious crisis arose on the Eastern Front.

to the Field-Marshal that he must again write to
H.M., or, in other words, to the Adjutant-General
on duty, for him to report to H.M.—it can't go on
like this. I am just composing the letter. There
was an amusing incident yesterday at breakfast.
Helfferich and Lewaldt sat drivelling away about
England, etc. At last I really could not bear it
any longer and said: " We can't go on much
longer with a damned slack Government like ours;
it is beginning to stink to heaven, etc." Their
faces! Lewaldt said he supposed I had read the
Kapp Memorandum. I said I didn't need any
memorandum; my own understanding was enough.

July 6, 1916.

Solf was here yesterday and to-day. However,
he had nothing much new to tell us. Food would
hold out. There were difficulties, but they could
be overcome. Very thick with Bethmann. Still in
hopes of an understanding with England. They're
all a band of brothers when it comes to hating
Falkenhayn; but so long as it's only platonic, and
no one will take a risk, I see no possibility of
success. The Field-Marshal has actually cut out
a few passages from my very mild and courteously
expressed letter. Whether it will be allowed to go
remains to be seen.

All is in perfect order here. The Russians are
attacking at a few points and senselessly wasting
their ammunition: very slight results and a futile
loss of life. Our positions are very well constructed
and nothing has any effect on them. For example,
yesterday 4600 shells fell on one Divisional Front.
Result: one man wounded.

Our child of sorrow of the last few days—
Woyrsch's Force to the south of us—is apparently

out of its worst difficulties, thanks to the reinforcements we have sent there.

In Volhynia and Galicia prospects are not very bright in one or two places, the cause being the unreliability of the Austrians and bad leadership on the part of the Germans. There's really nothing more we can do. As long as the position down there is not really critical they won't give us the supreme command.

July 7, 1916.

As I had anticipated, the letter — after much polishing and many corrections—was not sent off; the plan was to send the letter at the same time as a demonstration by the Chancellor was to take place. Eisenhart, whom we sent to the Chancellor, has now telephoned that he—the Chancellor—has, for some reason or another, decided to do nothing for the time being, so that the whole affair is hung up.

In spite of furious Russian attacks our whole Front is in the best of good order, but the Austrians, on the other hand, are still in a mess. The proper thing would be for us to be given the supreme command on the East Front, so that we could put things straight for them. After a long conference this morning Hindenburg did at least send a short telegram in this sense to G.H.Q. It will probably be no use, but we have relieved our consciences.

July 8, 1916.

Our wire of yesterday to Lyncker actually produced some effect. The area of our command is to be probably somewhat extended, and we are to take over part of the Southern Front. Under that arrangement we shall change our quarters—perhaps to Warsaw: an idiotic thing to do.

July 11, 1916.
General Grünert was here yesterday — he was Q.M.G. with us at the beginning of the war, then Chief of Staff with the 8th and 9th Armies here in the East, and then with the 2nd Army in the West. The 2nd Army was the one involved by the Anglo-French attack. Although he had predicted the date of the coming attack, and asked for reinforcements, none—as usual—were given him. Hence the first successes of the French. He was made a scapegoat and superseded, and was given a Division here on the Eastern Front. He is pretty savage with G.H.Q.

July 14, 1916.
G.H.Q. has not actually put Linsingen and Woyrsch under our command, but something at any rate has been accomplished. Every two or three days Herr von Falkenhayn asks what we think of the position there and what arrangements we propose to make. So something is happening. It has been a truly complicated business, but we are getting there.

July 18, 1916.
There can be no sort of doubt but that the general position is serious at the moment. For the first time they are making a simultaneous attack upon us and are consequently preventing us from moving our Reserves between the two Fronts, because they are being shouted for everywhere at the same time. Still I don't think the situation is one for real anxiety. We must just hold on. Even if we lose this or that position, or have to retire a few kilometres, there is no great harm. The main thing is to keep one's head calm and clear.
On our Front the Russians began an attack

yesterday in the neighbourhood of Mitau. Up till now we have beaten off all their attacks. Early this morning I pushed up a few Reserves, and I await the outcome with confidence.

July 19, 1916.

The prevailing depression is very natural. Most people do not realize that we have not won such an unconditional victory as the Pan-German papers make out, and that we shall still have to fight hard to hold what we have won.

July 20, 1916.

The Chief's journey to Berlin was entirely superfluous. The question of the supreme command was not touched upon, and only such matters were discussed as could have been perfectly well dealt with in writing. Probably Falkenhayn wanted to give H.M. the impression that he took Hindenburg into his confidence over all operations. As a result of it all, Ludendorff came back in a pretty savage temper. He had also talked to the Chancellor, but there is nothing doing there. Falkenhayn is confident that we can hold on in the West. Our Austrian comrades are the difficulty. We shall perhaps bring a few Austrian Divisions up here and so release a few German ones.

By the middle of August our fleet will be ready for sea again; the English fleet will not be ready for some time.

July 22, 1916.

A savage amount of work here. More discussions as to the extension of the supreme command over the Austrians, or at least a part of them: but, as usual, it was all brought to nothing by some idiotic scruples.

July 23, 1916.

I have not yet had a serious conversation with the Field-Marshal about Kapp. He cares absolutely nothing about Kapp's proposals. Ludendorff agrees, as I do, with a part only of his Memorandum. What Kapp wants is to get the Field-Marshal and Ludendorff to bolster up his U-boat theory, and there I can't help him. At present, none of us here have changed our point of view on this subject: " If we have enough U-boats, well and good." If we shall have enough by the autumn I don't know. The Chancellor's inclination to treat Kapp's Memorandum with contempt, like the anonymous one, is generally disapproved. Tirpitz I don't trust an inch. His own subordinates call him " The Father of Lies," and at present there is much contention as to who has told the most lies in all the negotiations over the U-boat question—Tirpitz or Falkenhayn.

Yesterday's exchange of letters and telegrams about the extension of the supreme command was simply comic. . . . However, we gave thanks for small mercies.

July 27, 1916.

I spoke with Bockelberg, who had travelled with the Field-Marshal and Ludendorff, immediately after Kattowitz. They reached Pless about eleven o'clock, and before their reception by H.M. they had a talk with the Chancellor, who had also betaken himself to Pless. Falkenhayn visited the Austrian Headquarters at Teschen yesterday — I assume to organize the opposition to the Field-Marshal's taking over the supreme command.

The fact that the arrival of the Turks in Galicia, even before they have got here, has been so loudly proclaimed is surely rather humiliating for the Austrians. A Division is actually on the way. Enver has long wanted to increase his prestige by taking a share in the war in Europe.

It would be very desirable, if it were practicable, to stimulate the Bulgarians to greater activity, especially against the Rumanians. The King of Rumania is determined to remain absolutely neutral, Bratianu has given the strongest assurances to our Foreign Office to that effect, and the Rumanian banks have been warned, for the present at least, to reckon in their operations and speculations on the continuance of neutrality for the next six weeks. However, one would like to make sure, and if the Bulgarians appeared on the Rumanian frontier with 4 or 5 Divisions the enthusiasm of the Rumanian hooligans would be sensibly damped.

July 26, 1916.

The position as regards the Austrians is still far from satisfactory. As a result, it is not impossible that the supreme command may be transferred to us, at least as far as, and including, Linsingen's army. I only hope the Field-Marshal will not let himself in for half-compromises. In this connection I have been feeling considerable anxiety, for he has been repeating since yesterday: " Yes, what my King commands, that I must do! "

July 30, 1916.

Falkenhayn's position much shaken, ours much strengthened.

July 31, 1916.

Yesterday we took over the command of Prince Leopold's Army Group,[1] and this evening we are

[1] Hoffmann writes on this point in *The War of Lost Opportunities* : " At the end of July, Field-Marshal von Hindenburg and General Ludendorff were again ordered to General Headquarters. The difficult position on the Eastern Front called for energetic measures. In particular the fall of Brody, news of which had just arrived, silenced such trifling scruples as

going to Brest-Litovsk, there to take over Linsingen's and the 2nd Austrian Army (Lemberg). Thus we have achieved what we could. As I wrote yesterday, the Field-Marshal and Ludendorff came back very well satisfied from Pless. Falkenhayn's star is sensibly on the wane. In the conflict, which at times became rather acrimonious, between Hindenburg and Ludendorff on the one side and Falkenhayn on the other, H.M. decided throughout in favour of the former. Falkenhayn did not subsequently appear at the Imperial dinner-table, which gave rise to a general hope that he was possibly so offended that he might take his departure. Unfortunately not; but in any case our position is now very much more secure. The task of putting all that mess straight in the south is of course naturally not an easy one, but I have no doubt that we can manage it.

BREST-LITOVSK, *August 2, 1916.*

Early yesterday morning, I am glad to say, we disembarked here. It was, I think, high time. The moment we arrived we took over the command of Linsingen's Army Group and, on the following day, of the 2nd Austrian Army as well. So our command extends from south of Lemberg to the Baltic. It is fortunate that in these days one does not lead armies on horseback.

August 4, 1916.

At 3 A.M. this morning we returned from our journey to Kovel and Lemberg. Our worthy allies'

there were." They could not yet decide to make a complete job of it and extend the Front of the C.-in-C., East, as far as the Carpathians: but they did at least decide to place under his command the whole front as far as the area to the south of Brody, including Böhm-Ermolli's Army Group.

Pflanzer-Baltin's army, the Austrian 3rd Army, and the Southern Army were formed into a new Army Group, under the Archduke and Heir-Apparent Karl. The German General von Seckt was assigned to him as Chief of Staff.

prospects do not look too good. We shall have to spit on our fingers pretty smartly, but I don't doubt that we shall pull it off.

Princely receptions, of course, everywhere, with guards of honour, and all manner of flummery and banquets, etc.

August 5, 1916.

On our Front, as far as the German troops reach, all is well. Only the Austrian 2nd Army in front of Lemberg makes me anxious. I shall not be easy in my mind until we have moved German troops down there.

August 6, 1916.

The command of this gigantic Front may be a very honourable position: but I should like it better if it involved less work. And the whole thing is continually on my nerves. Added to which there is eternal friction with G.H.Q.

August 7, 1916.

Surprises are never at an end here.[1] Yesterday at midday all was in excellent order on the Front of the 2nd Austrian Army: at 2 P.M. it was reported that the Russians had attacked with superior numbers; the whole army was in retreat, position very serious, etc. We took all possible steps to help them. Report from the Austrians in the evening: position not so bad as had been thought, on no account to move from where we were that morning. Report early to-day to the effect that the Russians

[1] From 8th-10th August, Linsingen's Army Group and the left wing of Gronau's army was again attacked. There were simultaneously attacks on the Austrian 2nd Army and the Archduke Karl's Army Group. The 2nd Austrian Army was broken through. Two German Divisions just placed at the disposal of the Eastern Command by G.H.Q. had to be moved down to stop the retreat of the Austrian troops.

had broken through at so-and-so and so-and-so, situation serious, etc. The fellows lose their heads at once. If we had a German Staff and a few German Divisions down there then peace would come upon the land. However, the last few days have been rather exciting.

I had a talk yesterday with the Director-General of Railways, General Gröner, a very clever man. He has lately come from the West, and he thinks the position there is now quite secure. The heavy fighting will go on for a time, but the crisis is over. The Entente is still making the most colossal efforts to knock us out by the spring. No one is very keen on a third winter campaign. Nor—speaking frankly—am I.

The situation looks rather ominous in Rumania. The King certainly is a man of good will, but English and French gold have been assiduously working on public opinion, which makes it more essential that the Austrians shall be made to stand their ground. It is a pity that G.H.Q. does not lighten our task. Personally I am absolutely confident. If Rumania is so stupid, then the Turks and the Bulgarians must be let loose upon the land. The Rumanian Army is bad and has no ammunition. The Entente's Salonika Army is bluff.

August 8, 1916.

Not a day without some special attraction. We had our Front in tolerable order. On the Sereth, where the Russians had driven back the Imperial Army in front of Lemberg, we were going to put so many German troops into the line to-day that we should have been able to attack to-morrow: then, farther south, there was an attack on the Archduke Heir-Apparent's troops who are not under our command. Seekt, who is Chief of Staff

WAR DIARIES

there, sent up a wail for help. So we had once more to entrain a part of our Reserves and send them southwards.

August 10, 1916.

. . . If, after the war, anyone comes near me with a Nibelung's oath of fidelity and an offer to die at my side in battle, I shall certainly knock his head off. . . . In the army group of our right-hand neighbour, the Archduke Karl, there was the devil and all to pay, and we exchanged friendly telegrams. We are still sitting in a train, as the furniture from Warsaw has not arrived.

August 14, 1916.

Continual friction with the Austrians, and almost more with G.H.Q. The day before yesterday the Field-Marshal telegraphed to H.M. at our urgent request, in reply to which he received the all-gracious instructions to mind our own business. I have said to Ludendorff and Hindenburg that in my view Hindenburg must at last take the matter in hand seriously and offer the alternative: Falkenhayn or himself. But he will not. And one can do nothing but worry. The comical thing about the whole business is: G.H.Q. do everything that we telegraph them to do, but it must look as if they had done it on their own. One needs nerves like ropes. The other day I was so sick of the whole thing that I asked Ludendorff to let me go as Chief of Staff to a Corps. He over-persuaded me kindly, and I am still here.

August 15, 1916.

The position is unchanged here. The Russians are apparently still shifting troops to the south so as to make the most of their success against the

Archduke Karl. In the meantime our Staff has investigated the mistakes that were made, and has so strongly reinforced the Archduke that from to-morrow he should be able to hold his ground. Thus we are gradually getting things straight again —and the whole affair was so unnecessary. Everyone could have foreseen it weeks ago, except Herr von Falkenhayn.[1]

August 16, 1916.

Our cry of despair that something must be done has had some effect—in any case G.H.Q. came to Pless this evening. Whether enough troops can be transferred to the East in any reasonable time to drive the Russians out of the Bukovina again seems to me very doubtful. Ludendorff and I have, in fact, an idea as to how it might be done.

August 17, 1916.

Nothing new here, for continual rows and disputes with Falkenhayn are nothing new. He wants to take reinforcements from a part of our line where they cannot be spared.

The visit we projected yesterday has come to nothing, though H.M. sent his most all-gracious thanks; he does not much value our visits. When Hindenburg and Ludendorff went to Pless they carried all before them. Falkenhayn did not appear at dinner and all the world thought that he would send in his resignation. He did nothing of the kind —he let the two of them depart and then got hold of H.M. again. I can only explain it by the fact that he gave him false information about the state of affairs, and about his and our proposals. Anyhow, H.M. twice decided against us—*i.e.* he first had a

[1] Hoffmann overlooks the difficulties connected with the distribution of forces in the face of the threatened attack on the Somme.

telegram sent to the effect that we should confine our attention to our own Front, and now he has rejected our protest against Falkenhayn's decision to take a Division away from us. Ludendorff had already sent off an orderly with a request to be allowed to resign, as Hindenburg wanted to pass the thing over. It was only Ludendorff's threat of departure that moved him to ask H.M. for an interview. H.M. refused, so a long dispatch went off to him to-day. What will be done depends on the answer.

We cannot at present get Hindenburg to ask to be allowed to resign—not even by Ludendorff threatening to depart. I have had to persuade him personally that he must not, in fact, let Ludendorff go—he must, for the time being, await the answer to the letter that is to be sent off to-day.

August 21, 1916.

Heavy fighting now in progress at one point of our Front on the Stochod. For two whole days I was rather anxious, but we have now been able to bring up enough Reserves there. The Austrian Front is like a mouth full of sensitive teeth. So soon as a breeze gets up there is toothache somewhere. Otherwise, nothing special. We are trying to scratch up some troops from anywhere we can, so as to get together some new Reserves, as one never knows what the next hour may bring. The letter to H.M. went off yesterday. It will not make very much impression. It could deal only with the purely local conditions on our Front.

The vast mistakes that G.H.Q. have made, and continue to make, cannot be spoken of openly. What is done cannot be undone; to talk of them would only make the nation discontented, and no power on earth will convince H.M., when he has once agreed to an operation, that it is wrong.

Verdun, for instance. The attack on Verdun was right if it was successful. But when it became obvious that the French were staking everything on holding it, and when it began to call for such sacrifices, not merely in men but in ammunition, it should have been given up. Everyone knew about the great French attacks on the Somme a month before the time, only G.H.Q. did not believe in them and took no precautions. When the Austrian disasters began 6 Divisions should have been put on the railway and sent across at once. Falkenhayn got on his hind legs and said he had none to spare. So things go from bad to worse, and now he has sent 12 Divisions—*i.e.* he has now had to send twice as many to repair the damage. That is the kind of thing that makes one so angry, and there are dozens of instances.

August 23, 1916.

H.M. has not yet answered our dispatch, and the Field-Marshal is in a state of great excitement. Two years ago this day he appeared with Ludendorff in Marienburg. God, what has happened since then! So much, that in Hindenburg's place I should act and speak very differently.

August 24, 1916.

H.M.'s answer to our dispatch came yesterday. It consists of a very gracious autograph letter to the Field-Marshal; no grasp of our difficulties and a number of observations that no one has ever disputed. So that's the end of that, and we might again have saved ourselves the trouble.

August 27, 1916.

. . . In addition to this we are anxious about the Austrians, who always come to grief: they can't seem to take the war seriously. . . . The officers on the active list occupy comfortable chairs in the higher Staff appointments—on the Lines of Communication or somewhere of the sort—and the clerks, actors and small officials, who figure as officers in the front line, know nothing and can do nothing. And if they are any use, and try their best, they have no sort of authority among the men. Besides, there are all these different races mixed up together—no less than twenty-three distinct languages. No one understands anyone else.

On the Polish question I have just heard that there has been an agreement with Austria-Hungary.[1] A Kingdom of Poland is to be established—in the main the old Congress-Poland with an Austrian Archduke as King. The new kingdom will, however, not be connected with Galicia, but is to maintain a military convention with Germany; in other words, we are to take their army in hand as well as their diplomatic representation. The settlement would have been published already, chiefly to enable Polish legions to be raised, but H.M. has still a strange hope of coming to a separate understanding with Russia, so that it is not thought wise to offend the Tsar over Poland. I have not much faith in a separate understanding with Russia, though it is true that there have of late been voices heard in Russia pointing out the futility of continuing the war.

August 30, 1916.

After our latest disputes with G.H.Q. we have confined our activities to the Ober-Ost[2] area, and

---

[1] On August 11th the Chancellor, von Bethmann-Hollweg, reached an agreement with the Foreign Minister of the Dual Monarchy, Baron von Burian, providing for the establishment of an independent Kingdom of Poland.

[2] "Upper East." The usual term for the Eastern War area and, being brief and convenient, here retained.—*Translator.*

have abandoned all further attempts to stiffen up the Archduke Karl's Army Group, etc. After the entirely unexpected entry of Rumania into the war [1] they all seem to have got into a state of nerves. The day before yesterday, after noon, Lyncker telephoned to Ludendorff asking the Field-Marshal and him to come at once to Pless: Falkenhayn, he said, knew nothing about it, and would be informed only after they had arrived. I at once said to Ludendorff that the time for the discussion of trifles was over, and that the Field-Marshal must go all out: he must say quite definitely to H.M.: "After the way Falkenhayn has behaved I can no longer merely offer advice. I am ready to pledge my reputation and popularity and to take over the difficult post of Chief of the General Staff of the Army in the Field. If Your Majesty agrees, then let Falkenhayn depart to-day—or else let me go back peacefully to Brest-Litovsk." He seems to have said something of the kind, for the telegram came yesterday. . . . It is a big jump for me: all the Army Group and Army Commanders are, of course, considerably my seniors (I shall actually become an Excellenz!), so I must be rather particularly careful.[2]

August 31, 1916.

I have no Commander-in-Chief, no G.S.O.,Ia (he is not yet appointed), and no Ib, as Ludendorff has taken Bockelberg with him, whom I can very ill spare. He is quite unsympathetic to me, but an uncommonly able man. So I am all alone in the

[1] On August 27th Rumania declared war on Austria-Hungary.
[2] On August 29th, Field-Marshal von Hindenburg was appointed Chief of the General Staff to the Army in the Field, and Ludendorff the First Quartermaster-General. Field-Marshal Prince Leopold of Bavaria succeeded Field-Marshal von Hindenburg as C.-in-C., East. Lieutenant-Colonel Hoffmann was appointed Chief of the General Staff to the Commander-in-Chief, with Lieutenant-Colonel Keller as G.S.O.,I, later replaced by Major Brinckmann.

world, and in addition to my official papers my writing-table is piled with congratulations and petitions.

September 3, 1916.

I cannot do more than hold on to what we have, and, for the rest, try to spare as many men as possible to help at other points. Then I shall have carried out my task. At present it is not easy. The Russians are violently attacking the army on our right and Linsingen's Group as well. We have beaten them off up till now, and I am quite confident of the issue as a whole. If things look rather bad at a particular point—well, we must just spit on our hands.

Yesterday I had my first quarrel with Seekt. He is Chief of Staff to the Archduke Karl and therefore not under my control. . . .

Well, I applied to Ludendorff and got my way, and all was peace in the land.

September 5, 1916.

All is in excellent order here, and on our right the position seems to be slowly improving. Mackensen's march into the Dobrudja with a few Bulgarian Divisions and a German force has made a paralysing impression on the Rumanians: they have not stirred for the last three days in Transylvania.[1]

In the West there is heavy fighting on the Somme.

---

[1] On August 27th Rumania declared war on Austria-Hungary, and Russian and Rumanian troops pushed forward over the borders of Moldavia and Wallachia as far down as the Danube, and into Transylvania and Hungary.

G.H.Q. was then confronted with the task of strengthening the Army Group of the Archduke Karl, and providing for a stroke against Rumania that would secure that part of the Front. As no troops could be spared from the Western Front, the C.-in-C., East, was instructed to withdraw troops from various points in his line.

South of the Danube, Field-Marshal von Mackensen received an order on August 28th to take over the German, Austro-Hungarian and

September 6, 1916.

The situation on our Front is, of course, perfectly satisfactory, but the Austrians on our right are still very shaky. I am continually taking troops out of the line and sending them south in support. I am in constant telephonic communication with Ludendorff, as I hope to get sanction for my proposals regarding the command farther south.
I continue on excellent terms with my C.-in-C.

September 7, 1916.

The Duke of Brunswick was here at midday. I did the honours as Chief for the first time. He was very charming and agreeable. This afternoon Prince Leopold went off for a three days' visit to the Austrian 2nd Army, which forms our right wing. On our immediate right the Army Group of the Archduke Karl is under the orders of the Army H.Q. at Teschen. We—*i.e.* Seekt and I—exchange views. I have already complained of him twice at Pless. In Bulgaria—*i.e.* for the Dobrudja offensive—Mackensen is in command.

September 10, 1916.

Hindenburg and Ludendorff have been on the Western Front for a few days. Ludendorff rang up just now and said that there was severe fighting

---

Bulgarian troops then posted on the line of the Danube and the Dobrudja frontier. There were also at his disposal: the Austrian Danube flotilla to the west of Orsova, some Bulgarian Landsturm in Donauschutz, a mixed German force at Rustchuk, a Bulgarian Division in the same place, and further unimportant Bulgarian forces as far as to the east of the railway line from Bulgaria into the Dobrudja. And a few German heavy batteries and a Turkish Division were on the way.

Field-Marshal von Mackensen was instructed to invade the Dobrudja with these forces. He began to march at the beginning of September: by September 6th Tutrakan was taken, and by the 9th, Silistria.

In the meantime the 9th Army was concentrated at Mühlbach, in Transylvania, and the Austrian 1st Army on the Maros.

in the West, but no cause for anxiety. Dreadful mistakes have been made and it is high time that matters were put straight.

September 10, 1916.

The programme of the very successful journey with H.M. was as follows: at 7 P.M. a guard of honour met H.M. in Kovel; reception, etc.; march past; after which H.M. distributed decorations, the first being a " Pour le Mérite " for me. Everybody—Lyncker in particular—congratulated me most kindly. Then dinner at Linsingen's Headquarters, where I sat between Lyncker and Gontard. On the next day a review of the 42nd Regiment near Vladimir Volynsk, followed by a speech by General Litzmann in the Royal train at Sokal. After this, breakfast in the train, at which I sat by H.M., and he very graciously drank my health. We then crossed over into our own Royal train and went on to Krasne to Böhm-Ermolli, where we were to meet H.M. the next morning (7.10). Another full-dress reception at the station and then on to Zloczov to Eben's Corps. From Zloczov we went by car to the Front, with soldiers lining the way on either side, cheering and looking fine. On a bit of rising ground, from where we could see the Russian positions, Eben made a speech, and then a review was held of all the troops in reserve, against the background of a wood with all its autumn foliage. Great enthusiasm. Address by His Majesty. Our men are really splendid. They had just been through weeks of heavy fighting and looked as though they had come out of a band-box. . . . Then back to Zloczov, where we again had breakfast in the Royal train. Then we parted. H.M. very gracious and in the best of spirits—as he had had nothing but good news during the entire trip (from the West, from Transylvania, and about the Imperial Loan). At parting he shook me very heartily by the hand and said: "Well, I hope you will carry on like this!" H.R.H. and I then went on in a car to visit the Southern Army, where my impressions were not very encouraging. At night I took a special train back to Brest-Litovsk, got through a part of the pile of work that had accumulated on my table, and the same evening took another special train back to Kovel, met H.R.H. there early yesterday morning, and then we both went to meet the Archduke Frederick. After exchanging a few resounding orations in H.R.H.'s saloon we got back here at midday yesterday.

September 13, 1916.

There is heavy fighting in the West. I am accordingly afraid that it may not be possible to withdraw the new formations from that Front, and that we on the Eastern Front shall have to supply the further Divisions needed for the Transylvania campaign. However, we shall manage it.

September 14, 1916.

We have now so many German and Austrian troops in Transylvania that there can be no question of any further Rumanian advance. I hope that the troops now arriving may be collected for a combined attack on one Rumanian Corps and destroy that: then proceed to the next, and so on.

England is, of course, skilfully working on the feelings of the Neutrals, more especially Spain and Denmark: but I have great hopes it will all come to nothing. For this reason it is most important that the campaign in Transylvania should be well conducted, so that we may finish off these Rumanian swine as quickly as possible. Good progress in the

Dobrudja. Our stroke there took the Entente by surprise, and there are only one Rumanian, one Russian, and one or, at most, two Serbian Divisions in that part, the latter being composed of Austrian deserters of Serbian nationality. It is important to reach the Bukarest-Costanza railway as soon as possible and prevent the Rumanians from using it. It is the shortest route between the Danube and the sea. Then, even if the enemy succeeds in bringing reinforcements up as far as that, we can still hold this short stretch of line with comparatively weak forces.

September 17, 1916.

I do not know what has happened to the Polish question. Civil authorities, like the Chancellor and the Foreign Office, do not make decisions as quickly as all that. Two days ago I had a long conference with Prince Lubomirski (from Lemberg), who wanted to see Prince Leopold and put the Polish case before him. The fellows are completely mad. I let the man talk and then told him to put it on paper and send it all to me in writing.

Yesterday the Russians began another attack, like men demented, on our extreme right wing, and on Linsingen's Front. We have repulsed them all here: but they have driven Seekt back in a few places, and we had a pathetic appeal from him early this morning. After a talk with Ludendorff on the telephone I sent one regiment and three batteries. The U-boat question is still in suspense. The opinion that it has no great prospect of success is becoming more and more general.

September 19, 1916.

I have just reported to Ludendorff, who calls up nearly every day, that all is in order here.

To-day he was badly in need of some more troops for another purpose, and I was able to say: "They can start this very evening." Even he was taken aback. It is, however, very interesting to manage with so few troops on such a gigantic Front and still be able to spare some for elsewhere. On the other hand, it is rather a self-sacrificing sort of affair. I would rather be the one who received the troops and was able to do something with them. Still, one cannot have everything, and must be patient.

September 22, 1916.

As far as the Danish question is concerned the English and a certain Germanophobe party in Denmark have very cleverly worked on the Danish Press to force Denmark gradually into an attitude of unfriendliness to Germany. However, the counter-measures taken by us — the transfer of troops to the Danish frontier, the construction of a fortified position there, the demand for repayment from Danish customers, etc.—have had a very cooling effect. The majority of the Danes are neutral. As long as the present Ministry remains at the helm Denmark will certainly remain unconditionally neutral.

September 24, 1916.

According to all reports the Russians appear to contemplate another determined attack upon us here. I am confident of the result, but the burden of responsibility is very great.

September 29, 1916.

Our Front extends from Zborov, on the railway from Lemberg to Tarnopol, to the Baltic, and consists of the 2nd Austrian Army (Colonel-General Böhm-Ermolli) and the three Army Groups of

Linsingen, Woyrsch and Eichhorn. Every Army Group is composed of several armies. In addition to which we control the administrative district called Ober-Ost, consisting of the provinces of Bialystok, Grodno, Vilna, Lithuania and Kurland. The entire area is as large as East and West Prussia, Posen and Silesia all together, or as large again as the territory under the Governor-General of Warsaw, which is not administered by us. At the head of it all is Ober-Ost, with a Central Administration in Kovno, and at the head of the individual administrative areas are Provincial Governors, with the necessary sub-Centres, civil officials and so forth. As Ober-Ost is at present established in Brest-Litovsk the Quartermaster-General, von Eisenhart, who remains at Kovno, carries on current business there. More important matters he comes to discuss here, or he sends the Departmental Minister concerned (Finance, Religion, Forests, Agriculture, etc.).

September 30, 1916.

I don't believe in this indecisive Peace by Christmas; not so much because I would not trust Bethmann to negotiate such a Peace, but because England would not at present agree to any sort of Peace we could accept.

Much liveliness here. The Russians seem at last to be making a determined attack on the 2nd Austrian Army and Linsingen.[1]

October 2, 1916.

That was a pretty bit of work in Transylvania. Our Rumanian friends must be feeling rather poorly to-day. I should like to see a few more of

[1] The Russians made persistent and furious attacks to the west of Luck, at Brody and Zborov, at Brzeczany and on the Narajovka, as well as in the Carpathians.

their Divisions destroyed and then offer them peace—that would be the best end to the business.

Ludendorff is going slow and concentrating on training troops, so as to be able to dispose of a large body of trained men in the spring.

October 3, 1916.

The Russians made further attacks yesterday: the I. Russian Guard Corps attacked seventeen times—all repulsed and our line intact. But I must see if I cannot scrape together some more Reserves from somewhere.

Item: H.M. is to appear within the next few days to thank the troops under Böhm-Ermolli and Linsingen.

Item: The Archduke Frederick then visits us, and not long after the King of Bavaria. I seem to be becoming a sort of Court Chamberlain. Ludendorff has just rang up to say that he would like to extend the area of our command still farther to the south, as our friends down there are playing the fool. I am honoured by his confidence, but it is getting rather much for me.

October 4, 1916.

So H.M. comes to-morrow. I shall go with the C.-in-C. to Linsingen's H.Q. at Kovel, so as to be there to receive him. We shall spend the night in the train at Kovel. On the 6th he will visit General von Eben, on what has hitherto been our extreme right wing, stopping at the various Headquarters on the way. On the 7th he will travel back to Pless; H.R.H.—my C.-in-C.—and I, after a few stops at intermediate points, will proceed to the Southern Army, commanded by Count Bothmer, which, as from to-morrow, is also under our command. This will make something like a Front. I shall have to spit on my hands, I can see.

October 5, 1916.

On the afternoon of the 7th, H.M. goes home again. H.R.H. and I will proceed by car to visit the Southern Army that we have just taken over. I shall put matters straight there and come back here the following night by special train. H.R.H. will stay over another day and show himself to the delighted populace.

October 12, 1916.

We all know that the Imperial Chancellor is a weak personality and should long ago have been superseded. Odd as it may sound, we have no one better at the moment. At least I know of no one. A soldier would be continually bothered by not knowing the ropes: Tirpitz, Helfferich—no, I know of nobody. It is just the same with the Foreign Office. There is no use in turning Jagow out unless the whole system is changed, and a change in the system would mean a complete change in our whole social organization. . . . I spoke to Plessen and Lyncker about Jagow and the Foreign Office. Both told me that they had several times talked to H.M. and the Chancellor about getting rid of Jagow; but they could not get away from the fact that he is cleverer than the others, and we have no more suitable man.

Prince Leopold is certainly much cleverer than —— but he is scarcely the star performer of the German political stage.

October 14, 1916.

As we have lost a part of our prepared positions, it is obvious that bad mistakes have been made. In the first place, further strong positions should have been constructed. Several fortified lines should have been constructed in the West, one behind the other, and more ammunition, etc., should have been available. These are our blunders, but they are now recognized, and Ludendorff is doing what is humanly possible to put matters right. More cannot be expected for the time being. H.M. has also been informed of all this. Hindenburg and Ludendorff see him every day, so that there is no longer any question of not being able to penetrate the ring surrounding him. The person responsible for the ammunition shortage has also been superseded, so at the moment I know of nothing more that could or ought to be said to H.M. about the Somme battle.

October 15, 1916.

It is clear that the only possibility of an agreement with Russia lies in a satisfactory solution of the Dardanelles question.

There is a mass of tactical work on hand, as in the next few days we are extending our area of command over the 3rd Austrian Army as well. Thus we shall be in control from the Baltic to the Carpathians. The Archduke Heir-Apparent, with Seekt, commands in Hungary and Transylvania, which makes a convenient break in the line.

October 17, 1916.

From the Carpathians to the Gulf of Riga I have my own saloon railway carriage, and more often than not a special train, automobiles, full-dress receptions wherever I arrive, and everyone in helmets on the platform when I depart, etc. I shall feel very strange when I take over my infantry regiment after the war. And yet I would not be sorry to do it to-day. The anxiety and responsibility are very great, and they make one so old.

October 20, 1916.

I am watching with curiosity how the Russians are going to help their threatened Rumanian allies. They are withdrawing troops along the whole Front, and will probably transfer them to the Carpathians, on the Transylvanian frontier, where they are making a thrust against the Austrians. Then we shall have to reply by taking troops out of the line and sending them down to the Carpathians in support of the Austrians, so that the Russians will then have Germans to deal with. The essential point in the whole business is to find out as early as possible at what parts of the line any troops can be spared, so as to be able to move them down by rail before the enemy can move theirs. We, of course, can move ours quicker, but one must always reckon to lose time on those meandering Austrian railways, with their infamous staff. Hence the delays in the campaign against the Rumanians: the German troops can never be got up in time.

October 25, 1916.

Generally speaking, our Front is quiet; we are going forward well in Transylvania and in the Dobrudja; only in the West our people seem to have gone to sleep again. The recapture of Douaumont, reported to-day, I can only ascribe to the fact that we have once again been taken by surprise.[1] There are no details.

November 3, 1916.

Nothing special here from a military point of view. We are regrouping some of the troops; the Austrians are howling for reinforcements on the Italian Front, and I am sending some.

[1] After the Somme battle had burnt itself out, the French attacked on October 24th on a Front north-east of Verdun. Fort Douaumont was lost. And on November 1st Fort Vaux had also to be evacuated.

November 4, 1916.

Ludendorff has just rung me up. To-morrow the proclamation providing for a Kingdom of Poland is to be issued, and in eight or ten days the formation of a Polish Army is to begin. The difficulty over the formula of the oath of allegiance has been solved. The Poles are to take the oath to the German Emperor as the Head of their Army during the war, and to the Emperor of Austria as Guarantor for the establishment of the Kingdom of Poland.

November 5, 1916.

I am, of course, much intrigued to know what impression the Polish Manifesto will make, and whether we shall really get any appreciable number of Polish recruits. The Operations Section at G.H.Q. has just rung up again to say that Ludendorff wants yet another Division from us — this time for the West, where, apparently, things are rather serious. Ober-Ost is like the widow's cruse of oil. It will be gradually emptied, though this time we can perhaps manage it.

November 7, 1916.

The supply of horses is causing extreme difficulty. We get no more from abroad and the losses can no longer be made good from home. We must consider every possible source from which horses can be spared. A few days ago one of the Army Groups sent in a request for 23,000 horses.

I have seen no foreign newspaper comments on the Kingdom of Poland—only the French wireless; they are incredibly abusive, so obviously they do not like it.

November 11, 1916.

My visit to Pless went off very well. Ludendorff himself met me at the station (I arrived at 3.36 in the afternoon) and we drank tea at his quarters. Of course we at once began to talk about Service matters. I explained just exactly how many more troops I could let him have, and he seemed very pleased. As we were going to his office, Ludendorff told me about his work and what he had achieved. After all it was high time that Falkenhayn, Wandel and Wild were got rid of, or everything would have burst up in the autumn. But by taking the situation in hand energetically he had pulled things round, and we were now on the up-grade. One of Ludendorff's measures will soon be generally known. A law regarding compulsory labour will be put before the Reichstag. "Every German must work." In that way we shall be able to deal with the shortage of munition-workers, and the munition question is still the decisive one. A law providing for the rationing of the population of Germany on the military scale is now being worked out. Ludendorff is in conflict with the Chancellor and the Admiralty—with the former because he will not turn Jagow out, and the latter because they have no sense of realities. Ludendorff was the moving spirit of the U-boat campaign in the Polar Sea, which has been so successful—not the Admiralty at all.

Position in the West: heavy fighting, but no need for anxiety. As the nerves of the troops in the West are more badly shaken than in the East, we must arrange for some exchanges; there will be no difficulty about this.

Then General von Cramon, German Intelligence Officer in Teschen, came in, and we had a talk about the Polish Legion and Polish Army. Ludendorff, of course, fully realizes the disadvantages in which a Kingdom of Poland may involve us, but we need reinforcements and must take the disadvantages as well. The question as to who is to be King is still undecided, and there is no hurry. Anyhow, a King cannot be chosen before there is an Army and a Government to support him.

Then appeared Conrad von Hötzendorf, with a few officers of his Operations Section. We discussed the progress of the operations in Transylvania and whether I could spare any more troops for them.

H.M. was in Pless, but he was ill. Ludendorff did not believe in the illness, and was of the opinion that he had frightened him with his Labour Law, etc., and that H.M. had evaded any further proposals on a plea of illness. Everyone here is amazed that Ludendorff tells H.M. everything and puts the true situation before him, extenuating nothing.

November 19, 1916.

There has been a devil of a rush here to-day again—one incessant stream of visitors since 7.30 this morning: and Pless calling up every five minutes and demanding troops for the Salonika Front. The Bulgarians are howling for help. However, I have refused: I can't do any more. Ludendorff can scrape together some troops from the West Front.

November 20, 1916.

Ludendorff wanted a few more troops—I am now stripped to the bone—all for Rumania, where things are going well. It is to be hoped that Mackensen will cross the Danube to-day or to-morrow.[1]

---

[1] Field-Marshal von Mackensen's operations in the Dobrudja had led to a complete success. The Rumanian Army in those parts was completely defeated, and Costanza was taken on October 23rd. The advance was then stopped. Mackensen received instructions to re-group his forces, and in the second half of November to cross the Danube south of Bukarest, and thus combine operations with the 9th Army, which, after its victories in Transylvania, was drawn up in the Szurdak Pass ready to invade Wallachia.

November 25, 1916.

There is much liveliness opposite our Front, and the Russians are possibly going to attack at some point in order to relieve the Rumanians. The beloved Entente has left these Rumanian ruffians completely in the lurch, and quite right too. I have great hopes that we shall get to Bukarest.

I have long known that Ludendorff was a possible candidate for the post of Chancellor. I discussed it with him in Pless also, and I told him that I knew no one but himself who was fit for it.

November 26, 1916.

I have invited the Commander of the Polish Legion and his Staff to dinner the day after tomorrow. The Legion will be withdrawn from Baranovici to Warsaw and the neighbourhood. The New Polish Army will be formed out of the Legion.

H.R.H. brought very little news back from Vienna: however, perhaps he did not want to tell me any. He has got no further with the Polish question. The Austrians have too much regard for their prestige to be willing to give up the Governor-Generalship of Lublin: on which account I see trouble brewing over the Polish Legion.

December 13, 1916.

The Peace question [1] has, of course, caused great excitement here. England will move heaven and earth to suppress the whole thing. It is certainly noteworthy that, although the Italians' preparations for an attack on the Isonzo have been ready

[1] On December 12th the Peace offer of the Quadruple Alliance took place.

for the last fortnight, in spite of the fine weather they have made no move. Moreover, a somewhat strange decree has been issued by the Austrian Emperor, so that for some days past I have had the impression that Austria and Italy are negotiating.

Russia and England are having differences about the delivery of war material. It is not beyond the bounds of possibility that some negotiations may take place, but I don't believe that England is ready to make peace now. However, perhaps our broaching the question of peace will have the effect in America (if the proposal is rejected by England's influence) of making people more reasonable over the U-boat question.

December 14, 1916.

I have some heavy work on hand, and I am shortly sending an officer to Pless to put before Ludendorff a proposal for the development of the operations against Russia.[1] I have an idea and I am anxious that Ludendorff should know about it. Whether it is feasible is, of course, impossible to say from here.

[1] In this connection Hoffmann writes in *The War of Lost Opportunities*: "About Christmas I wrote a letter to General Ludendorff in which I explained that in my opinion the offensive in Rumania, that had now become a purely frontal advance, would come to a standstill on the Sereth in the New Year. If it was desired to continue the campaign and finally put Rumania out of the war, in that case, in my opinion, there was only one thing to be done, and that was to give up the attack in the south and make a thrust from the north. If G.H.Q. was in a position to send 4-6 Divisions to the C.-in-C., East—it would be simplest to send some of those now fighting in Rumania—I thought we could carry the movement through. I proposed that the reinforcements and all the troops that could be collected from C.-in-C., East, should be concentrated in the neighbourhood of Zloczov; the Russian position to be broken through at that point and the offensive to be carried through Tarnopol along the main line to Odessa. The bulk of the Russian Army in the Carpathians would thus be brought into an untenable position, and I believed that the operation would lead to a great success.

General Ludendorff did not feel in a position to promise reinforcements. "For the moment no troops could be spared from the West, and in the present state of the Rumanian and Hungarian railways it was impossible to transfer troops quickly from Rumania."

December 16, 1916.

Before the New Year I shall move the administration from Kovno to Bialystok, so as to have it nearer. In the dispute over the control of the administration I have won all along the line. The administration remains not merely under our authority, but is to be extended over the whole Ober-Ost area.¹

December 21, 1916.

It is clear that matters are not going as well as might be wished; but the Conservatives are making all this fuss, not because they are afraid that anything may go wrong with the Fatherland, but much more from fear that their political predominance may suffer. We cannot dictate a German Peace. To do that we should have had to win the battle on the Marne, or at least, after it, to have put Ludendorff, not Falkenhayn, in control. So we must cut down our demands on one side or another, however regrettable that may be. It is no use banging on the table or playing the strong man.

December 27, 1916.

I have a great deal to do. By the 1st, Ludendorff wants to have before him schemes for all manner of different possibilities. Personal reports on officers come in at the same time. In addition, the extension of the administrative area involves much work. The Peace offer is, as was to be expected, rejected by everyone. More especially the Russians emphasize the fact that there can be no talk of peace until they get Constantinople.

¹ There were movements on foot to withdraw the control of the administration from the C.-in-C., East, and place it immediately under the Quartermaster-General. General Ludendorff decided that matters should remain as they were. The Administrative Departments were moved from Kovno to Bialystok so as to be nearer Headquarters at Brest-Litovsk.

The Italians, however, I can't understand. Why on earth don't they attack on the Isonzo? They have been ready for weeks, and remain inactive in spite of the fine weather.

December 30, 1916.

The Chancellor's Peace terms are, so far as I have been able to ascertain them, better than I should have given him credit for.[1] He certainly should not accept anything less. They are more or less my own. Of course I cannot tell whether we could get better terms, or whether the U-boat war may reduce England to such extremity that she may be forced to be more accommodating. On the other side the military situation in the West is certainly secure, but not brilliant. Everybody, including the Generals, have been asleep for so long over there, and there was, and is, so much leeway to make up — infantry training, heavy artillery, airmen, etc. However, it is to be hoped that we are now out of the wood.

January 6, 1917.

I have had the most troublesome time of late. And, in addition, a horde of visitors—the Q.M.G., Generals, Chaplain-General of the Dutch Army inquiring into "spiritual welfare" arrangements, Turkish princes, Generals on their way through— my head is positively swimming.

January 9, 1917.

I had a letter from Ludendorff yesterday. He complains of the Chancellor and the Foreign Office; neither of them know what they want.

My view of what we want has not altered for the last two years. I do not want Belgium, more

---

[1] Following upon the Peace move there had been an exchange of views on Peace terms, to form the basis of instructions to the German Ambassador in Washington, Count von Bernstorff.

especially because of the unpleasant addition to our Central and Social Democratic parties that it would involve. I want only so much of France . . . as they will redeem for 25 milliards. Belgium, too, must pay a war indemnity. Until it was paid we could keep control over the Belgian railways. Only Liège we must keep as a matter of prestige.

As against this, we want Lithuania and Kurland in the East. Our frontiers against Poland must be improved from a military standpoint — for which purpose Ossowiec is absolutely essential to us.

Vilna we do not want — that may be left to Poland, who can push her frontier as far to the East as she likes.

Bulgaria should get Macedonia and the Dobrudja. Austria to have a good slice of Serbia, but she *wants* a further division of Poland, if we do not agree to the whole of Poland coming under Habsburg sovereignty. Rumania must pay.

The question is how we are to secure these terms. My view is that it is possible to bring Russia to her knees, if the necessary troops can be placed at our disposal on the Eastern Front. In the West we can only remain on the defensive, and, if we have the necessary number of U-boats, there is always the intensified U-boat campaign: that point is beyond my judgment. In any case, it is the only means of putting pressure on England, though we should have America to reckon with. If there are not enough U-boats, then we must just hold on until the distress is so great in England, and more especially in France, that they are ready to negotiate. At present we must get enough troops and ammunition in hand to be able to resist the great offensive in the spring. It will certainly come, but we have enough Reserves to be able to face it with equanimity.

January 11, 1917.

Nothing special here. The Russians are very lively on their entire front; they naturally want to prevent us bringing up troops and sending them to Mitau, where a few days ago, as the result of the failure of a Landsturm battalion, they took a few of our trenches. They know us well enough to be afraid that we shall bring up Reserves and turn them out again.

January 15, 1917.

I am all against Bethmann-Hollweg — mainly, indeed, on account of his want of decision. He must do something; what he does is less important than that something should be done, but nothing *is* done. Neither he nor the Foreign Office know what they really want—that is what is the matter. If he wants Belgium he should say so; if not . . . he should say so too. But in either case he is afraid of one party or the other, so he will not speak out either way.

January 16, 1917.

Kapp was here yesterday. He explained the whole miserable incompetence of our Government. This time we were in pretty general agreement: an intensified U-boat campaign, and, as the Chancellor does not seem to know what he is about —as witness his futile vacillation in always postponing it—he should be superseded. That is what the large majority of the people wants. However, Kapp overestimates my influence in the matter. I gladly promised I would write. The question of a successor is a difficult one. His candidate is Tirpitz. The worst of it is that I do not know another at the moment. Ludendorff cannot yet be dispensed with, and he has not yet sufficient grasp of the political interrelations of the various States. Moreover he has hitherto had too little to do with policy. It would therefore be desirable that Tirpitz should merely keep the place warm, and that Ludendorff should succeed him later. These were the main points of our conversation.

H.R.H. Prince Henry is coming to-morrow. I can't guess what he wants, but I assume that he wants to become Duke of Lithuania and Kurland — perhaps also King of Poland. Everyone who has been here until now has wanted something or other.

January 17, 1917.

I laughed heartily over Witting's lucubrations. Who was it that was always shouting that we should have to go to war at last, that we could not go on standing this sort of thing, etc.? Why, Herr Witting! Of course we could have knuckled under again in the summer of 1914; in which case the Entente would have certainly struck in 1917, that being the earliest date by which they could have been ready. To that extent, I agree, we began the war. The unfortunate thing was simply that our military leaders failed. The difference between Witting and me now is that I will have nothing to do with a Peace patched together by international banking interests. I want a victory. It is still possible—not of course in the sense in which we understood the word earlier—*i.e.* the entire capture or destruction of the enemy armies—but we could, for example, take Petersburg, and so force the Russians to make peace, or bring England to her knees through the submarine campaign.

Undated.

This was my trip in brief: went with Seekt and Hell to Pless; usual kindly and cordial welcome from Ludendorff and Hindenburg. Ludendorff then explained the general situation and his own views. Of course the position could not be rightly estimated until the U-boat war had begun. Our —very modest—requests for the Eastern Front were, in general, granted.

I then had a private talk with Ludendorff about Bethmann-Hollweg and the Foreign Office. Hindenburg and Ludendorff are at considerable loggerheads with the civil power. Bethmann-Hollweg, Helfferich and Zimmermann recently came to Pless for a conference and Hindenburg did not invite them to dine. At Ludendorff's request I then had a further half-hour's private talk with Hindenburg about politics. At the end of it he was prepared to speak to H.M. provided I would put all I had said to him in writing. For the moment it is not practicable to replace Bethmann-Hollweg just because the U-boat campaign began to-day. We must wait a few weeks more and then he must go.

February 5, 1917.

America's prompt answer points to the fact that there is, in fact, a secret understanding between Wilson and England. America would, therefore, certainly have come in, according as events turned in any way to our advantage. Well, it's a good thing to have the situation cleared up at last.

February 8, 1917.

In the next few weeks we are combining the administrations of Lithuania and Vilna-Suvalki (up till now two separate large administrative areas) into a Greater Lithuania, with a capital at Suvalki. This arrangement will probably cause a political sensation, as the Poles must regard it as directed against themselves, which, in point of fact, it is. We shall produce clear evidence to show that the ancient government of Suvalki, which Napoleon in his time turned over to Congress-Poland, should not be allowed to fall to Poland, but remain independent.

The attitude of the European neutral States towards us over the U-boat question is unexpectedly favourable. I have had excellent and reliable news on the point, that will also damp Herr Wilson's fervour a little.

February 11, 1917.

That there is a movement in various circles against Ludendorff — military circles as well — is known to him and to me. At the moment Ludendorff cannot be superseded—that is quite impossible, as Hindenburg would go too, and the consequences of such a step would mean the End. So we are unperturbed.

February 14, 1917.

How far the Rittmeister is correct in his observations on France and French politics I cannot, of course, judge. I do not greatly believe in the possibility of overtures to France and a separate Peace. Besides, at the moment, the French are too much strung up by the hope that they may yet win the war.

As regards N. and D., I have never much trusted either of them during the war, especially not D. I fancy S. too is a member of the gang. For the moment it is not possible to get rid of D., but Ludendorff is arranging to get N. removed.

It is very odd to think that a fortnight ago I asked Prince Isenburg to induce Erzberger to come here again. Erzberger is complaining about our administration in Lithuania, and I want to show him that his information is false. In any case I am curious about future developments. If he could come here I should, of course, talk to him about political questions, Ludendorff, etc.

February 16, 1917.

Nothing special here. A few days more and my troubles are over. It is not a pleasant feeling to be so entirely without Reserves. In the West things are slowly getting livelier; but I do not expect the great attack until the middle of March. Whether our Russian friends will be far enough advanced by then remains to be seen; but in any case I am ready for them.

From the reports in the newspapers the U-boats seem to be doing well. In order to produce an effect we must sink 800,000 to 1,000,000 tons of shipping in the next three months. I think that will be enough. This will produce such a state of nervousness that a great many ships will not put to sea at all.

There is very encouraging news from the interior of Russia. It would seem that she cannot hold out longer than the autumn.

February 22, 1917.

In the West they are all complaining of the cold. There are no dug-outs and they are lying in shell-holes. It would be more sensible to give up the present fighting area on the Somme and the Aisne and retire a few kilometres to the next well-prepared position. We should thus transfer to the other side the privilege of lying in the mud without proper shelter. Whether Ludendorff will do this I don't know, but I hope he will.[1]

[1] On March 16th, in the West, the so-called Alberich movement began. The entire salient of the German position between Arras and Soissons was evacuated, and, along the chord of this arc, the so-called Siegfried position was occupied.

February 23, 1917.

It is natural that the Poles should carry on a strong propaganda for the inclusion of Lithuania and Kurland in the Kingdom of Poland. I am at the moment engaged in an extremely acrimonious correspondence with Warsaw, the Foreign Office, and the Imperial Chancellor, to get them to put a stopper on this Polish propaganda.

February 28, 1917.

There are four conflicting elements in this area —German, Polish, Lithuanian and Lettish—and no politician in the world can bring them together. All we can do—while the war is on—is to say: " The Germans must come first, and the others will be treated with absolute impartiality." All three of them hate us because each of them wants to predominate: nothing will alter that. My conscience is clear in the whole business, as is obvious from the fact that I have invited the various representatives to come here and look into the circumstances for themselves.

We all know that Ludendorff is no politician, he is too impulsive. He always wants something to happen at once, while the politician must know how to wait.

March 2, 1917.

There is nothing in the French newspaper-cuttings that I did not know before. Every sensible soldier knows that Ypres and Verdun were Falkenhayn's greatest crimes.

March 4, 1917.

Our small affair on the Stochod yesterday went off well — 9000 prisoners, including 4 regimental commanders, 15 guns, 200 machine guns and trench mortars, are a very pretty result. I had reckoned on 3000 at the outside. The Russian Army is deteriorating.

The Russian Revolution is, from the military point of view, a great piece of luck for us, and our withdrawal in the West is extraordinarily unpleasant for the Entente; they wanted a speedy success and hoped to obtain it after their colossal concentration of men and material on the Somme. For the moment time is on our side.

I have just arranged for Erzberger's and Richthofen's travelling permits to be sent to them from here. I have heard no more of Zimmermann's blunder over Mexico; in point of fact, the blunder consisted in being found out: in itself, his action was, of course, perfectly right.

March 5, 1917.

For the rest, a state of violent activity continues on the whole Russian Front. The Russians are constructing a large number of new positions and they certainly will not attack until these are ready. Generally speaking, this is to our advantage. I am gradually disengaging so many Reserves that I can look forward to further developments with equanimity. It was extremely fortunate for us that the Russians left us entirely at peace during the last few weeks. If they had attacked at certain points during the last three weeks I should have been in a damnable mess. And this feeling tends to get on one's nerves in the long run — which partly explains my bad temper these last weeks. In addition to which I had a passage of arms with the authorities at Warsaw. They go on with their Polish propaganda—and what our Lithuanians say is all one to them.

March 10, 1917.

I had a letter from Frau Ludendorff about my influence over her husband, and asking me to use it. Now the trouble is that in trying to influence anyone by letter one cannot meet his objections. One can influence a man in political questions only by talking to him. . . .

I can see from the papers and the debates in Parliament that the outlook at home is bad.

All reasonable people are agreed that we cannot starve England out by the day after to-morrow; on the other hand, the shortage of raw material (ore, pit-props, etc.) in England, and of coal in France and Italy, is likely to be so great in the course of the next three or four months that the various Governments will have to consider whether it would not be more sensible to negotiate. We must take care that the Entente does not win any considerable success in the field during this period —such as Verdun, or the first few days' fighting on the Somme.

March 12, 1917.

I have just written a letter of some length to Frau Ludendorff (she had applied to me to work for Nicolai's dismissal), so my spare time is all used up.

March 14, 1917.

The situation here is unchanged.

There seems to be serious disorder in Petersburg. I think it will probably end in an open conflict between the Duma and the Government, which might easily bring down the Tsar. Whether it will have any effect on the conduct of the war cannot, of course, yet be seen, but it is by no means out of the question.

March 15, 1917.

Our 1st Adjutant, Captain von Trotha, said to me just now before he left me: " Well, sir, your work's up to full strength, anyway "; and he was right. Such time in the morning as H.R.H. has left me is completely taken up by appointments with General Staff Officers and Adjutants. Erzberger and Richthofen are coming to lunch. In the afternoon I am expecting the A.Q.M.G. with seven officers to discuss various important questions of administration. General Riemann is coming before dinner with various requests regarding personnel and tactics. In addition to the above-mentioned, General von Bernhardi, who has been visiting one of the Divisions here, and Prince George of Bavaria are coming to dine. After dinner I shall receive the two Deputies—I have had no time for them before: and I fancy that interview will last until midnight. Then I have to look through the evening mail, and all the incoming reports. There are many days when twenty-four hours are not enough. To-morrow Erzberger and von Richthofen are to lunch with the Prince at Szkoki, and in the afternoon I shall send them in my private saloon, with an orderly officer in attendance, to Escherich at Bialovicz.

There is actually serious disorder, and street-fighting, in Petersburg. I don't know the facts yet, but I suspect that the Government wanted to send the Duma home, and that they would not go. We have no further news yet. What repercussions, if any, this will have on the Russian Army cannot yet be foreseen. I am far from being an optimist, but the cutting of railway lines, strikes, burning of factories, etc., must at least gravely endanger the output of munitions, and thus weaken the Russian Army. We must wait and see. In the meantime I am having a leaflet printed to explain the cause of the troubles to the Russian soldiers in the trenches. Otherwise the poor fellows would know nothing about it, which would be a pity.

March 17, 1917.

Erzberger and Richthofen sat with me the day before yesterday from 10 P.M. until 1.45 A.M., yesterday morning from 8 to 10 and yesterday afternoon from 3.30 to 5 o'clock. They then left for Berlin, travelling straight through, via Warsaw. My proposed journey to the Front and to the occupied territories had to be put off owing to lack of time. It was all very interesting, especially to hear Erzberger's views and expositions. He is a very clever man, with an amazing fund of varied information. Yet, in spite of it all, I was rather disappointed with the visit, for they neither of them threw a really fresh light on anything. It was just a succession of opinions and wishes, of course deserving of respect—but no more. I promised—this was the main object of the visit—to pass it all on to Ludendorff, and this I will do to-morrow; I cannot deal with it to-day, there are too many arrears of work. Of course we also talked about Kurland and Lithuania, and I was astonished to find that Erzberger shared all my views on this point; so I asked him to inform me direct of any complaints that looked like being more than usually vocal, so that I can investigate each one thoroughly.

March 18, 1917.

It is not advisable to be too optimistic about the Russian Revolution at present. There has been no trouble with the army as yet. The Grand Duke Nicolai Nicolaievich has once more become Commander-in-Chief of the entire army. His aim will be a victory, and then a march to Petersburg with the victorious troops to hang the revolutionaries and make himself Tsar. On that account he will very soon make a great effort to win a victory. Things may, of course, work out differently. The whole business is naturally very encouraging for us, as a domestic convulsion of this kind is never a very practical proceeding for a State at war.

March 19, 1917.

In the West the withdrawal has now been carried out. I consider it an excellent piece of work. The French and English have to start their preparations for the great Spring Offensive all over again; they are lying in the open, unprotected from our artillery fire and from the weather, and in front of a fresh line of defence which we constructed months ago. And as it is considerably shorter, we shall save a good many Divisions, as well as artillery.

March 21, 1917.

I think Erzberger is wrong in arranging a meeting with Ludendorff for the end of the month in Berlin. I told the two of them repeatedly that I was perfectly willing to pass on a number of ideas and hints to Ludendorff (as in fact I did yesterday in a letter of several sheets which I sent off by old Israel), but that I must point out to them it was naturally very difficult to exercise any influence on a third party by means of the written word. A personal interview was better. I would therefore ask Ludendorff to let me know when he was next coming to Berlin, and I would try to meet him there. I could not fix a date, as I did not know when Ludendorff would be next in Berlin. I probably cannot manage the end of the month, as the C.-in-C. is going to Munich on a fortnight's leave.

It goes without saying that there will be an attempt to negotiate with Russia. It will be difficult, because at present no one knows who holds the sovereign power in Russia, and the whole affair might be wrecked by too much precipitation. However, that is no reason for me to hurry to Berlin, as the establishment of any such relations is not my business, and it will not take place in Berlin. So far as I know, the steps to be taken in the matter will be discussed upon the occasion of the Chancellor's visit to Vienna.

March 23, 1917.

There is always something up somewhere, and yet we live in perpetual boredom here. We sit and wait while things happen to other people, instead of being able to do something ourselves.

March 26, 1917.

Israel, whom I had sent to Kreuznach, brought me back a long screed from Ludendorff. He, of course, disagrees with Erzberger's and Richthofen's views on various points, especially over the Chancellor and the Foreign Office. He writes very pointedly on both subjects. The Nicolai business cannot be dealt with yet, although he does not trust the man either, but he will not be able to do anything until later on.

March 28, 1917.

There are four problems at the moment which are giving me endless trouble and driving me nearly crazy. But the stupid thing is that all our affairs and decisions go straight up to H.M., as there is no one else over us, and in all such matters the Cabinet is incredibly petty, and irritating beyond measure.

April 2, 1917.

Yesterday evening Erzberger sent me a very interesting memorandum on Russian and Italian relations: from which I observe that I was, generally speaking, right.

April 6, 1917.

Wilson's message is very interesting. England's expressed attitude now is: " We are not making war against Germany or the German people, but only against the House of Hohenzollern and their Prussian adherents." Very astute in itself, but also a promising sign for us. The idea that Germany must be crushed and destroyed has been gradually given up. It is astute in so far as they are speculating on the assistance of the Social Democrats. In point of fact, I think I can see the Internationale hard at work in all this.

April 12, 1917.

The loss of positions in the West is of course very unpleasant. But these are inevitable mishaps for which we must be prepared. Two Divisions, as I have just gathered, went to sleep, did not expect the attack until later and allowed themselves to be taken by surprise. Yesterday's news from Ludendorff suggests that he hopes that the affair may be localized. We must keep calm and just hold on, and whether we do so a few kilometres to the east or west is of no importance.[1]

April 28, 1917.

I had a heart-to-heart talk yesterday with the Burgomaster of Bremen, Dr Buff. He shares the

---

[1] On April 9th the English attacked at Arras on both sides of the Scarpe and overran the German front lines. It was the opening bar of the great battle of Arras.

The battle was still at its height when, on the 16th April, the French began their attack on the Aisne and in Champagne.

view of all sensible men that the Chancellor must go, only he knows of no successor. Buff made a most excellent impression on me.

April 30, 1917.

Nothing to report here. We are showering newspapers and leaflets on the Russians and trying to get at them in various other ways. Whether anything will come of it remains to be seen. In any case, for the time being we need no munitions, and they can all go to the Western Front; which is very fortunate, as the consumption there is enormous. All seems to be going well at Arras: at Rheims the French will certainly attack again. In any case, the Russian Revolution is a godsend to us, for if there had been heavy fighting in the East at the same time we should have been up against it.

May 2, 1917.

Richthofen's estimates are greatly exaggerated, the French cannot hold out for three years more, nor can the English, for by that time they would not have a single vessel left. So, as the saying goes: "Do not drive young horses over-hard." I think it quite out of the question for Ludendorff to take any part in a matter of politics. Nor, indeed, is it necessary, for if left to themselves these people may have some views of their own.

May 12, 1917.

Nothing special here. We are giving the Russians much good advice, telling them to behave sensibly at last and make peace, but they don't yet seem very anxious to do so. Yesterday, for the first time, there was a rather more important interview, for which some of our officers proceeded to Dünaburg, to the Russian Headquarters there. But nothing much came of this either.

May 19, 1917.

I had a visit from two Reichstag Deputies, the Conservative von Winterfeldt and the Social Democrat David—the latter of the two was by far the abler and more interesting man. We all enjoyed talking to him. They are now to see something of our Ober-Ost Command and its administration.

There is nothing to be said against the Chancellor's speech. The questions of the Conservatives, having regard to the present state of affairs, showed once again incredible political crassness, and the Chancellor extricated himself from the affair pretty well.

May 20, 1917.

In the West the great offensive seems to be at an end. During the last few days the French and English have made only partial attacks, and the French newspapers are openly expressing their indignation that the great offensive has been broken. Of course it is not beyond possibility that they will have a try at another point. The new Generalissimo Pétain must show what he is made of. However, perhaps he thinks it better to leave well alone and puts his hope in the spring of 1918.

May 24, 1917.

I have not much use for my suggested rôle as scapegoat between the Chancellor, G.H.Q. and Parliament. Such a position is neither one thing nor the other, and leads to no result. Stein's manœuvre was unfortunate, though the outcry over him was excessive. He certainly intended nothing by his phrase " Greek gifts," least of all to provoke the Reichstag.

May 26, 1917.

The Russians are making violent counter-propaganda against our efforts to paralyse their army by suggestions of peace. It seems that Kerenski has gone to the Front, and he is perhaps trying to get them to attack again. Well, they may, for all I care. The Italians are attacking with great energy on the Isonzo and the Austrians have lost a few positions. I do not consider the situation serious at present—of course we shall have to help them again.

May 29, 1917.

Yesterday Erzberger sent me a report from Russia according to which the situation there is growing more and more unmanageable. He takes a very optimistic view of the future. Well, people say he was always too optimistic, but in any case I prefer him a thousand times to Witting and his friends. After a general review of the earlier policy of the Government one can only say: "The Russian Revolution was a surprising piece of luck, which you did not deserve!" Still, there it is, and Russia is collapsing. The great question now is, which will come first—the breach with America or the Russian collapse. The latter, I think. I am very curious to know how England will answer the Russian request for a restatement of war aims. If she refuses, that will be a proof that our U-boat war is not so effective as we hope, but if she shows signs of reconsidering the point, then we shall know that the U-boat war is producing results. It is an excellent opportunity of finding out.

Still nothing fresh here. A few days ago, as a result of our propaganda at the Front, we got an opportunity of getting into direct touch with an Army Staff. General Dragomiroff, the Commander-in-Chief on the Russian Northern Front, sent a request for a few German officers to come to see him. He went on to explain that this was not his own wish, but that the soldiers had compelled him to write. In any case I did not want to let the opportunity slip and I induced H.R.H. to write a letter to Dragomiroff, which was, of course, very galling to the Russians. He acknowledged the letter, but did not answer. To-day we have printed the letter, with an explanation of its object — a request for an armistice with a view to peace—in a leaflet, and scattered it over the entire Russian Front.

June 1, 1917.

An armistice is, in fact, in being at many points on the Russian Front: at other points firing is going on—it is indeed a strange war.

I am very curious to know what is going to happen in the West. I cannot suppose that the English are going to give up their great offensive without a word or an effort. I think they are going to collect their forces again somewhere else, perhaps in conjunction with a landing. The West is strong enough in Reserves to face such an event with equanimity—thanks to the Russian Revolution.

June 7, 1917.

The Russians are becoming more energetic in their counter-propaganda. Alexieff had promised to attack, but in the meantime he has been superseded and Brussiloff put in his place. Whether he will manage it remains to be seen. In any case we have made all necessary preparations. I regard the thing as a piece of folly : they can't possibly break through, so it is simply a senseless waste of life in England's honour.

It was apparently Hertling that backed up the Chancellor last time. We shall make another attempt very shortly. Hertling has the King of Bavaria entirely in his pocket. Zimmermann does not want to stick to his office. On the contrary, I think he would be only too glad to go, as soon as he was told that it was essential in the interests of peace. There is no point in my going to Berlin to talk to a dozen people. There is no point in talking. These fellows must do something. I myself am a soldier, so I can't go and say: "Your Majesty, please dismiss the Chancellor." The politicians in Berlin can, but they don't do it.

June 8, 1917.

I have read Braun's articles. They are in general agreement with the views of reasonable people— viz. that after the war we must come to an understanding with Russia and Japan. That is just as much in the interests of the other two as in our own, so as to provide a counterpoise to the enormous commercial predominance of the Anglo-American alliance.

June 9, 1917.

Administrative questions that have to be disposed of quickly, letters to Erzberger (who wants money from Ober-Ost to distribute in Lithuania), to Witting, who wants me to mediate for him in certain railway matters, etc., and, in addition, a mass of purely military business. It is not beyond the bounds of possibility that the Russians will attack at one point or another; what Reserves and war material we have must, consequently, be shifted to where the enemy is making preparations for an attempt. No sooner are we settled than the West comes along, takes our men away, and gives us in exchange troops that are sorely in need of a rest after their experiences there—and so the whole business begins again.

June 11, 1917.

I am not furious about St., I shall receive him quite affably. Letter from Erzberger, this time less optimistic about Russia. The English are doing all they know to keep Russia steady and induce her to attack. Apparently they are successful; at any rate, at certain points in the line it looks as though their friends were going to try their luck again. We are quite on the spot with everything needed to deal with them.

June 12, 1917.

There is still much liveliness opposite us. Kerenski has pledged himself completely to the English, and, I imagine, undertaken to attack again in the next few weeks.

June 13, 1917.

I had a very interesting letter from Erzberger about our awkward foreign relations. Very sensible, and not so wildly optimistic as he usually is. His information comes from the General of the Jesuits and the new Nuncio in Munich—two unexceptionable sources. Still, I fancy that both of them—Italians in the last resort—want to create a depressing effect, so that Germany's demands may be as moderate as possible.

June 15, 1917.

I have now taken the river-fishing energetically in hand, and we are daily getting supplies of the most excellent pike, etc., by the hundredweight. It is a pity that we are too far from where it could be packed and sent home. If the catch increases I shall start a fish-smoking establishment.

June 16, 1917.

A brief anecdote, tending to show the good sense and acuteness of our Foreign Office. A certain von Maltzahn, Counsellor of Legation, is to be appointed to Ober-Ost and is due to arrive here any day. I received the following telegram to-day: " Counsellor von Maltzahn arrives Warsaw 18th at 6 P.M. Please make arrangements for his journey to Brest-Litovsk: sgd. Stumm." I really wanted to reply: " Please instruct von Maltzahn not to make a mistake and get out at Warsaw, but to stay in his compartment: will then unavoidably arrive destination Brest-Litovsk." These people are really too . . .

June 19, 1917.

Apparently the Russians are really going to attack us in Galicia. Well, let them. Ludendorff has put a little more artillery at our disposal, and I can face any further developments with equanimity.

June 25, 1917.

The Russians are keeping absolutely quiet. I have not heard a single gun, nor, in spite of the fine weather, seen a single airman. I don't think they will attack again there in the near future. Whether it will come off in Galicia I do not know. I think it possible, but I still have my doubts. In any case all my preparations are made: " Let them come and we'll give them a welcome! "

June 26, 1917.

As regards the removal of " certain people," Erzberger told me yesterday on the telephone that his patience too was at an end, and that he was for a change. He will give me his reasons in writing.

June 29, 1917.

I had a frank discussion with the Minister Lentze, Drews, and three Privy Councillors, which lasted until shortly before one o'clock: by that time we had reached an agreement on all points. It was half-past two before I had looked over the correspondence, etc., that was waiting for me. The work does not diminish unfortunately, it increases.

I just sit and wait to see whether Brussiloff will attack in Galicia or not. It is to be hoped he will —and I hope I shall be able to provide him with a pleasant surprise. But at present we cannot tell whether he can get his Comrades out of the trenches or not.

According to what Drews, the Under-Secretary, told me, another crisis with the Imperial Chancellor is imminent — I hope it may hasten his fate. Ludendorff is going to a conference at Vienna in a day or two.

June 30, 1917.

I sit and wait (like children waiting for Father Christmas), wondering whether the Russians will attack at last. But we have no luck. They make half-hearted attempts at a sort of attack, but until now they have not really brought one off. It is a pity—it would have been a good show. We had provided such a delightful surprise for Herr Brussiloff.

July 1, 1917.

The Russians are attacking us in Galicia. I hope they will keep it up for eight or ten days, so that we can give them a proper dressing-down.[1]

---

[1] The C.-in-C., East, planned for the second half of July an attack on a large scale along the Lemberg—Tarnopol railway. G.H.Q. had placed 6 Divisions at his disposal for this attack.

On July 1st the Russians broke into the Austrian positions between

July 2, 1917.

The Russians are really remarkable people. At the bottom of my heart my only anxiety was lest they might not be induced to attack in Galicia, and so prevent us carrying out a very neat counter-operation. Instead of which they have been attacking for the last few days with such fury and with such a concentration of troops as we have never seen in the East: 7-8 Russian Divisions against one of ours. Which is rather more than I like. . . . In any case the position here is, at the moment, very interesting. I am not anxious in the least, but we must be very careful, because even a trifling Russian victory would, of course, influence public opinion among all classes in favour of the war.

July 6, 1917.

We shall have to wait ten days or a fortnight before my " surprise " can come off. Meanwhile I hope the Russians will press their attacks.

July 7, 1917.

All in perfect order here. Heavy fighting yesterday. The Russians attacked in positive hordes—all beaten off. My preparations for the " surprise " are proceeding according to plan.

Zborov and Brzeczany. The situation was restored by the German Divisions which had just come up.
After a powerful attack on July 4th against the Southern Army, which was repulsed, on the 6th and 7th powerful Russian attacks were launched against the Austrian 3rd Army south of the Dniester. The 3rd Army retired behind the Lomnitza and Kalusz fell into Russians hands.
The German troops intended for the break-through at Zloczov had to be diverted to the 3rd Army : and by these means the Russian advance was brought to a standstill.
The German attack near Zloczov began on July 19th and led to a complete success. Tarnopol was taken on the 25th, and the whole Russian Front was shaken. In the first days of August, Galicia and the Bukovina were cleared of Russians.
While this operation was still proceeding, preparations were started at Mitau for an attack on Riga.

July 11, 1917.

Much work and much trouble over our worthy allies. Heavy fighting in Galicia, but no cause for anxiety.

July 17, 1917.

Yesterday's news has quite relieved my mind. Litzmann has retaken Kalusz, and there are now such strong German reinforcements in those parts that nothing need worry us.

The weather has also improved, so that I hope to take rather more vigorous action in the next two or three days. The Austrians have grown more and more . . . dear to me in the last fortnight. They are really impossible. . . . Not content with running away, they lie and send false reports, and with it all they are quite unashamed, and make difficulties wherever they can. I should like to go to war with *them*.

July 18, 1917.

If the weather holds, I shall proceed to the offensive at a certain point. It won't be so big an affair as I had hoped, because I had to use too many troops to stop the Austrian retreat in the neighbourhood of Kalusz.

July 19, 1917.

Our little surprise at Zloczov made a good beginning yesterday. We broke through the Russian positions on a twenty-kilometre Front, and I hope we shall make good progress in the next few days.

July 21, 1917.

The affair is developing according to plan. I should like a few more prisoners. The fellows ran away so frantically that we could not catch any of them. Only 6000 up to date, and only 70 guns.

I can't of course predict how things will go, but I hope all right.

We are still sitting in the train at Zloczov, and shall stay here till the end of the month. I don't want to let the operation get out of hand.

July 23, 1917.

We are succeeding beyond expectation down here. Unfortunately we have made only a few prisoners — they ran away too fast — and only 50 guns.

On the other hand, I am worried about Eichhorn's position up in the north. The Russians are attacking heavily at Smorgon and Dünaburg, and yesterday they broke through our line at one point. Steps have been taken to deal with the situation.

Well, once more I am glad to be a soldier: politics leave me cold.

The Emperor of Austria was here yesterday, and he behaved himself in the sort of way that falls just short of direct discourtesy. There was of course no question of any thanks for the reconquest of a province for him.

July 25, 1917.

H.M. came early yesterday morning and pressed the " Pour le Mérite," with oak leaves, into H.R.H.'s hand and into mine. I then gave him an account of the situation. Next we went in a car towards Tarnopol to see Prince Eitel Friedrich, who took Tarnopol this evening with the 1st Guard Division. In H.M.'s car were His Royal Highness, Prince Fürtensberg, and My Insignificance. In the evening, at dinner in the Royal train, I sat on H.M.'s left. He was of course in a brilliant humour.

To-day he visited the Southern Army. I had work to do and let H.R.H. go with him alone.

Ludendorff has sent me a number of very good Divisions, which helped us to win the battle in a style I could have scarcely dreamed of. We are going forward well, and the Russians are on the run as far south as the Carpathian Front.

There is now no decoration left that I should care for.

July 26, 1917.

All proceeds according to plan; we reconquer Galicia and the Bukovina for the Emperor Karl and he has not yet once said " Thank you."

Our Emperor was about all day yesterday, and to-day he has gone to Tarnopol. Yesterday I was again invited to dine with H.R.H. H.M. was again extraordinarily gracious and friendly, shook hands with me three times when I took leave of him, etc. An invitation has just come for me to dine again this evening. The day after to-morrow we shall go home again (H.M. is going on to Vilna to-morrow).

July 28, 1917.

Yesterday we dined with H.M. for the fourth time. I sat on his right, and he was as gracious and friendly as he had been all day. He left for Vilna at ten o'clock. They were very good days, but I am glad they are over. I am not much of a courtier.

We are leaving this afternoon, and shall be home again on the morning of the 29th. Our work down here is practically over. I should not have dared to hope that the operation would be so successful. I certainly believe that in the next few days we shall succeed in throwing the Russians and Galicians over the Galician and Bukovina border. Then we shall necessarily come to a stop, because we shall be so far from the railways that are still intact that we shall not be able to bring up supplies and reinforcements. Then we must try something else—if Ludendorff will let me have the troops. I have just had another admirable idea.

July 30, 1917.
Our operation progresses: on the Galician Front we shall reach the frontier at every point to-day. It will be another two days before we take Czernovitz. . . .

July 31, 1917.
Much work, and a great deal of worry. The Russians are defending themselves very obstinately in the Bukovina and progress becomes daily more difficult. Still, I hope we shall take Czernovitz all the same.

August 1, 1917.
Ludendorff has just rung up. He is satisfied with yesterday's great Entente offensive in the West.[1] The losses are of course considerable, and we have lost a certain amount of ground, but—and this is what I care about—he needs no troops for the West.

Our operation here is coming to an end. I still wish we could get Czernovitz.

August 2, 1917.
I could really do with a few days' leave—I am gradually beginning to feel the strain and anxiety of three years of war—but it can't be done. I have to carry the entire responsibility for the Eastern Front—no one regards the Prince as responsible—so I can't get away for the time being. H.R.H. is going to Bialovicz to-morrow—the shooting season has begun.

[1] The great Flanders battle began on July 31st in the West.

Something very pleasant happened yesterday evening. H.R.H. ordered champagne at dinner, stood up and announced in a neat speech that H.M. the King of Bavaria had conferred on me the Cross of a Knight of the Military Order of Max Joseph. He made some very nice remarks about me, and concluded by calling on the company to drink my health. The Military Order of Max Joseph is the Bavarian " Pour le Mérite," and they very rarely, and reluctantly, give it to non-Bavarians. H.R.H. proposed me for it, without saying anything, and the whole manner and method of the announcement was very charming.

A report has just come in that detachments of our troops have entered Czernovitz. I hope the Russians have not too utterly destroyed the place. As far as our Command is concerned, the affair is practically at an end—we are now on the frontier of the Bukovina and Galicia, both of which provinces we have reconquered for the Emperor of Austria. Whether the Russians will make any serious counter-attacks I cannot yet say; it is not probable, but it is always possible. In any case, I hope that the situation is clear until the middle of August, and that we can turn our attention to something fresh. We ought not to leave the Russians any peace until they collapse. Propaganda and guns must work together.

August 4, 1917.

Nothing special here. Czernovitz was taken yesterday, and with that my interest in the operation comes to an end. Now the Archduke and Mackensen can take on the business.

August 5, 1917.

Our operation is practically at an end and I am devising something new.

August 9, 1917.

According to a newspaper report the Emperor of Austria has conferred on me the Iron Cross (Class II.)—a distinction that I can hardly regard as adequate to the services rendered.

The Emperor of Austria has made General von Kövess a Field-Marshal for the taking of Czernovitz —I have already said to Fleischmann, and will say it again in writing: " The idea of the Galician battle was mine and mine alone, and was carried out entirely in accordance with my instructions."

August 10, 1917.

There are some troop movements going on, and as they all come through Brest, if they can, everyone wants to know where he is to be sent. I hope the information I give them is correct and that no one will make me look a fool. There ought to be some sort of insurance against the loss of military reputation in such circumstances.

August 11, 1917.

Our nerves were rather on the stretch yesterday. Seekt, Chief of Staff to the Archduke Joseph, had started an offensive in continuation of our victory. Now we are being overwhelmed with appeals for help. I am against this, as a campaign in the Carpathians in support, or *ad majoram gloriam*, of the Austrians is futile. The railways are so bad that we could not get the troops down south, and, what is worse, we could never get them away again. The negotiations are going on at this moment. I do not want to give up my new plan—I want to carry it through in any circumstances, supposing the situation in the West makes it in any way possible. Ludendorff never leaves me in the lurch and has not done so this time: he shares my view. If all goes smoothly we may see a very pretty bit of work about the middle of September.

August 13, 1917.

The position is unchanged. All depends on whether we can hold on to our troops or not. Mackensen is calling for help, so is the Archduke Joseph, likewise the Chief of the Operations Section, who wants more troops for the West, but until now Ludendorff has been obdurate and refused them all. Unfortunately it is still some time until the beginning of September, and anything may happen. This waiting gets on a man's nerves.

August 14, 1917.

My military heaven is rather clouded over. I am afraid I shall have to give up some troops to the West. The English and French are apparently launching big attacks in Flanders, on the Aisne, and at Verdun, on both banks of the Meuse. I shall be very sorry if, as a result of this, nothing comes of our scheme, but I am afraid the prospect is poor. Insurance against loss of military reputation is becoming an absolute necessity.

August 15, 1917.

After a long silence I had another letter from Erzberger yesterday. The man is gradually becoming a public danger. He writes that he has been in Switzerland, where he has been negotiating with the Lithuanian leaders. He has apparently made promises to these people which are quite inconsistent with our views, and some of which could not possibly be made good: for example, he has promised them an independent kingdom. The Lithuanian is just about as capable of governing himself as my daughter Ilse is of educating herself. I have just rung him up to tell him so very politely. I have no intention of quarrelling with him, though his ridiculous Peace resolution is enough to make one do so.

August 18, 1917.

Ludendorff has just rung up to say that the need in the West is very urgent. Everyone is asking for troops. For the present he will not take any away from me. The question is what will be the outcome of the French attack at Verdun. If the need becomes very great there, then there is no help for it: we shall have to give up troops. I see that clearly —it can't be helped.

August 21, 1917.

Ludendorff rang up early yesterday morning: "I'm very sorry, I must have some troops." Very well: I sent out all the orders. In the afternoon he rang up again: "Perhaps I can manage": so I cancelled all the orders. To-day we shall probably get counter-orders again. I cannot blame Ludendorff: he would be only too glad for me to carry out my plan, and would like to leave me the troops. But it is, of course, more important that the Western Front should stand firm. The great French Verdun attack is, so far as the main objectives are concerned, a failure—only the "Mort-Homme" has been lost.

August 26, 1917.

Yesterday and to-day we had a crowd of guests. Turkish officers, high Staff officers passing through, Duke Johann Albrecht of Mecklenburg (who would like to be Duke of Kurland as well), all swarming around here. Dryander is coming shortly to hold

Divine Service on the Eastern Front. In the meantime there will be visits from Deputies of the Reichstag and Press representatives. I often hardly know how to manage them all.

September 10, 1917.

We got back yesterday afternoon. The first part of the Mitau offensive went according to plan.[1]

The Russians expected our attack farther to the West: they appear to have been convinced that they could not stand their ground on this side of the Düna, and had consequently made all preparations for a retreat to Riga. Our thrust was delivered near Uexküll and took them utterly by surprise: they immediately realized that they could no longer hold Riga and prepared to retreat beyond that city. We changed their retreat into something like a rout. Guns, boats, field-kitchens, and material of all sorts, were left standing and lying about everywhere. Unfortunately we made fewer prisoners than I had hoped, as the great majority of their troops, whom I had hoped to cut off, had just been evacuated from the bridge-head.

We should of course have liked to continue our advance in the direction of Petersburg, but unfortunately we had to stop, as Ludendorff, with the best will in the world, could not let us keep the necessary Divisions. He needs them, and Austria needs them,[2] so we must resign ourselves. H.M. has been here for three days, as gracious and kind to me as ever. As there are no more Prussian war decorations that could be conferred on me he has

---

[1] On September 1st the passage of the Düna was forced and Riga taken. After this preparations were made for the capture of the bridge-head of Jacobstadt and the occupation of the islands of Ösel, Moon and Dagö. The first operation took place on September 21st, and the second from 11th to 18th October: both were successful.

[2] In the meantime, on the Italian Front, the 11th battle of the Isonzo had started. The Italians had some success north and south of Gorizia.

given me his signed photograph in a gun-metal frame. H.R.H. applied for me to be promoted General: but Lyncker would not hear of it. It was no more than I had expected, so I was not disappointed. I greatly enjoyed my visits to Riga. Both on the first occasion, when I went alone with H.R.H., and especially when the Kaiser made his entry, the enthusiasm of the German population was most moving. We did not feel as though we were entering a conquered city, but a German city just set free. The marvellous weather and the magnificent panorama of Riga added to the effect.

September 11, 1917.

Russia seems to be all upside down again—the two Commanders-in-Chief, Korniloff and Kerenski, are actually fighting for the Dictatorship. I don't believe any other nation in the world has suffered such a state of affairs during a war.

We have more visitors: the Burgomaster of Lübeck, in addition to eight Reichstag Deputies. I am more excited about the last than the first.

Friend Erzberger has had a bad Press lately. Personally I think he has made a fool of himself. I have the impression that the Emperor Charles and, more especially, the Empress Zita have been making use of him against us, and to the advantage of Austria.

September 13, 1917.

Russia seems to be in a dreadful mess. Korniloff and Kerenski are fighting for the Dictatorship. It is such a pity we could not carry our offensive any farther. A German advance on Petersburg now would bring about the complete collapse of Russia.

September 14, 1917.

Colonel von Wrisberg, the most important man we have in the War Office, was very interesting on the subject of the situation in the Reichstag, and the Chancellor's incompetence to manage it. He had not a good word for Erzberger—no one has at present—who had, he said, allowed himself to be hopelessly entangled by the Emperor Charles and the Empress. The news of the domestic situation in France sounds excellent. The country is sick of the war, and the accounts we get from responsible and impartial persons in Switzerland are most encouraging, from our point of view.

September 29, 1917.

I do not share the anxiety that Ludendorff's position may be shaken. I know that Nicolai does not like me. I duly got him his job on the General Staff, and there is always something burdensome about a feeling of gratitude—it easily changes into dislike.

October 6, 1917.

A good half of the German people is convinced that if we hold on firmly we shall win an easy victory. I take a middle view: I am convinced that we cannot be conquered, but, on the other hand, that we are not in a position to win a complete victory over the English. On these grounds I am for a Peace by compromise, but not for one that means annexation.

October 10, 1917.

News came in the day before yesterday that the Emperor of Austria wanted to visit the Linsingen Army Group, and would like to take the opportunity of seeing H.R.H. Prince Leopold. As the

Prince does not come back from leave until to-day I decided to go to Kovel and meet the Emperor. After my experiences at Zloczov I did not look forward to doing so, but I was completely surprised. The Emperor was uncommonly friendly, invited Linsingen and myself, after he had reviewed the troops in Kovel, to go with him to Vladimir Volynsk and join him at lunch. I sat opposite him and we had a good talk. He is not exactly a shining light, but much cleverer than a Monarch needs to be.

Nothing special here. The Reichstag debates are a regrettable storm in a teacup. The excitement over the propaganda in the army is ridiculous. The Lecture Organization — combined with legal and other advice for the men—is not political, and of course will be conducted just as before. The Parties seem to have come to terms again with Helfferich. I can only laugh at the whole business.

October 12, 1917.

Our friend the Chancellor has postponed his visit here for forty-eight hours. I thought his attack on the Independent Socialists was foolish.[1] Either the three Comrades were so deeply involved in the Navy Treason case that they could be imprisoned, or he should have kept his mouth shut. On the other hand, the Reichstag impressed me less than ever throughout the whole affair. The attack on Helfferich reminded me irresistibly of the shootings at Hornberg.[2] Either refuse a man his pay, so that he has to go, or don't raise the subject at all.

[1] The Chancellor, Dr Michaelis, had made a sharp attack on the Independent Social Democratic Party in the Reichstag. The question raised was the connection of the Party with insubordinate elements in the High Seas Fleet. The Majority Parties in the Reichstag supported the I.S.D.P. against the Chancellor.

[2] A German proverbial phrase for invariably missing the mark.— *Translator.*

October 13, 1917.
A few days ago there was an attack by certain Deputies against the administration of the C.-in-C., East. Colonel von Brandenstein, who came to report on the debates, tells me that, besides the Social Democrat Ledebour, friend Erzberger has been incredibly abusive. These gentlemen take the view that all products of the occupied area belong to the inhabitants, and that it is an incredible piece of brutality on our part to send foodstuffs home from the occupied area. Only what is freely offered by the inhabitants should be taken for the use of the army and the population at home. We cannot of course accept this point of view. In Erzberger's case this is not a matter of conviction but a party move.

October 14, 1917.
It is very inconvenient that H.M. is not in Berlin at the moment, but on a visit to our Eastern Allies in Sofia and Constantinople. His visit to the Sultan is however essential, I believe, as our popularity in Turkey has considerably fallen off owing to lavish expenditure of American money.

October 18, 1917.
A report has just come in that we have successfully occupied the island of Moon. The Naval people were much more use, and more intelligent, than I had expected. They gave us more help than their officers thought they could promise when the affair was being discussed.

Now we have to take Dagö, and then we shall come to a stop once more. Anyhow we took about 10,000 prisoners at Ösel and about 50 guns. At the beginning of the war it would have been a great victory.

I met the Chancellor in Vilna and found him,

as I have said, better than I should have expected after his late performances in the Reichstag. He is not imposing, he makes no great impression upon further acquaintance, and he looks at all political questions rather from the point of view of a Finance Minister than a Statesman — still, compared with Bethmann, he has the advantage of at least speaking his mind clearly and calmly. We were in general agreement in all our political views, and in particular as regards the extent of the future Eastern Province. The question is whether he will stick to what he alleged to be his views.

October 19, 1917.

The propaganda for Falkenhayn is very amusing, but too late. At the time it must have been very difficult for him to find anyone to write this sort of stuff for him. The operations against Ösel, Moon and Dagö are making good progress. We have provisionally appointed a Governor for all three islands, although we have not yet got Dagö. On Moon we have captured a General with 5000 men. The Russian Army is in a bad state—what a pity we can't take advantage of it. If I hadn't had to give up those Divisions we should have got to Lake Peipus.

October 26, 1917.

One of the armies in the West was again too optimistic and helped the French to success, which will greatly encourage them to enter upon another winter of war. It is too bad! Every time there is a great success in the East, or one of the other theatres of war (*e.g.* Ösel and Italy), the West puts an extinguisher on it.[1]

[1] Since September 20th the third Flanders battle had been raging in the West, and in the course of it there were several serious crises. On October 22nd the French stormed the Laffaux salient—south-west of Laon—and completely shattered some German Divisions.

October 28, 1917.

There is heavy fighting in the West, the English mean to win a victory at all costs: which is a good sign. Good progress in Italy.¹ Many more than 60,000 prisoners, and more than 500 guns. We cannot yet foresee developments. I fancy that the Italians will very soon evacuate Gorizia, and go back behind the Tagliamento.

Yesterday I had a very interesting political interview with three gentlemen from Riga. The Livonians are more imposing than the Kurland Barons—they made a most excellent impression on me.

A report has just come in that the Austrians are already west of Gorizia, so the Italians must certainly have evacuated Gorizia yesterday. That city was the sole achievement of their eleven Isonzo battles.

October 30, 1917.

A telegram came in yesterday that H.M. had promoted me Major-General. I had ceased to count on it. H.R.H., upon the occasion of the capture of Ösel, Moon and Dagö, had telegraphed to Hindenburg and again asked for me to be promoted. Hindenburg and especially Ludendorff brought very strong pressure to bear and overcame the Cabinet's resistance. I gain two years and four months' seniority by this; the Colonels of April 1914 are now due for promotion, while my Colonelcy dates from August 1916. I am of course delighted with such an acknowledgment of the fact that we on the Eastern Front have really done our bit during the last year. Michaelis has gone. I hope Hertling will succeed him. I know of no other.

¹ The attack on Italy at Tolmino had begun on October 24th.

November 13, 1917.

I have a great deal to do. A long interview yesterday with Waldersee and Falkenhausen, neither of whom will take orders from the other, etc.[1]

November 20, 1917.

I have much to do, both over the scrapping of the whole administration, and also the complete *détente* on our Front has meant a great deal of work on the military side. We can take troops out of the line, drill and train them, etc., for I don't believe the Russians will ever pull themselves together for another attack on us.

November 21, 1917.

We cannot get a clear view of the Russian situation as yet. I have requested that the Imperial Chancellor should answer the Bolshevik peace-offer in his speech on the 29th. He can quite safely say: " Certain persons in Petersburg have sent out a wireless inquiry about peace. The German Government cannot tell whether the inquiries emanate from those who do in fact represent a Russian Government possessing the power to conclude a Peace. If they do, then the offer should be conveyed to us in the proper manner through the ambassador at Stockholm. We are ready to enter into negotiations." In this way we should deprive the Entente of their opportunity for counter-propaganda. At the moment they are of course saying to the Russian soldiers: " Now you see what the Germans are like, you offer them peace and they do not even answer you." Whether the Chancellor will do this, I cannot of course say.

[1] There had been a change in the administration of the area under the control of the C.-in-C., East. At the head of it were now a specially appointed Governor-General, General Count von Waldersee, and a high civil official, the Under-Secretary of State, Freiherr von Falkenhausen.

I had a long interview with Waldersee and Falkenhausen yesterday and drew up a scheme for the new government of the occupied territory.

November 26, 1917.

Here I sit advising the Russians to declare an Armistice. Whether they will I cannot yet say, and we have no clear picture of what is likely to happen in the interior of Russia in the immediate future.[1] Anyhow I have collected here during the last three days all the people I could who may be able to help me: Rosenburg of the Foreign Office (the most agreeable and sensible fellow they have got), a representative of the Naval Staff, a few Austrians, etc. At the moment they have nothing to do; they just sit around and make work.

November 27, 1917.

I hope we shall manage to finish off this business. Negotiations are going forward over the entire Front. Fighting has stopped at many points, and I hope we may establish a proper Armistice on the entire Front. I am expecting representatives of the Austrian G.H.Q. and the Austrian Foreign Office.

February 17, 1918.

To-morrow we are going to start hostilities again against the Bolsheviks.[2] No other way out

---

[1] In November the Bolsheviks had seized power; on November 26th the Government sent out an inquiry by wireless as to whether the German G.H.Q. were ready to conclude an armistice. G.H.Q. answered that they were. On December 2nd the Russian Armistice Commission crossed the German line at Dünaburg and went on to Brest-Litovsk. The C.-in-C., East, was authorized to conclude an Armistice, and on December 15th the Armistice was signed. It was to last until 12 noon, on January 14th, 1918.

[2] The Peace negotiations at Brest-Litovsk dragged on until February 10th, without any agreement having been reached. A separate Peace had been concluded with the Ukraine. On February 10th, Trotzky

is possible, otherwise these brutes will wipe up the Ukrainians, the Finns and the Balts, and then quietly get together a new revolutionary army and turn the whole of Europe into a pigsty. Of course, with the forces at present at our disposal here, I can't run a victorious express train to Petersburg, but I hope to achieve something all the same. I am very curious to see whether the Russians will defend themselves at all, or whether they will clear out without a fight. The situation in the Ukraine is not encouraging. The Ukrainian troops are, like the Russians, totally disorganized by revolutionary ideas, and they, too, simply want to " go home." The whole of Russia is no more than a vast heap of maggots—a squalid, swarming mess.

February 18, 1918.

To start hostilities again was certainly the right thing to do. The Foreign Office was against it, mainly from anxiety as to its possible effect at home. Whether we shall succeed in overthrowing the Bolsheviks sooner, we must wait and see. The situation in Russia must, indeed, be appalling— the most patient race in the world could scarcely stand such a state of affairs for long.

The Poles have apparently gone quite mad over the question of the Cholm district. There are strikes and all sorts of troubles in Warsaw. They let their political imagination run away with them. They have not moved a finger for their Kingdom, and yet, like children, they want everything.

stated that he would make no definite Peace, but that Russia regarded the war as at an end. As a result, a week later, the German Eastern Army began a general advance; the consequence of this advance was that the Russians expressed themselves as ready to continue the negotiations and conclude a Peace. Peace was made on March 3rd, and was followed on March 5th by the conclusion of a preliminary Peace with Rumania.

February 19, 1918.

We started our advance yesterday: took Dünaburg in the north, Luck in the south; and Trotzky and company immediately wirelessed from Petersburg that they were willing to sign a Peace.

February 20, 1918.

Events are moving here. The Russian Army is more rotten than I had supposed. There is no fight left in them. Yesterday one lieutenant with six men took six hundred Cossacks prisoner. Hundreds of guns, motor-cars, locomotives, trucks, and several thousand prisoners, were brought in without any sort of fighting at all.

Yesterday, in accordance with my instructions, I sent a wireless message to Herr Trotzky to the effect that his offer had been received, but that he must confirm it in writing to the " German Commandant at Dünaburg." Last night a reply came in at once that a courier was on the way with the document. He seems to be in a devil of a hurry—we are not. Unfortunately, our advance is very slow; we are short of horses for transport and the roads are bad; it will be some time before we can get to Lake Peipus.

February 21, 1918.

Our advance proceeds. Yesterday we marched across the ice from the islands into Esthonia. The Bolsheviks ran before we reached them. Up to yesterday evening we had captured more than 1500 guns, which were standing about all over the place on railway stations ready to be sent back.

Trotzky's written offer to sign a Peace has now come in. For the time being I have no notion how the Chancellor will handle the business. Anyhow, every day's delay is in our favour.

There is also a hitch in the negotiations for peace with Rumania: this is not so much due to the Rumanians as to the fact that we and the Austrians cannot agree over the spoils. We of course want considerable commercial privileges in connection with the petroleum wells, etc., and the Austrians are crying aloud to Heaven that they are getting nothing.

It seems that Kühlmann is going to Vienna to-day to join Czernin, and then they are both going on to Bukarest. At least that is what I hear—I can't guarantee its truth.

February 22, 1918.

Early this morning the ultimatum was sent off to Trotzky. It must be admitted that the Foreign Office and G.H.Q. have worked well together. It contains everything we ought to insist on. Whether Trotzky will accept it seems to me more than doubtful. But the position of the Bolshevik regime is probably so shaken that he will have to snatch at it. Our movements are proceeding according to plan. It is the most comical war I have ever known—it is almost entirely carried on by rail and motor-car. We put a handful of infantrymen with machine guns and one gun on to a train and push them off to the next station; they take it, make prisoners of the Bolsheviks, pick up a few more troops and go on. This proceeding has, at any rate, the charm of novelty.

February 25, 1918.

I am expecting the Peace Delegations to come in one by one to-day and to-morrow. Whether Trotzky will take the road to Canossa in person, or will send someone else, is not yet certain. The negotiations here will last three to four days at the most, as this time the Comrades must simply swallow what we put before them.

March 1, 1918.

The first meeting is to be at eleven o'clock to-day. According to my information the Russians will protest, but will agree to all the demands contained in the ultimatum. Any additional demand they will certainly refuse.

I have endless work to do. I hear from Bukarest that Rumania is, at the moment, taking a very high line, and that prospects of peace are, for the time being, slight. The situation will change in our favour as soon as we have fixed up peace here.

March 7, 1918.

Nothing fresh here. We are waiting to see if Russia will duly ratify the Peace—they must do so within a fortnight. Otherwise we shall certainly march on Petersburg. In the meantime Lenin has summoned a great congress at Moscow for the 15th. Our operations in the Ukraine are going forward. We are, of course, moving more slowly than at first, as our Bolshevik friends are now beginning to destroy the railways.

March 8, 1918.

In the Ukraine we are still advancing—chiefly in the direction of Odessa, and then from Kiev to the East; in Esthonia and Livonia there is a sort of guerrilla war. Apart from this, for weeks past, everything that is not absolutely immovable has been put on the train for the West. I wish I could be there, but I haven't a chance. Even the greatest personages suffer from jealousy, so I don't think that Ludendorff is likely to let me have my finger in the pie.

Erzberger's story is, of course, pure imagination. It may be assumed that the Russians secretly hope that their Peace terms may be reconsidered at the general Peace. None of them said so.

March 12, 1918.

More serious trouble here. Mumm, who is to go as our diplomatic representative to Kiev, arrived yesterday, and also a Polish mission (General Musnicki). I have sent Brinckmann to Kiev to treat with the Ukrainian Government there. The difficulty in the Ukraine is simply that the Central Rada has only our rifles behind it. The moment we withdraw our troops their authority will collapse at once. The cause of this is the land problem. On the land question the more moderate Social Democrats, who compose the Rada, are just as idiotic as the Bolsheviks—*i.e.* they also have confiscated the landed estates and given them to the peasants. Consequently the agricultural industry in the Ukraine is ruined. The bulk of the land was represented by the large estates. The peasants have now divided and taken over these properties, but they will not risk cultivating them, because they do not know whether they will in fact be left in possession of the land. Everyone is rolling in money—roubles are printed and almost given away. A cigar costs six roubles at Kiev, and a cup of tea with sugar five roubles, dinner twenty-four roubles, and so on. The peasants have enough stocks of corn to live on for two or three years, but they will not sell it.

The Petersburg Government migrated to Moscow yesterday, so as to take a vote there on the ratification of peace. I think they will ratify, but I have got out of the habit of prophecy.

March 13, 1918.

Endless trouble with the Austrians in the Ukraine. They want to enter Odessa alone, and are behaving with their usual meanness when the knife is not at their throat.

March 14, 1918.

I don't yet know whether our worthy Comrades in Moscow have decided to recognize the Peace or not. It almost looks as if not, as otherwise they would have already wirelessed. In that case we must, of course, take Petersburg. Yesterday some more Russians suggested a visit. A representative of the Monarchistic parties has arrived in Vilna to ask our help for the restoration of the Monarchy. It costs nothing to give the man a hearing, so I have invited him here.

I am having the most frantic trouble with the Austrians in the Ukraine. It is a pity that the Italians do not attack. One can deal with the Austrians only when they are in difficulties.

As regards Eastern affairs the Reichstag—especially Erzberger—are making a mess of things. The Chancellor is shortly to receive a Lithuanian deputation, and I am afraid that they will then do something foolish in Berlin. It is possible to make something of Lithuania only if it is closely associated with Prussia: any sort of independent Lithuania would be hopeless. Whether Erzberger is too stupid to see this, or whether Roman interests would not allow such an increase in Prussia's influence, is more than I can say.

March 21, 1918.

I can't raise much excitement over Falkenhayn.[1]

[1] After his recall from Turkey, General von Falkenhayn had received a command on the Eastern Front.

He will have no more important strategic problems to solve here, and personally I have nothing whatever to do with him—I deal with his Chief of Staff.

Much trouble with the Lithuanian Government. Comrade Erzberger has roused the National Assembly to fury against us, and the Chancellor seems to defer to Erzberger's most lunatic suggestions. These people want to go back on their resolution of December by which, in return for the recognition of their independence, they bound themselves to a close association with Germany, a military convention, etc. They now insist on independence first of all. I hope the Chancellor does not give way.

March 22, 1918.

The conquest of the Ukraine proceeds slowly but surely. I also believe that we shall get such supplies of corn as we absolutely need. At the same time it seems to me doubtful whether we shall succeed in helping the Austrians in time. We don't want ours till June: they want it in April, and we can't get it so quickly.

March 23, 1918.

There are serious riots among the dockers in the Black Sea ports, which are apparently giving trouble to our troops. I have no further information, as the troops in those parts are under Mackensen. Our movements in the Ukraine are proceeding according to plan.

Yesterday we had a visit from Lindequist, the ex-Secretary of State, with a German clergyman, representing the German colonists in South Russia and the Crimea. The clergyman talked a good deal about the right of self-determination, and, on this ground, suggested the union of the Tartars of the Crimea and the German colonists, thus combining the Crimea and the adjoining provinces into a German colony. I told him I had no objection.

There would be no object in my discussing the Lithuanian question with Erzberger, as our views are too far apart, and he has done too much harm already.

March 25, 1918.

I think it possible that the lately published Memorandum by Lichnowsky was disclosed by Witting: he let me see it too.

March 29, 1918.

G.H.Q. has produced a considerable upset here. As the establishment of transport facilities in the Ukraine is of the very first importance, it was decided that General Gröner, the former Director of Railways, should be sent there. As it was also felt that he would not get on with Linsingen (who is difficult), Linsingen was removed from his post and replaced by Eichhorn. Gröner becomes his Chief of Staff, so Keller also, the former Chief of Staff of that Army Group, is left high and dry. The Eichhorn Army Group (our Northern Army Group) is to cease to exist as a unit, and the three armies of which it consisted are to be under the immediate authority of Ober-Ost. This method of creating a sphere of authority for Gröner was simple, but a trifle high-handed. I have never regarded Linsingen as a great commander—still, for the last three years he has been one of our most distinguished Generals. I find it rather difficult simply to send him a telegram to the effect that "H.M. has no further use for your services."

April 3, 1918.

I had a great deal to do to-day, as Waldersee came in for a long talk. There was no particular point in our discussion, as G.H.Q. and the Chancellor were not yet in agreement about Livonia, and so many authorized and unauthorized persons had got their fingers into the Lithuanian pie that nobody knows what will be the end of it.

There is a further advance in the West, and they all seem confident. We have not details of any kind. Everything and everybody (even from the Staff) that could be spared has been shifted to the West. I often think that it is really a pity that Hindenburg and Ludendorff did not get me a Division. The command of a Division in the West at present would, anyway, be much more interesting and offer much better prospects than my dead post here. However, following the proverb, "Never interfere with your military destiny," I shall do nothing, but calmly await further developments. I must just live on recollections.

April 4, 1918.

All proceeds according to plan in the Ukraine. We have now occupied the whole of the Crimea, and on the East we have nearly everywhere reached the boundary of the Ukraine. All we need now for the complete control of the Black Sea are the ports of Taganrog and Novorossisk, and those we must have.[1]

April 8, 1918.

I am expecting a number of visitors to-day. The future Commander-in-Chief of the I. Polish Corps, General Dowbor-Musnicki, is coming to

---

[1] Our operations in the Caucasus area were also conditioned by our needs in regard to war material. We had accordingly to get control of Baku and the Baku—Tiflis—Batoum railway in order to cover our shortage of oil. By agreement with the Chancellor, Colonel von Kress was sent to Tiflis to represent G.H.Q., together with an escort of two companies. As the English tried, by crossing the Caspian Sea, to get possession of Baku, Colonel von Kress was reinforced by one Cavalry Brigade and a few battalions.

confer with representatives of the Governor-General of Warsaw and a member of the Regency Council. He would have preferred to go to Warsaw, but Ludendorff would not allow it. I would have let him go; it is useless to annoy people over such trifles.

April 9, 1918.

We have taken Kharkov. I could never have dreamt a while ago that German troops would enter that little hole.

The discussions with the Poles were very interesting. They really have quite lost their heads. They are visionaries, who spend their time dreaming, and do not, or will not, understand realities.

April 24, 1918.

We are progressing slowly, but according to plan, in the Crimea. We have taken Simferopol and we shall shortly attack Sebastopol.

No news from the West, except that our great airman, Rittmeister von Richthofen, has been killed.

April 26, 1918.

In the Ukraine the situation is coming to a head. The Government is making further difficulties, and I am afraid that we shall have to look for another. The storming of Mount Kemmel is the most important event in the West. From that point we can control the whole stretch of country towards the north, so that the English will certainly have to give up Ypres.

April 29, 1918.

There is the devil to pay in the Ukraine. However, Eichhorn has the situation well in hand, so that I think we shall emerge from it without serious trouble. Part of the Government there has established an anti-German League. Eichhorn has accordingly arrested these gentlemen. A wife of one of the Ministers (as might be expected) played a great part. She also is under arrest. It will, of course, cause alarm in certain quarters. If the Government retires we shall have to set up another; however, it will certainly be better than the existing one. Eichhorn is being most bitterly attacked in the Reichstag; but everything he does in the Ukraine is the result of most careful consultation between the Chancellor, the Foreign Office and G.H.Q.

I am in two minds at the moment. Shall I go to Kovno or shall I stay here? I think Kovno would be better for the future, but the situation in the Ukraine is so obscure at the moment that it is really more practical to be rather more on the spot.

April 30, 1918.

From the political point of view the chief event is that the Ukrainians have at last overthrown their Government. They have summoned a General to be Hetman of the Ukraine and Dictator.[1] As this gentleman stands by the Brest-Litovsk Peace and other agreements regarding the delivery of corn, etc., this is very likely to our advantage. On the other hand, as a result of the change of Government, Eichhorn's not very tactful treatment of the former Ukrainian Government may perhaps be forgotten —not that any blame attaches to Eichhorn personally, but certain minor personages behaved like the bull in the china shop.

May 1, 1918.

The difficulties of arranging for our prisoners of war to cross our lines at certain points take some

[1] Hetman Skoropadski had been a General Commanding in the Tsarist Army.

dealing with, and it is one of those tasks that must involve minor hardships. Everyone thinks he is the only one, and must be sent home at the earliest possible moment. There were about 1,500,000 Austrian prisoners and about 100,000 of ours. These are now all streaming back. In addition, there are about three to four million of the population of Poland, Lithuania and Kurland now wandering home again: part of them were carried off by the Russians, and part fled before our advance. The railways are hardly a practicable means of transport as we have too few locomotives. We must get rid of the Austrians as soon as possible, otherwise we shall have to feed them. So we can't provide a special train for everybody. I grant that it is trying and tedious to have to wait eight or ten days, but it can't be helped.

Nothing special from Kiev. The change of Government has been smoothly carried out and the city and the country are quiet. It is only the Foreign Office and the Chancellor who are anxious. God! It is really pitiable how afraid people are of the Reichstag! I have been only indirectly informed of the whole story, but of course I shall have to take up an attitude of opposition to the Foreign Office.

May 2, 1918.

The Don Cossacks have telegraphed to the German Emperor, asking him to help them against the Bolsheviks. . . . They are quite fond of us now. I am against mixing ourselves up in the affairs of the Don province—our Eastern movement must come to an end some time.[1]

---

[1] The Entente made a stand against Bolshevism. They organized formations of Czecho-Slovak troops in Russia on the Siberian border and gradually moved them forward to the line of the Middle Volga.

In the north, Entente troops moved up the Dvina from the White Sea,

May 6, 1915.

G.H.Q. is in direct touch with Kiev and believe they understand the position there better than we do. I am afraid that this will lead to the collapse of the Ukraine which cost us so much trouble to create. The efforts of G.H.Q. and Eichhorn are, though they do not know it, driving the Ukraine back into the arms of Great Russia. At the moment this does not greatly matter, but for future purposes I should have thought it useful to have preserved the Ukraine as an independent entity. I shall call attention to this again to-day, so as to clear my conscience, but it will not be much use—my political insight is no longer esteemed as it used to be. Well, I must try not to mind.

May 7*th*, 1918.

Dr Rohrbach, the well-known writer, came to see me yesterday on his way to Kiev. Interesting man, a Balt by birth, pan-German, and oddly enough well disposed to the Poles. I had a good talk for the first time for weeks, and learned a few things I did not know. He shares my anxieties about the Ukraine and promised to use his influence in the right direction at Kiev and later on at home.

May 21, 1918.

I have had long conversations with the famous Dr Rohrbach, who is just back from Kiev, and with

and southwards from the Murman coast along the Murman railway. On the Dvina the advance was very slow. The Murman railway was destroyed by the Bolsheviks. On the west of the Lower Volga the Don Cossacks under General Krasnoff were in conflict with the Soviet troops. German G.H.Q. entered into relations with General Krasnoff to prevent him joining the Entente.

In the Kuban province, between the Don Cossacks and the Caucasus, General Alexeieff was fighting Bolshevik troops with his volunteer army. Alexeieff was under English influence.

Olszewski. Rohrbach confirmed my fears that the Ukraine is steering straight towards a new Greater Russia. I hope that Brinckmann, whom I have instructed accordingly, may be able to use his weight against this. I have asked Rohrbach to let me have his full impressions in writing so that I may put the matter forward officially. Olszewski was very sensible. I had already agreed with Waldersee and Falkenhausen how far we could meet his wishes.

May 22, 1918.

Yesterday there were further negotiations with the I. Polish Corps of General Dowbor. As the Warsaw Regency Council has allowed itself to be involved in conspiracies with the Polish troops and the Ukraine, all still existing Polish formations must be disbanded and disarmed. I had not thought that Dowbor would have given way without a fight, and we had, accordingly, pretty strong forces ready for any emergency. He was, however, astute enough to accept all our conditions.

May 23, 1918.

The Ukraine still causes me anxiety. The men at present in control there are steering straight for union with Great Russia. However, that beautiful land is now fortunately in such a mess that the Hetman may perhaps think twice before he makes a move. For example, the partition of the land in Russia is by this time practically accomplished. The land has been taken away from the landlords and given to the peasants. Thus any future Government, whether the Monarchists or the Cadet Party get into power, is in a very difficult position. If they take the land away from the peasants the Revolution will start again, and they will find it hard to suppress it even if they can create a new army, for the soldier is a peasant. If, on the other hand, they leave the land to the peasants, they are founding their authority on the basis of a broad, illiterate democracy, without any higher stratum from which they can get officers and officials. So that the Russian problem is, I am thankful to say, by no means simple. We have information from all sides to the effect that the Bolsheviks will soon collapse from incompetence, but I don't think they will yet awhile. There is no one to take their place, as there is no army to support a new sovereign power.

May 25, 1918.

Nothing of any great importance has been happening here. The Peace negotiations between the Ukraine and Great Russia are slowly getting under way, the Don Cossacks have entered into an alliance with the Ukraine, with a view to getting their and our help against the Bolsheviks. I should have no objection to pushing farther and farther eastwards —I should like to get to India, except that the distances grow more immense, and our army does not.

I hear little or nothing from the West. I had thought that the lull would be over, and that they would be on the move again by now, but it seems that the preparations are not yet made. In any case, our troops there are ready for any developments.

May 26, 1918.

The Chief of Staff of the Dünaburg army has just rung up to say that they arrested sixty people there yesterday who had planned a large anti-German conspiracy—a peasant rising, murder of officers, etc. A good part of them were agitators released by the Bolshevik Government.

May 30, 1918.

I paid my call on the local Bishop yesterday. Like all important Catholic ecclesiastics, he is a clever, cultivated man. In contrast to his Vilna colleague, he is a thorough Lithuanian, and well disposed to the Germans.

The Entente is making colossal efforts to stir up trouble over here in the East. Their agents are trying to stir up the peasants—especially in the Ukraine.

June 4, 1918.

I have the impression that in the West our advance has gradually come to a stand on the Rheims—Soisson line. The French have apparently brought up all their available Reserves—as we hoped they would do. A continuation of the offensive here would thus mean very heavy losses—if I were in Ludendorff's place I would break it off at this point, and make a thrust at a place where the French have now no Reserves.

June 5, 1918.

The position here is unchanged. The I. Polish Corps (Dowbor-Musnicki) is being gradually disarmed and sent home, the negotiations at Novorossisk over the remains of the Russian Black Sea fleet are still in suspense, and the Peace negotiations in Kiev are proceeding very slowly. At home the Government, especially the Foreign Office, are in a state of terror over the possible antics of the next Reichstag. It is really pitiable.

The situation in the West is as I had thought—*i.e.* our offensive has gradually come to an end again. We must now wait patiently until another can be started elsewhere.

June 16, 1918.

It is not in our power to end the war, we are simply forced to go on fighting. Kühlmann is no fool. If he saw a means, or an opportunity, of getting America out of the business he would have long since seized it. The idea that America might make peace, if we took a step to the left in our domestic politics and transferred the sovereign power to the Reichstag, is in my opinion erroneous. On the contrary, we should go to the dogs, from a military point of view, if people like Erzberger and Richthofen were allowed to have a say in military matters. There is no help for it, we must set our teeth and hold on.

There has been all manner of fighting in the Ukraine in the last few days. Near Taganrog, 10,000 Bolsheviks from the Kuban province made a sudden landing and attacked our troops in Rostov. The Würtemberg Landwehr there were very much annoyed. South of Kiev there were a few Bolshevik peasant risings, but they were suppressed in a few days.

June 17, 1918.

The Austrians have actually attacked, and they report 10,000 prisoners. Anyway, the whole thing is a *succès d'estime*. I would never have thought that they could have induced their men to attack. They are so utterly sick of the whole thing.

The position in the West is good. The French are in a complete quandary. I hope we may have a few more long-range guns ready: I anticipate a strong moral effect from a more vigorous bombardment of Paris. The tone of the French newspapers is already different from what it has been in the last four years.

There is a great deal of work here as usual,

and not much satisfaction to be got from it. To-day I am expecting the Saxon Minister, von Seydwitz. The newspapers have been discussing the proposal for the union of Saxony and Lithuania under one crown, and now the Minister is coming to look into the position. I think the whole thing is lunacy. The Lithuanians themselves will make all manner of difficulties, and the Saxons have not enough officials to fill all the posts in the Administration. The King is, of course, extremely enthusiastic over it.

June 18, 1918.

A certain deputy, Michalkiewicz runs the administration of Lithuania in Vilna; he is a true blue Pole of the most besotted kind, and gives us a great deal of trouble. We have been trying for months to get rid of the man and to get in a Lithuanian in his place. The Poles, whose influence in Rome is greater than that of our Foreign Office, know how to put difficulties in our way. But when Michalkiewicz recently used the Corpus Christi procession for a large Polish demonstration Ludendorff's patience gave way, and we have orders to remove Herr Michalkiewicz. This will be done to-morrow, and will no doubt give rise to a great outcry. I should have thought that, if our Foreign Office had displayed a little more energy *vis-à-vis* the Curia, it would have been possible to secure his recall. But if nothing came of this, then I share the view that it is right to remove him by force. We must show these people that we mean business.

June 20, 1918.

Public feeling in France and Italy individually seems to be falling below zero, which is very encouraging. Their only hope now is America. Any considerable defeat before America's help makes itself felt will, I think, mean the fall of Clemenceau and Lloyd George. That would be an important step towards peace.

June 26, 1918.

Kühlmann has made an ill-advised speech. I assume that he will probably disappear. The difficulty is, who will be his successor? There are so few that are fitted for the post. And the regrettable thing is that Kühlmann probably meant something quite different, and does not deserve to be dismissed.

I laughed over Stresemann's flaming speech of protest. I often think of his and Bernstorff's demeanour at Witting's some while ago, and now he is a fanatical Pan-German, Militarist, and Annexationist.[1]

June 29, 1918.

As regards politics, it seems as though the Parties of the Left in the Reichstag want to keep Kühlmann: whether they will succeed seems to me doubtful. The Chancellor's visit to G.H.Q. has nothing to do with the Kühlmann crisis: he had been summoned there some time ago. It seems to me significant that our Ambassador in Christiania, Hintze, has arrived in Berlin. He has long been H.M.'s candidate for the Foreign Secretaryship. Hintze has been a naval officer, and a military attaché in Petersburg, and is regarded as a clever man. I do not know him personally, but judging from his dispatches he is rather unpractical.

[1] Secretary of State von Kühlmann, in his speech in the Reichstag on June 24th, had stated in general outline his views of a possible Peace, and in doing so had stated that the war could hardly be brought to an absolute end by a military decision alone, without diplomatic negotiations.
This observation finally led to his resignation and replacement by Admiral von Hintze.

July 3, 1918.

According to our representatives in Russia, the days of the Bolsheviks are numbered. I cannot be so confident of their fall, as I do not see who is to succeed them. Whether the Monarchists have the necessary courage and energy remains to be seen.

July 5, 1918.

The political and military situation is, generally speaking, unchanged. Every day we get several telegrams, "The fall of the Bolsheviks is imminent," but I do not feel so confident. It would be too stupid of the others to assume control before the beginning of the new harvest, as the essential condition of every new Government is to remedy a shortage of food. I do not yet entirely understand the speeches by the Social Democrats in the Reichstag against G.H.Q. I do not understand what Scheidemann's object is. Perhaps I shall find someone to explain it to me on my way through Berlin.

July 7, 1918.

In my opinion the Entente as well as the Cadet Party are behind this crime [the murder of Count Mirbach in Moscow]. Many hope that this may lead to a renewal of hostilities between Germany and Russia. I am sure the Bolsheviks had nothing whatever to do with it. They have promised to do everything they can to catch the murderer. We must wait and see whether they are successful.

July 20, 1918.

I had a tremendous rush in Berlin. Everything settled to my satisfaction at the Ministry of War. I could not agree with the Quartermaster-General about our situation in the East. In the afternoon

I met Kühlmann at the hotel, and had a very interesting talk with him. Towards the evening Your Friend, among others, came to see me.

The general feeling in the Foreign Office about the late resignation is not encouraging. They are all so uncertain. None of them dares to do or say anything until he knows the attitude of G.H.Q. on the matter. In many respects this is not without its advantages, but it leads to a good deal of uncertainty. The best thing would be for Ludendorff to become Chancellor; that would clear things up.

July 23, 1918.

The affair in the West is a nuisance, having regard to public feeling at home—though from the military point of view it is of small importance. Although the troops in the field were warned by G.H.Q., which foresaw the French attack, the troops allowed themselves to be surprised.[1]

July 27, 1918.

Our great administrative transformation is now in progress. Our Ober-Ost administration is coming to an end almost entirely, and will be divided between the administrations of Lithuania and the Baltic provinces. It is a good move, apart from the question of personnel, which has been badly handled. For example, in agreement with G.H.Q. and the Q.M.G., we had proposed Count Waldersee for the newly created Military Governorship of Lithuania. The Military Cabinet opposed this and appointed General von Harbou, who has never been in Lithuania before. By way of compensation,

[1] On July 18th the French counter-attack at Soissons began, which led to the evacuation of the Marne salient. The evacuation was carried out according to plan in the night of July 26th-27th.

he is to have a new Chief of the Administration who has never done any political work. We shall have to keep pretty wide awake to see that these fellows don't make fools of themselves. It is an excellent thing that the three Baltic provinces should at last come under a single administration. Gossler, however, is to be at the head of the combined administration, and I don't think he is fit for it. We seem to have an unlucky touch in personal matters. However, the whole reorganization is a step in the right direction.

Now we have got a new job too over the Russian propaganda. I had long been abusing the authorities for conducting our propaganda on the wrong lines. So G.H.Q. have skilfully got out of the difficulty by simply handing the work over to us. If only I had my old Intelligence Officer, Major Hey, it would be a very simple matter. But now I have got Prince George of Bavaria instead, so I must get on to the job myself.

July 28, 1918.

The position in the West is, as I have said, from the military aspect, extremely unimportant, but the effect of the retreat on public feeling at home is extremely unfortunate.

Lyncker, who has been ill several times lately, has left the Cabinet, and has become President of the Imperial Military Court. His successor is not yet known. Some time ago I should have been glad, as I was not on very good terms with Lyncker, but latterly he had been invariably open to reason, and agreeable to me, so that I am really very sorry he is going.

Waldersee gave up his post yesterday. I am very sorry. Besides, it was very stupid to take him away from here.

WAR DIARIES

August 1, 1918.

All my enjoyment of the excursion, the lovely woods and the fresh air, was clouded by the news of Eichhorn's murder. It is the most damnable thing. The Social Revolutionaries are going back to their vilest Nihilistic times. From the purely personal point of view I was very upset. I was very fond of old Eichhorn and he of me. He often wrote to me, whenever he was seriously troubled over any matter. I also knew Captain von Dressler very well.

August 3, 1918.

I am overwhelmed with work. Now that Waldersee has gone, all the administrative officials want to see me. Until the major part of the administration is divided between Lithuania and the Baltic provinces this place will be full of people coming and going all day long. And trouble of all kinds.

August 6, 1918.

It is, of course, not impossible that the Russian Social Revolutionaries will try their hand at further murders, and it would be foolish not to take precautions. Those chiefly in danger are, of course, our people in Moscow, Kiev, Odessa, and such places in Russia itself (as compared with Ukraine) where there is much street traffic. Although we are not in much danger here, I have got a large number of Security Police about the place. Visitors are carefully watched and escorted, and the streets barricaded.

August 8, 1918.

If the English move farther south along the Murman railway we shall unquestionably have to go to Petersburg. We cannot let the English occupy Petersburg and Kronstadt. I do not imagine a march to Petersburg would be very difficult. However, we must be prepared for everything.

August 9, 1918.

In the West there seems to have been a further small mishap. Apparently we have again allowed ourselves to be surprised. Otherwise I can't understand what did happen, as we have plenty of troops, etc.[1]

The situation here is gradually coming to a head. The Entente has organized a vast propaganda in Russia. Whether we can still cope with it seems more than doubtful. However, we will try.

Our Embassy is to be shifted from Moscow, as it is too unsafe there. I should have proposed Kovno, but the Highest Authorities do not agree, so it is to come to Dünaburg or Pskov.

August 12, 1918.

Nothing new here. Yesterday I had a very interesting interview with a Russian Monarchist, a German Russian, on the situation in Russia and probable developments. He thinks (as I said months ago) that we were unfortunate in neglecting to make propaganda for ourselves and against the Entente, and that England is consequently ahead of us. He regards the English occupation of the Murman area as dangerous for us, and he considers that we must certainly deal with it in some way. Either the Russians must turn them out or we must. I hope that influential quarters may take this to heart: it rather looks as if they may.

[1] The 2nd Army was heavily defeated on August 8th between Albert and Moreuil.

August 14, 1918.

The position here is unchanged. The treaty with Russia is so far ready that Comrade Joffe has gone to Moscow to get it signed. I shall be curious to see what happens then. We cannot in any case tolerate any further English advances in Murmansk. Either the Russians must throw them out or we must. The affair in the West seems to be a wash-out. The only advantage is that the Reichstag was not sitting. The —— would, of course, have lost their nerve again, and talked the most appalling rubbish. That is clear from the fact that the *Berliner Tageblatt* demands that the Committee should meet.

Erzberger is behaving like an idiot again over the question of the Lithuanian crown. He has written to the —— that they need not be afraid—he, by the favour of God, Herr Erzberger, will see that they get their Urach[1] for King. The man is a public danger.

August 15, 1918.

Our Military Attaché from Moscow[2] was here to-day; he had come back with the Embassy. It is noteworthy that, to a man who has lived in all that beastliness, and been in the closest possible contact with the saner elements and heard their execration of Bolshevik rule, the political situation in Russia looks quite different from what it does to us here. In Moscow the entire Peace of Brest-Litovsk is regarded as a crime against humanity. How could the Germans have had anything to do with such brutes? It was unworthy of a great

[1] The Duke of Urach: a connection of the Royal House of Wurtemberg. —*Translator*.
[2] Major Schubert. He and the leader of the Delegation, Secretary of State Helfferich, were both agreed that Germany must break with the Soviets. Hoffmann took the same view. As to Hoffmann's attitude, see *The War of Lost Opportunities*, chapter xvii.

Empire, etc. These people forget that the Bolsheviks were the only party who made us an offer of peace, and that it was only as a result of the Armistice and the Peace Treaty that we succeeded in so disintegrating the Russian Army that it collapsed, and we were able to transfer 1,000,000 men from the East to the West.

August 18, 1918.

Ludendorff seems to have got his way over the Polish business; with any luck, we shall get at least 1,500,000 more Polish subjects, and, therewith, the embittered enmity of the new Polish Kingdom. Well, it's all one to me.

August 19, 1918.

It is obvious that Ludendorff under-estimated the enemy, after the first great successes. However, the retreat seems to have been caused by gross carelessness on the part of the troops. At one point where the French attacked they were actually getting in the harvest—so it is said.[1] It is the old, old story that the rank and file are always careless. At the moment I consider that our position in the West is secure.

I can only repeat that the blunder lay in the premature shouts of victory, the award of the Star with Rays to Hindenburg, etc. As a result of all this the nation was wrongly led to believe that all would be over in a few weeks: so that the disappointment was doubly severe.

My only hope now is that the English will try to bring off a coup from the Murmansk in the direction of Petersburg. Then we must attack. It is too boring here, and the whole thing is getting on our nerves.

---

[1] A myth. The cause was a surprise tank attack, under cover of mist.

August 22, 1918.

Yesterday I had a very interesting conversation on Russian affairs with one of the former Russian Generals who had retired to his estate in the area occupied by us, and I at once telegraphed the gist of it to G.H.Q. I repeated what I had been saying for weeks: we shall have to attack, otherwise the English from Murmansk will get us in the rear. If the Entente set up a Tsar in Russia, then Russia will be closed to us.

They have unlimited money and are working feverishly. But I hope we shall attack in time. G.H.Q. and the Foreign Office seem to me to be convinced of the importance of the affair.

August 23, 1918.

Solf's speech is very astute. I laughed over only one thing: he says roughly what Kühlmann had said; they shouted "crucify him" at Kühlmann, but nothing is too good for Solf. Hintze seems to me cleverer than Kühlmann and understands better how to deal with Ludendorff. I am curious to know the result of the Polish negotiations—I have heard nothing at present. But I am especially interested to know what will come of the point in dispute between Ludendorff and myself—*i.e.* whether we actually take that broad strip of buffer territory or not. I have always thought, and still think, it would be a political blunder, and a disaster, for us to annex one more Pole than was absolutely necessary.

August 26, 1918.

Yesterday I had a very interesting interview with one Herr von Maltzahn, Deputy and Provincial

Councillor. He was for a long time with the Crown Prince, with whom he keeps up a constant exchange of views. He gave me his impressions of the West, where he was lately at Ludendorff's H.Q., of Rumania and of conditions at home. He had had an interview with Ludendorff at the request of the Conservatives, who were considering how best to encourage public opinion. I then explained my views on the East, and asked him to make them known and support them, which he gladly agreed to do. I think it absolutely essential that we should attack soon. If the Entente sets up a Tsar without our co-operation we shall be eliminated from Eastern Europe for the next half-century. As our trade with the West will be negligible in the first few years after the war it is doubly important to keep the East open and an access by land to Asia. I hope that our convincing appeals may get some attention in the long run.

August 28, 1918.

I am waiting to see whether the Foreign Office does not come over to my view—at present they don't seem inclined to. I have suggested to G.H.Q. that I might perhaps take a train to Berlin one day and talk to the Secretary of State. I have not yet had a reply.

August 29, 1918.

I am in an evil temper. Everyone is apparently too blind or too stupid to see the growing danger in the East. I don't mean in the military sense— I don't think the Entente will succeed in ever getting a Russian army on its legs and inducing it to fight us—but politically we shall be pushed out of Eastern Europe—and for a long while too. I look everywhere for some means of getting a finger into the pie later on, but I see no prospects.

September 3, 1918.

I talked to Hintze in Berlin, and, besides him, Radowitz, Winterfeldt, Richthofen, Erzberger. . . . I also had an evening at the Club, and met a crowd of princes, etc., there.

My general impression was not at all encouraging. Public feeling in Berlin is not good. For the most part people are saying what I do. We started the summer badly. All those laurels in advance, and all those jubilations, and then a retreat, make a bad impression.

The Secretary of State is definite and lucid, and I should say clever and well informed beyond the average. He has a certain self-confidence that is not displeasing—he knows everything. So long as he is right I don't care. To my astonishment I found that we were in agreement about the position in Russia and the necessity for an attack there in good time. We disagreed only on small matters, and the date. He thought we could wait a little longer. I consider waiting dangerous. G.H.Q. has also much emphasized the difficulties, apparently. It almost looks as if Ludendorff did not want to stick fast in the East. I also got the Prince to sign a long telegram, yesterday evening, in which I expressed my view. So that I have relieved my conscience. If, after all that, they do not do what I advise, I can help them no more, and must just wait and see what happens.

Anyhow I explained my view of the position in the East to everyone in Berlin. I see no military danger, but I see a gloomy commercial future for us in the East if we let the Entente get in with them and do nothing ourselves.

September 4, 1918.

Yesterday evening our plenipotentiaries to the Federal Council were here. I took the opportunity to explain to these gentlemen after dinner my views about the East. For the most part they had been hopelessly taken in—they all thought that the Bolsheviks were charming people and that all was in excellent order.

September 5, 1918.

Yesterday I had a visit from an important Russian banker, who made a deep impression on me. He was the sort of man who appears in modern novels —a superman: either the greatest genius, in the spheres of trade, industry and industrial policy, or a colossal swindler. He offered himself and his organization (as he would have me believe), Banks, Railways, Press, Priesthood, Senate, etc., in our support. I, of course, accepted, but I don't yet know what it will cost. It seems that he has a capital of 500 millions, against which there are, of course, gigantic debt charges. Probably he sees that a continuance of the Bolshevik regime will involve a gigantic smash, which he can avoid only if we invade Russia and he remains in power by supporting us.

September 7, 1918.

The position is unchanged here. Apparently G.H.Q. and the Foreign Office cannot yet decide to make a move here, so that I feel gravely anxious. As a result of the English plot there is a Red Terror in Moscow and Petersburg. The better classes are being arrested by thousands and shot by hundreds. I have no sympathy with these people—on the one hand all these sections of the population wanted war and must now reap what they have sown; on the other, it was their own idiotic incompetence that got them into this mess. The worst of it is that we are made responsible for all this misery—" we supported the Bolsheviks, we are their allies." This idea, which is gaining ground in Russia, is arousing an insane hatred against us. This is a matter of indifference for the time being, but we shall suffer for it industrially later on.

I had a letter from Helfferich to-day: he was sorry he had not met me in Berlin. He had heard my views of the Russian situation and was entirely in agreement with them. Good!

September 10, 1918.

According to all the information from Russia we are generally regarded there as allies of the Bolsheviks. Bolshevik and German is the same. That means great danger to our whole future. All our propaganda will not help us in this connection—deeds are what is wanted; people will not be consoled with empty phrases. I hope the authorities will still come to their senses in time.

September 11, 1918.

Nothing special here. Yesterday the first instalment of the Russian indemnity—gold and paper—reached Orska on our front line and was taken over by the Reichsbank. The Bolsheviks are clever and know how to touch us. Now, as they have begun to pay, the Foreign Office and the Reichstag are, of course, strongly for supporting the Bolsheviks, without regard to what the future may bring. The state of affairs in Petersburg and Moscow is indescribable. I shall now say and do no more—I shall forward all reports that come in; I have made my views known everywhere.

September 13, 1918.

The situation in Russia has undergone a change, in so far as, since the Russian victory at Kazan, the danger from the English is not so acute as before. We need not now take action—speaking from the purely military point of view—at once. But the feeling against us grows more and more intense. The whole Intelligentsia hates us, because we look on and do nothing. The Rumanians appear to be coquetting with a renewal of hostilities, as indeed Burian has openly stated. Well, it is only the Rumanians that will regret it.

At G.H.Q. Ludendorff has reorganized his Staff. The former Chief of the Operations Section, Lieutenant-Colonel Wetzel, has been given the command of an army, and Heye is shifted to G.H.Q. I have not yet discovered the reason for the change, Personally I am much attached to Wetzel, and think a great deal of him. But if a change was necessary the choice of Heye is a good one. He is uncommonly able, and marvellously industrious and conscientious.

Until six months ago there was a chance for original ideas on the Western Front, now it is merely a question of defence. And for that purpose Heye seems to me the best choice. By the same token my friend Hell has again done well for himself. He fell into disfavour at the time of the Peace negotiations—he got on too well with Kühlmann. . . . He has commanded the 28th Division with distinction in the West and has now been appointed to Heye's former post—the command of an Army Group.

September 15, 1918.

A few days ago, in Odessa, two men and a woman called upon the Austrian authorities, as well as our

General Staff officer there, and asked for permits to go to the Crimea for a few days to attend a wedding. In the course of the interview one of the men made himself known as the Crown Prince of Rumania. He had only four days' leave from his father, but he wanted to be present at a friend's wedding, and he must be allowed to go through incognito. He was told that it could not be managed, apart from the fact that in the present state of communications he could not get to the Crimea and back in five days. He then gave up the idea and stated that he wanted to go back home. On the following day he appeared again, and stated that as he was not allowed to go to the Crimea he had achieved the object of his journey on the spot—he and the lady accompanying him (Mademoiselle Zizi So-and-so) had got married. What a family!

For some time past I have been taking a lively interest in Rumania and the Rumanian situation. These people think that we are in such a bad way in the West that they can be impertinent. Well, they —and their ladies, more especially the Queen—will find they are wrong.

September 16, 1918.

To-day again I am feeling rather low after the Austrian Emperor's feeble Peace offer. . . . It was made at almost the worst moment for us. Of course that dangerous creature the Empress Zita is behind it—she hates us.[1]

I have only heard rumours about the origin of the affair. It seems that the last time the Emperor Karl was at G.H.Q. it was agreed that they should wait until the present fighting in the West was over:

[1] Austria-Hungary, in spite of the German Government's objections, issued a Peace offer to the Entente on September 14th. It was answered with offensive contempt.

then, as Austria stated that she neither could nor would go on fighting, Peace negotiations would be opened through a Neutral Power; the Emperor Karl, however, did not abide by this arrangement, but took the initiative himself. On our side everyone is furious. I don't think anything will come of it, at least nothing tangible. If the other side condescend to answer they will make such absurd conditions that there is no sense in negotiating. The only advantage that may come of the whole business is an increased inclination towards peace in England and France. Well, we must just wait and see.

I must particularly emphasize the fact that what I have just written is not definitely known—it is merely a rumour. Very likely it all happened quite otherwise.

September 18, 1918.

I have for the time being given up hope of doing anything here—all my thoughts and efforts now are devoted to sending as much help as I can to the Western Front. The heavy attacks in the West continue, and in fact they seem to be preparing new ones. The Entente seems to be making every effort to force a decision this autumn. In such circumstances all our interests here are of secondary importance—all our strength must be concentrated in the West.

September 27, 1918.

The military position is far from good. In Palestine the Turks are retiring, without even fighting—perhaps there are not any more Turks. Down in Macedonia the Bulgarian Front is completely broken: and we hear rumours of separate negotiations, etc. We are, of course, sending troops at once,

Austrians, and German Divisions (the latter of course from here), and I hope a complete collapse may still be avoided. It's a bad business, anyhow. There is heavy fighting in the West. And the state of affairs in Berlin is not encouraging. Hintze seems to me to be a nonentity. The Chancellor's position has grown very shaky. Perhaps Solf will succeed him. Erzberger prophesied to me in Berlin last July that there would be a crisis over the Chancellorship: but I think it disgusting that it should come now, when the position is not favourable as it was then. It may perhaps be urged in excuse of our parliamentary friends that they were not in any way prepared for the Bulgarian collapse, as no one had foreseen it. Party intrigues there seem to have led to a shocking break-up of the army.

September 28, 1918.

The outlook is bad everywhere and sometimes I feel quite distracted. In Bulgaria the Tsar seems to mean well—it is to be hoped he may succeed in turning out the present Premier. Our Divisions are on the way, but in the present state of the railways it all takes time.

In the West the position is again very serious. I rack my brains trying how I can release some troops. We are gradually getting pretty thinned out here.

September 30, 1918.

There is heavy fighting in the West. I cannot understand how Ludendorff could have so underestimated the enemy Reserves. We are racking our brains here, of course, trying to think how we can help. But we are very near the bottom of the cask. I can't scrape much more out of it—only a few Divisions.

October 1, 1918.

The position is, of course, serious, but I have definite hopes that we may either put matters straight again — *i.e.* that King Ferdinand stays where he is and turns out Comrades Malinoff, Lukoff, etc. — or else that we may be able to construct a new Front with Austria. The most important point is the West. If we hold on there—and of that I have no doubt—we can quite well deal with the situation in the East.

Radical changes at home. . . . Hintze and Hertling go—and probably a few others, to make way for some of our parliamentary friends. Chancellor, probably Fehrenbach; Foreign Office, Stresemann; Under-Secretary for Home Affairs, or Labour, perhaps Ebert the Social Democrat.

If they had been sensible and given the franchise two years ago things would not have gone so far.

It seemed like a piece of historical *esprit d'escalier* when the Head of the Eastern Department, Geheimrat Madelung, came here yesterday, to get me to explain the position in Russia again and the reasons for my view that we ought to take definite action here, etc. He looked very astonished when I told him he had unfortunately come six weeks too late.

October 3, 1918.

The position—military and political—is serious. Of that there is no doubt. We have let slip too many opportunities and the Parties of the Right were too much in a rut. The main blunder was Ludendorff's, in still believing last spring that he could win a victory and thus using up too many troops, that we so sorely need now. But that is the story of spilt milk, on which there is no more to be said. How the situation at home is to be dealt with it is not yet possible to see. A Government based on the Social Democrats and the Centre would not be strong enough, and Social Democracy and National Liberalism are difficult to get under one hat.

Bulgaria is finally dropping out: it is merely a question of conditions. Are the Entente troops to be allowed into the country or not? And we must take our measures accordingly. We have at present enough troops in Serbia to hold up any advance in that part. It may be assumed that Rumania will again join the Entente. But if Austria holds fast we can deal with that too. We could, for example, retire from the Ukraine and use all the troops now stationed there against Rumania. Besides, I see other means of holding on in the East.

The decision lies, as it always has done, in the West. For a time the situation there looked very black, but the last two days it has improved. Generally speaking all the attacks have been repulsed, and the enemy has suffered very heavy losses. Moreover, his Reserves are not inexhaustible. If we can manage to hold on in the West for the time being—and I am confident we can—the others will listen to reason. So, as I have said, the position is serious, but there is no need to throw up the sponge.

October 6, 1918.

The development of the political situation at home is discouraging and disquieting. The humiliating Peace offer to Herr Wilson will not raise the spirits of the army in the West—on the contrary only the Entente will get a new impetus from it. Here in the East everything is to be reorganized —civil governments, self-determination and all the rest of it. I am very much on the stretch. I hope we shall not have to give up the control of the large estates, as in that case the provisioning of the country would be endangered.

I am not yet quite clear that Solf is the right man to represent us in our foreign relations. It is to be hoped I may be wrong. He is, of course, quite definitely better than Hintze. I am also curious about Excellenz Erzberger.

October 7, 1918.

I am waiting to see what answer the Almighty Wilson will make to our request—I imagine he will impose such conditions that it will amount to a refusal. I am also waiting to see what will happen in the occupied areas. As civil governments are now to be established here, I am more than curious to know how the new Imperial Chancellor will set about it. I don't like the look of things.

October 8, 1918.

I don't in the least know why I was wanted in Berlin. I was neatly side-tracked on every possible issue, even on those affecting the Eastern provinces —why, I really do not know. Since Ludendorff and I parted company (mentally, I mean), he has had no more luck, and perhaps that is why I am disliked. The abominable thing about this general collapse is that it need not have happened. Our troops are just as good as they ever were. We could hold on in the West—we only need to appeal to the men—and I will hold the East, if I must, without troops. But they have all lost their nerve.

October 10, 1918.

There was a Crown Council, yesterday evening, to discuss Wilson's reply. I am very glad I was not there. I should not have liked to have shared the responsibility. I think they have all lost their heads, and that the position is not so tragic as all that. Of course everything either stands or falls by the situation on the Western Front. What the outlook there is like, and how many Reserves we still have, I don't, of course, know. I have no fears for the West, even if Austria breaks down. In that case we should simply curl up like a hedgehog.

October 21, 1918.

I have still not been able to get any information about our Note. I don't think this is because it contains anything startling, but because it has to be first considered in all responsible quarters— Ministers, Federal Council, Reichstag — so that they may make suggestions. I hope it won't turn out too flabby a document in the end.

The military position in the West is developing as Ludendorff foresaw.

There was a certain amount of shooting yesterday here in Vilna. The Poles insisted on holding a political demonstration and the police had to interfere. The police were perfectly right, but of course there will be another outcry.

October 23, 1918.

I shall probably make a trip to Reval and Narva one of these days. I should like to have seen those parts once. Besides our policy up there is all on the wrong lines, and I should like to see for myself what ought to be done. We listened to the Baltic barons and to no one else, and the Esthonians and the Letts won't play. I warned our people of this foolishness years ago.

October 25, 1918.

Nothing new here. It was only to be expected that the Note would be reported to be offensive and uncompromising. But I have yet to learn that

Wilson has rejected our proposals. I really think that he attaches some importance to a continuance of the negotiations.

October 25, 1918.

Herr Wilson's answer has just come in. It is not agreeable—it is just about what was expected. My advice to our people would be: " Never mind the Armistice, let us go on negotiating without it."

October 26, 1918.

The situation, and the state of public opinion, is not cheerful. I do not know what we can reply to the American Note. Wilson says: " I will now consult my allies and they will then inform you of their conditions." So we must wait until we hear them. If the terms are unacceptable—and I imagine they will be so—we must just try to hold out. It is a bad time—I sometimes feel quite desperate—it could all have been avoided. We could not have lost the war and we might have won it.

October 27, 1918.

There was a telephone message yesterday to the effect that Ludendorff had resigned and left the Front.[1] I am not quite clear why — apparently the dispute arose through a secret instruction of Hindenburg's to the Commander-in-Chief of the Western Armies, which in his absence was issued everywhere—even here—as an open telegram and thus became known. I suspect — though I can't

---

[1] After the publication of the Third Wilson Note, G.H.Q., believing themselves to be in agreement with the Government as to the interpretation of the Note, had issued a message to the troops, in which it was incidentally stated: " Wilson's reply demands military capitulation. This we, as soldiers, cannot accept."
This message was the ostensible cause of Ludendorff's dismissal which followed on October 26th.

prove it—that Nicolai and Bauer were behind all this. Whether it is simply stupidity, or whether they were trying to force a Military Dictatorship on the country at the last moment, I do not know. In any case they have done no service to Ludendorff or to the German people. Even though Ludendorff is undoubtedly responsible for the collapse—he should never have carried out his offensive—it will be difficult, indeed almost impossible, to replace him. Anyhow Lossberg—who, I expect, will succeed him—has no easy inheritance, he will have to bear the entire odium of a dishonourable Armistice and Peace.

I don't know whether Hindenburg will stay; I hope so; it would have a bad moral effect on the people and the army if he went.

October 29, 1918.

Well, Austria has capitulated unconditionally. I hope at least that we may thus get the German lands of Austria for Germany and so compensate ourselves for what we shall have to give up.

There is not a cheerful prospect anywhere. Gröner went to Berlin early and I suppose we shall hear of his appointment to-day. I am very glad that I have been passed over.

November 11, 1918.

I earnestly hope that, in general, it may be possible to prevent disorder. It must be made possible, otherwise the German Empire will go down. Nearly everyone realizes that. Consequently we must now all work to this one end. The Armistice conditions were such as might have been expected after a complete collapse. One of them was that we are to evacuate the Eastern Provinces. How soon this can be done I can't state even approximately. A Soldiers' Council has been formed here also, which has hitherto been functioning in a peaceable and sensible manner—and with which I am in touch. I had a long conversation with the head of it yesterday, and he gave me the distinct impression of a man trying to do his best in a quiet and orderly manner.

November 12, 1918.

The Revolution has been carried out here peaceably for the most part. Soldiers' Councils have been founded everywhere, whose main concern is, strangely enough, lest the senior officers should want to go home. How they have got this idea is a mystery to me — I have never dreamt of such a thing. On the contrary we must all do our utmost to get the Eastern army home in an orderly manner. We must, of course, begin with the evacuation. I am sorry for the people whose territory we are handing over to the Bolsheviks, but I cannot restrain our men — they want to get home. The forcible transfer of authority has, of course, made the troops rather unsteady. The majority think they are relieved of their military oath, and they want to go home. The Soldiers' Council here is trying its best to counteract this view—whether they will have any success in the long run remains to be seen. The Polish rising causes me further anxiety. The Poles have seized Warsaw and the railways, and are trying to invade our provinces. The general nervousness, of course, gives rise to the most incredible rumours everywhere about Polish attacks. I do what I can to keep my head.

November 13, 1918.

Of course the men all want to get home, and it is very hard to make people understand that to carry out the evacuation in an orderly manner will take many months. Besides there are negotiations pending with the Entente, who want to send troops here, to keep order after our departure. I should welcome this, as such a proceeding would have a calming effect on the situation in Germany.

November 14, 1918.

The worst of all is the dilatoriness of the Home Authorities. We cannot get decisions about a quantity of important questions; so we have to decide many matters for ourselves as best we can. For instance, I am at present negotiating with the Polish Government to try to get them to prevent, or at any rate keep within limits, the formation of Polish bands in the south of the occupied area.

November 18, 1918.

I heard yesterday that Ludendorff was abroad. In spite of all his blunders he is a devoted patriot, and it must be a dreadful thing for him to fall from such a height and eat the bread of strangers.

November 19, 1918.

I am again very much annoyed at the behaviour of G.H.Q. Our troops here in the East belong to the oldest classes: and we have got most of the Alsace-Lorrainers. Any serviceable troops were taken away from us. The older men, naturally, want to get home. Discipline and order don't, for the most part, exist, although the Soldiers' Councils are, to their credit be it said, doing their utmost. Now, of course, in spite of all this, G.H.Q. want the Eastern army to be brought home as slowly as possible. If they had so instructed us from the beginning we could have managed it easily, but first they let things slide and then try to pull them back: it can't be done. Well, we must struggle along, I suppose.

November 21, 1918.

The main idea to get into people's heads is that we can get peace and public order only through a properly elected Government. Independent Social Democrats and Spartacus groups will produce a state of affairs like that in Russia, where everyone—and most of all the workman—is discontented, and every sort of industry is at a standstill. If Spartacus groups appear, then we shall inevitably come to a civil war, as in Russia. Besides, the Entente will send troops to keep order. We should then have to suffer the last horror which, among all our disasters, has hitherto been spared us: " War on German soil." So vote for a supporter of Ebert or a bourgeois Democrat!

November 23, 1918.

I still believe that the reasonable elements in Germany will conquer—if only because we can't take all our orders from Berlin, and because otherwise the Entente will refuse to make any kind of Peace with us. So far as is possible under present conditions I view the future calmly and confidently.

November 25, 1918.

At this juncture the essential question is whether the reasonable adherents of the Ebert-Scheidemann movement can keep themselves in power. If the Spartacus group gets hold of the Government, then the consequences are obvious.

Undated.

The troops are giving us rather more trouble just now. They are all wild to get home, and, in spite of the advice of the Soldiers' Councils, which have remained calm and sensible throughout, there is no holding them. The worst of it is that, if the men here behind the lines go off, our advance troops, especially those in the Ukraine, are left in the air. We are doing our best to shift the more reasonable elements among the troops back to the rear, so that they can take over the defence of the railway line against our other friends, the Poles: but we are in for a few trying days.

November 28, 1918.

There is pretty sure to be an inquiry into my conduct if the Spartacus movement wins. However, from all I hear, the more moderate element is likely to come out on top. Besides I am quite indifferent to any inquiry, since I had nothing to do with the outbreak of the war, nor with its prolongation: and I had no hand in the collapse in the West.

November 29, 1918.

I imagine that yesterday's inquiry from the Foreign Office arose out of the newspaper notice regarding my internment. I had in the meantime telephoned personally to say that the whole thing was a stupid and mischievous lie. I can explain how the rumour got about. On the first day of the Revolution there was great excitement here, as the rumour had spread among the rank and file that Ober-Ost was going home. It so happened that our train, with the saloon car, had been drawn up at the station platform, and the explanation given to me was that it was to be washed and cleaned out. The men still believe that we intended to clear out and leave them in the lurch, if they had not been on the look-out to stop us. This rumour naturally spread. After we had disbanded the Alsace-Lorrainers a few days ago one of them probably gave a somewhat embroidered version of the story to a correspondent, and that accounts for the telegram from Zurich. I only wonder at the stupidity of the newspapers for printing the news, though a simple telephone inquiry would have convinced them of its falseness.

December 2, 1918.

The newspaper paragraph about my being handed over to the Entente leaves me quite cheerful. I should like to see any court of law in the world—even the most venomous tribunal in England or France—that could bring any charge against me.

The situation in Germany would be unpleasant if the Liebnecht crowd came into power in Germany (not merely in Berlin). The people in Berlin are wrong if they think the decision rests with them alone.

December 3, 1918.

The position is difficult, but I hope that the return home of the Eastern army may be smoothly carried out. The Soldiers' Councils are reasonable for the most part and do their best: but the mass of the troops can think of nothing but getting home. They will be surprised to find, when they do get home, that they were mostly better off here than they will now be back in Germany.

December 4, 1918.

I feel confident that the population of East Prussia will remain sensible, even if the Spartacus crowd get to the top in Berlin. The returning troops from the West should produce a calming and sobering effect.

December 14, 1918.

Our quarters will probably not be shifted to Königsberg. G.H.Q. wants to hand over Ober-Ost to the entire defence of the Eastern frontier, making all the other commands subordinate to us. In that case we could not, of course, remain in Königsberg, but should presumably have to move to Frankfurt-on-the-Oder. The War Office have not yet decided. I had raised some objection to this, as it is not a grateful job; but orders are orders.

December 16, 1918.

The War Office have not yet decided whether we are to move to Königsberg or Frankfurt-on-the-Oder. The new regime does not function as quickly as the old. I had a long letter yesterday from Brinckmann, from Spa. I am glad I am not staying there, and I am even more glad to have no hand in the negotiations.

The situation here in Kovno is pretty well in order, but the outlook on the Baltic is not at all pleasant. Our men refuse to fight and are putting up no resistance at all to the Bolsheviks. As a result the evacuation is becoming very disorderly. There is also further trouble threatening to the south. The Poles in Warsaw have gone completely crazy; they have broken off negotiations there and shown our Ambassador the door.

December 17, 1918.

So we are to move to Königsberg. What is to happen then—whether we are to demobilize after we have got the greater part of the Eastern army home, or whether we are then to take over the defence of the frontier—is still left open.

December 18, 1918.

On the Baltic and in the Ukraine the situation is becoming more and more serious, but the Poles, on the other hand, are quite quiet.

December 20, 1918.

Hindenburg has solemnly protested against the military resolutions of the Berlin Congress of the Representatives of Workmen's and Soldiers' Councils; whether this will produce any effect remains to be seen.

December 21, 1918.

Yesterday I had two long interviews with one Biedermann, deputy for Nordhausen, and, at the moment, an Under-Secretary of State. He alleged he was an old friend of Lenin, Joffe and Radek. According to a telegram published in yesterday's papers he has also received money from Joffe, to bring about a revolution in Berlin. He came here with a representative of the Foreign Office to do what he can to help the Russian prisoners of war on their way home. I quite think this is his desire, but I suspect that the main object of his journey is quite different—namely, to get more Russian money. There are still 22 millions of Joffe's deposited with Mendelssohn's, in Berlin. But they are sequestrated, and consequently the Spartacus people can't touch them.

December 22, 1918.

Opposite the 8th Army on the Baltic, the Bolsheviks, and opposite the Kiev Army Group, Petlura's Republicans are giving us trouble. Still, I hope we shall succeed in getting the Eastern army (or the horde that now passes as such) back home in reasonable order, but it is growing more and more difficult. These fellows are too stupid and won't listen to reason.

December 25, 1918.

We are conducting, at this moment, very interesting negotiations with the Poles. They have offered to hold Vilna against the Bolsheviks, if we let them send their troops through from Warsaw to Vilna. I am in favour of it, as our troops will fight no longer. I don't yet know what the Government's decision will be.

December 26, 1918.

On the political side, the Spartacus people in Berlin, and the Bolsheviks in Russia, are making the greatest efforts to get together. The Bolsheviks are afraid that, without German help, they cannot maintain themselves against the Entente, and against the classes that detest them at home, especially the peasants. Hence this outcry. At the moment I don't think the Spartacus movement dangerous. But if, in spite of everything, the people in Berlin get the upper hand the Entente will occupy Berlin —which is not a pleasant prospect; but it does offer some sort of guarantee.

December 27, 1918.

The political outlook is not at present very encouraging. I don't think the Berlin Government can maintain itself, if they continue so vacillating and timid. The weaker we are at home the harder will the Peace terms be. For the time being I don't think the Entente has the slightest inkling as to the outlook in Germany, or they would have soon put an end to this nonsense. The Entente still has the idea that we have a properly organized army, and that the disorders in Berlin were a put-up performance.

December 28, 1918.

The events in Berlin are, of course, very depressing, but we must calmly await developments. For the time being the reasonable elements still seem to have the upper hand. It was, of course, inevitable that the Liebnecht people would do all they could to prevent the meeting of the National Assembly.

December 29, 1918.

In Berlin the Majority Socialists seem to have pulled themselves together a little. They have organized for to-day a great demonstration against the Liebnecht people.

December 31, 1918.

Everything seems quiet in Berlin for the time being. We are rather in a mess here unfortunately. We shall not be able to hold Riga.

The troops will fight no more.

THOUGHTS ON 1914

THOUGHTS ON 1914

In approaching the problem of the Great War the first question that forces itself on everyone is: Who was responsible?

Who was responsible for the fact that all the peoples of the earth fought for years with modern weapons and killed millions of men, and that the old order of things in Europe so collapsed that its peoples have not yet, eight years later, been able to recover?

The clause in the shameful Treaty imposed on us at Versailles, burdening Germany with the entire responsibility, a statement which the conquered were compelled to confirm in writing, is of no assistance to an historical inquiry. The revelations made subsequent to the war by all the Cabinets concerned, the *Memoirs* of a large number of statesmen have, indeed, meanwhile proved that the statement that Germany alone was responsible for the war is not in accordance with the facts.

Neither the German people nor the German Emperor willed the war, and did not need it. Were there, then, any peoples in Europe who could have desired a war or considered such a war necessary?

This question must be answered in the affirmative: France and Russia. France's vanity could not get over the defeat of 1870-1871 and the loss of Alsace-Lorraine, and from the Peace of 1871 the people were educated in the idea of revenge. Read the books used in the French schools on this subject: not merely the history-books but the reading-books for the smallest children are full of stories of the chivalrous, generous people of France, invaded by Eastern barbarians and robbed of two of their fairest provinces. For decades France was on the look-out for allies to help her to achieve an aim that, since 1871, she had never for an instant forgotten: the reconquest of Alsace-Lorraine and the recovery of "la Gloire" that had been lost in the campaign of 1870. France wanted the war, and worked for it with the fanaticism of a people brought up in a fixed idea.

Russia needed the war. The general situation in that gigantic Empire, the corruption of the official classes, the want of an educated middle class, the unsatisfactory agrarian position—in a word, a state of affairs from which only a genius could perhaps have extricated Russia—was driving the country steadily towards revolution. Only a victorious war could revitalize Tsarism and, in conjunction with fundamental agrarian reforms, save the Empire. It must of course be a victorious war. For the consequences of the 1905 defeat by the despised Japanese had shown that the inevitable and immediate result of defeat was revolution.

The situation, therefore, in the two countries threw France and Russia into each other's arms. But the Dual Alliance was confronted by the Triple Alliance of the Central Powers — it needed reinforcement. The wooing of England began; and German responsibility may undoubtedly be said to date from this time.

Those in charge of German policy should never have allowed the two great antagonists, England and Russia, to come to an agreement in spite of the many points on which they were at issue. It could easily have been prevented, for England herself much preferred an agreement with Germany to the Russo-French Alliance. Time and time again during Bülow's Chancellorship, feelers were put out by England to see whether an agreement could not be reached on all questions that interested England and Germany, for Germany's increasing trade and the building of her fleet were causing anxiety in England. Where the responsibility lay for not concluding an understanding between the two countries it is, of course, hard to say. Whether Bülow shared the unhappy Herr von Holstein's conviction, that an agreement between England and Russia was, and would remain, out of the question, and influenced the Imperial Master in this sense, or whether he could not force himself to give a definite direction to German policy for the next decade, only the Imperial Chancellor, Prince Bülow himself, could say, presupposing he is still quite clear in his own mind why he cold-shouldered the English suggestions. But, quite apart from the English efforts to reach an agreement with Germany, Prince Bülow had two opportunities of securing Germany's political future for a considerable period. He saw both countries hard pressed, one over the Boer War and the other over the Japanese War. No use was made of either of these opportunities in the interests of Germany. We got no thanks from either of them; on the contrary, in certain circumstances at least, doubt was cast on Germany's honour and good will. Whereupon H.M. the German Emperor gave Colonel von Lauenstein, Chief of the Military Commission with the Russian Army, an autograph letter to the Tsar Nicholas, in which he assured the latter of his friendship, and added that, in case of need, he might have no hesitation in withdrawing his troops from the German frontier and sending them to the East. In that event Germany would maintain peace in all circumstances. The thanks we received for this document may be read in the Official History of the War by the Russian General Staff. The letter is mentioned with the comment that no reliance could, of course, be placed on such an assurance—viz. the word of the German Emperor.

What our Foreign Office had regarded as impossible did, in fact, befall: England and Russia entered into an alliance against us. Then came a period of feverish preparation; France in particular put forth all her strength and actually reintroduced three years' compulsory service. This could not be a permanent measure. It pointed inevitably to the fact that Germany's enemies reckoned with an imminent, definite date for the war against Germany. What did we—" who were guilty of the war "—do in reply to this? We did not even arrange to enrol all our available men in the army. The Army Bill, brought in after a considerable delay, was so modest that even members of the Left Party in the Reichstag proposed that its scope should be enlarged.

If we had had two more Army Corps in peace time probably not a single Russian soldier would have set foot on German soil. Of course I would not absolutely maintain that the Marne disaster could have been avoided, as bad leadership, rather than shortage of men, was responsible for that.

Equally it should have been our duty to use strong pressure on Austria - Hungary to improve the Imperial Army.

That Italy would not fulfil her undertakings in the event of a European War, and place herself at the side of her allies, was not generally believed in Germany, and not at all in Austria. If General Pollio had been living at the outbreak of the war, and if, too, our diplomacy had not made Italy's breakaway so easy for her, it would have perhaps been possible to hold her down.

The Entente, called into existence as it was for an attack on the Central Powers, was of course a structure that, in view of the different interests of the parties, was intended to hold together for only a short time. The only question was whether there should be a further year's delay, so that certain deficiencies in equipment—*i.e.* the heavy artillery for the Field Army, in which Germany certainly had the advantage—could be made good. Then, on one ground or another, a pretext would have been found for war. Germany would never have begun it. There has never been a greater lie in history than Germany's war guilt. Our guilt—I say it once again—consists only in our geographical position, the ability of our manufacturers and merchants, and the incompetence of our diplomatists.

When, on June 28th, 1914, the Austro-Hungarian Crown Prince and his wife fell under the bullets of the Serbian assassins only a few suspected the risk of war it would involve. Unfortunately, the story of the murder and its originators is not yet fully cleared up, and it is not possible to judge whether the forces at work behind the scenes sent the assassins out in the hope that, in the thunderous political atmosphere of Europe, the deed would produce the desired war. The forces behind the murder perhaps felt nervous lest the negotiations carried on in 1914 by Kühlmann, then a Counsellor of Embassy, whose result was to be agreed by the end of July and signed on 4th August, might lead to a German-English understanding, which would make their intended war of aggression on Germany for ever impossible. If that be so, diplomacy certainly did everything to further the scheme. The brusque style of the Austro-Hungarian ultimatum to the Serbian Government, whether or not they were guilty of the Serajevo crime, lit up the political situation as though with a lightning flash, and Europe slid into the World War.

How far this war would spread and how long it would last no living man suspected in those first August days of 1914. The late Field-Marshal Count Moltke had in fact constantly pointed out that the power and resources of modern States was so great that they would not be content to give in after a first defeat, and that a modern war might consequently last seven, nay even thirty, years; but nobody believed the old soldier: they preferred to believe the modern bankers and industrialists, all of whom said that in these days a war could not last longer than from three to four months. Lord Kitchener expressed the view that the war would last three weeks, or three years. By that he meant that either the German Army would overrun France in a few weeks and force her to make peace, or the French would succeed in holding up the first onrush of the Germans, and then the war would last a long while. As Japan joined in, and as England and France saw themselves forced to bring in their coloured auxiliary troops, the war became something more than a European war, and the longer it lasted the more nations were forced to join in.

Whether it was wise on the part of the Entente to engage in military enterprises in the Colonies as well, and, for example, to teach the black man to shoot the white man, and maltreat and imprison his wife and child, was at the time very seriously doubted in England itself. The prestige of the white races received an inevitable blow; and England and France will, at no very distant date, have to suffer the consequences. The fighting in China, the attempts at independence and the insurrectionary movement of the yellow peoples of Asia are before our eyes to-day. It will be only a few years before the black peoples will follow with a demand for equal rights and the abolition of white supremacy.

If the population figure of the Central Powers is compared with the enormous numbers on the side of the Entente, the superiority of the latter is seen to be overwhelming. At the beginning of the war a rough estimate would be 130,000,000 on the one side, and 730,000,000 on the other. At the close of the war twenty-five States, with a round 1,350,000,000 inhabitants, were at war with the Central Powers. The comparison of the number of troops under arms at the beginning of the war was of course rather more favourable to the Central Powers. Against the 3,000,000 soldiers of Germany and Austria-Hungary, France, Russia, Belgium, Serbia and England could put, roughly, 5,500,000 into the field. I have, however, intentionally laid stress on the gigantic numerical superiority of the populations, to show what a reservoir of man-power the enemies possessed for the enlargement of their armies and the creation of new ones. The Central Powers had the advantage that, their troops being confined in a narrower space, they could be more quickly concentrated against a given point, and could strike before the Entente was in a position to make use of their numerical superiority.

The plan of campaign of the Central Powers had, therefore, to aim at securing a decisive success by a concentration of forces; any loss of time in the process was damaging and must be avoided. The plan of our great Chief of the General Staff, Count von Schlieffen, made proper provision for this fact. His proposal was to divert the bulk of the German Army against France, and drive through Belgium with a powerful, deeply echeloned, right wing. We should have to allow for the fact that this would add Belgium to the number of our enemies, but the

French eastern frontier was so strongly protected by fortresses that the process of forcing it would, in all probability, have taken too long.

The left wing of the German Army was to be based on Metz, and in the course of the German advance this fortress was to form for us the pivot of the turning movement. On the extreme left wing only weak forces were to be posted to protect Alsace against a French attack, and in case of necessity Southern Alsace was to be evacuated. The thrust of the powerful German right wing must cause any French troops pushed forward into Baden or Alsace to be hastily recalled to France. The considerations put forward by Count Schlieffen in support of his scheme are elaborated in the Imperial Archives (vol. i., p. 55), and their effect is entirely convincing. Why his successor, Colonel General von Moltke, departed, at first slightly, and then to an increasing extent, from the Schlieffen plan is incomprehensible. The Imperial Archives offer no explanation, and such of Count Schlieffen's colleagues as are still alive throw no real light on the point. It is, of course, true that Schlieffen's 1905 Memorandum deals only with war against France and England. Russia was at that time weakened by the Japanese War and the Revolution, and was not worth consideration as a serious army. But when Russia regained her military strength after the war, and when, by the help of French loans, she constructed her strategic railways and improved the armament and equipment of her forces, the General Staff was, naturally enough, faced with the question: " Is the Schlieffen plan still correct, as we now have to deal not only with France and England, but with the Russian millions ? " Some supported the proposal that we should remain on the defensive in the West and send the bulk of the German Army against Russia, and thus free and secure our rear. I have never been able to understand this notion. Of course, if we moved strong forces to the East, it would have been quite a simple matter to attack in a southerly direction from East Prussia, join hands with an Austrian offensive moving up from the south, and separate Poland from Russia. But, in the issue of the war, this would have helped us little, or not at all, for when the time came for attack, at the conclusion of our advance, we should only have come into contact with the garrison troops of the Western Governments of Russia. The bulk of the Russian Army could not possibly have been in position by that time. We should have been beating the air—in the first few weeks of the war the massing of the German Army in the East could have served no useful purpose. On the other hand, when the Russian deployment was over, we should have had to reckon with the advance of the Russian steam-roller. These considerations point inevitably to the Schlieffen plan. Only by carrying out that plan, as exactly and quickly as possible, had the German Army any chance of winning a victory. If we had stripped our left wing and supported our right wing with every man we could spare, broken through the enemy Front by the capture of Liège, lengthened our right wing in the course of our advance until it reached the sea, interrupted—or, at any rate, delayed—the junction between the English and the French armies, and then continued the advance of our right wing to the west of Paris, we might have looked for a speedy and decisive victory against the French Army, if we could have forced the French to a decisive battle.

END OF FIRST VOLUME

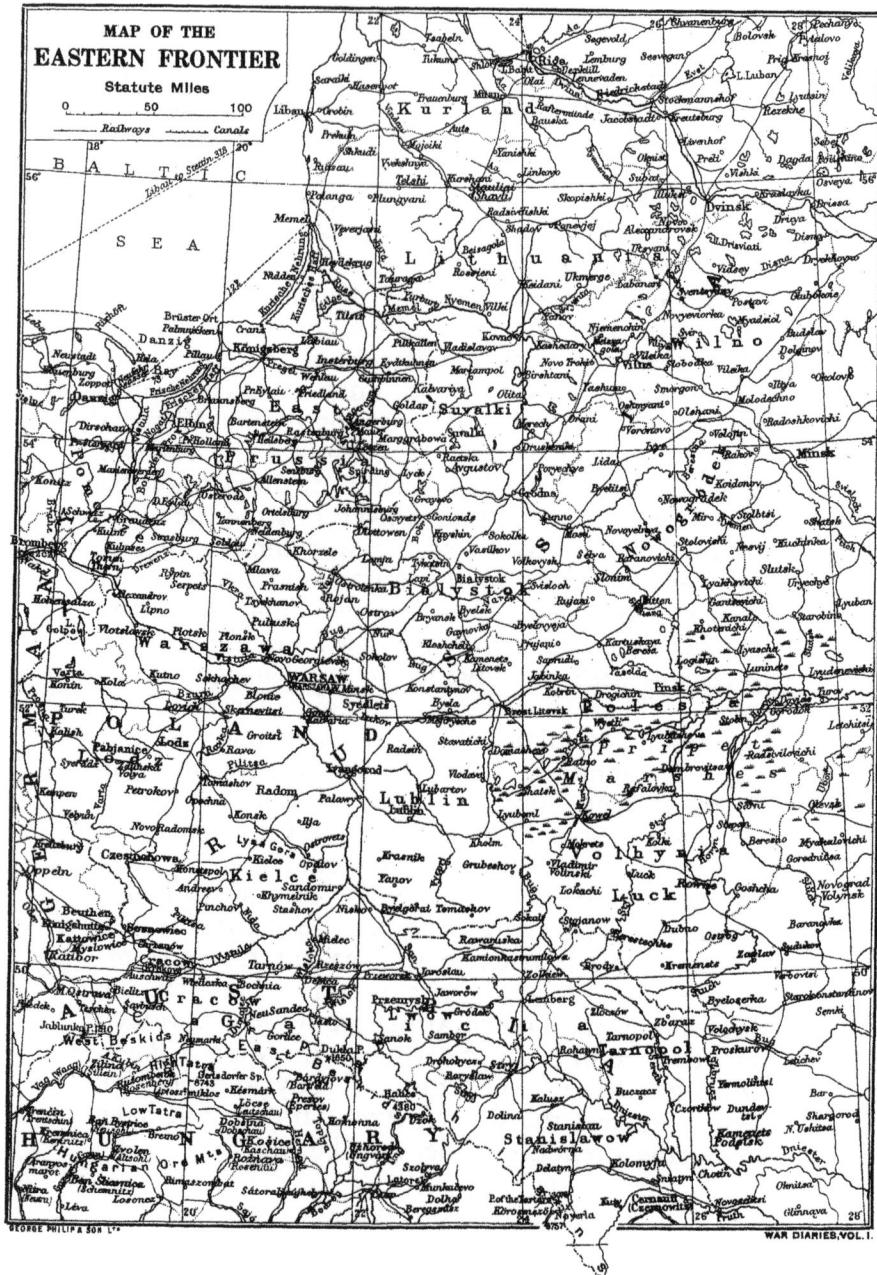

INDEX TO VOLUME I

ABDUL HAMID II., Ottoman Sultan, 200
Alexeieff, Chief of Staff to Russian G.H.Q., 182, 217

BATOCKI, von, President of the War Food Ministry, 119, 120
Bauer, Colonel, Chief of Section on the Staff of the C.G.S., 245
Below, Otto von, G.O.C. 8th Army; later G.O.C. 1st Army, 62, 68
Bernstorff, Count, German Ambassador in Washington, 164, 223
Beseler von, Governor-General of Warsaw, 76
Bethmann-Hollweg, Theobald von, Chancellor, President of the Prussian Council of State and Foreign Minister, 116, 130, 132, 145, 153, 166, 168, 201
Biedermann, member of Reichstag for Nordhausen, 252
Bockelberg, von, Major, G.S.O., Ib, Eastern Command; later on the Staff of the C.G.S., 60, 62, 75, 136, 146
Böhm-Ermolli, General von, G.O.C. 2nd Austrian Army, 49, 138, 149, 152, 154
Bothmer, Count, G.O.C. German Southern Army, 154
Brandenstein, von, Colonel, 200
Bratianu, S.S.C., Prime Minister of Rumania, 1909-1919, 126, 137
Braun, Magnus, Freiherr von, Regierungspräsident, 183
Brinckmann, Major, G.S.O., Ia, Eastern Command, 146, 209, 218, 251
Brussiloff, General, G.O.C. Russian S.W. Front; after the Revolution Commander-in-Chief, 182, 186
Buff, Dr, Acting Burgomaster of Bremen, 178
Bülow, Bernhard, Prince von, Imperial Chancellor, 1900-1909, 259

Burian, Stephan, Baron, Austrian Foreign Minister, 1915-1916, 145, 236

CADORNA, General, Chief of Staff of the Italian Army, 119
Cambon, French Ambassador in London, 94
Chelius, von, General à la Suite, attached to the Governor-General of Belgium, 121
Clemenceau, 223
Conrad von Hötzendorff, Franz, Count, Field-Marshal, Austrian Chief of Staff, 1906-1911 and 1912-1917, 21, 22, 160
Constantine I., King of the Hellenes, 1913-1923, married to Sophie, Princess of Prussia, sister of the Emperor William II., 90, 91, 99
Cramon, von, General, German Military Plenipotentiary for Austria, 159
Czernin, Count Ottokar, Austrian Foreign Minister, 1906-1918, Head of Austrian Delegation at Brest-Litovsk, 207

DELBRÜCK, Clemens von, Secretary of State, head of Civil Cabinet, Oct.-Nov., 1918, 97, 103
Dernburg, Bernhard, Secretary of State, 89
Dowbor-Musnicki, G.O.C. (proposed) the I. Polish Corps, 213, 218, 220
Dragomiroff, G.O.C. 5th Russian Army, 181
Dryander, Court Chaplain, 195
Dürr. Adj.-General to the Grand Duke of Baden, 81

EBEN, von, G.O.C. I. A. C., 149, 154
Ebert, Fritz, member of Reichstag, and subsequently President of the Reich, 240, 248

## 268	INDEX

Eichhorn, von, Field-Marshal, murdered at Kiev, 30th July 1918, 75, 83, 108, 153, 212, 215, 217, 227
Eisenhart-Rothe, von, General, Q.M.G. Eastern Front; subsequently Chief of Commissariat Dept. to the Army in the Field, 91, 108, 133, 153
Eitel Friedrich, Prince of Prussia, 189
Ernst August, Duke of Brunswick, 148
Erzberger, Matthias, member of Reichstag; Secretary of State, 1918; later Finance Minister, and Chairman of the Armistice Commission at Versailles, 84, 169, 172, 175, 177, 178, 181, 183, 184, 194, 197, 209, 210, 211, 221, 233, 239, 242
Escherich, Forestry Officer, 174

FALKENHAUSEN, Freiherr von, Under-Secretary of State, 203, 218
Falkenhayn, von, Col.-General, C.G.S. Army in the Field, 22, 49, 60, 61, 70, 71, 72, 81, 87, 88, 94, 97, 101, 102, 105-108, 114, 119, 121, 130-138, 142, 143, 146, 159, 163, 171, 201, 210
Fehrenbach, member of Reichstag, 240
Ferdinand, King of Bulgaria, 239, 240
Ferdinand, King of Rumania, 63, 136, 140
Fleischmann, von, Rittmeister, Austrian Liaison Officer to General Staff on Eastern Front, 117
François, von, Lt.-General, G.O.C. VII. A.C., 19, 40
Franz Ferdinand, Crown Prince of Austria, 261
Friedrich, Archduke, C.-in-C. Austro-Hungarian Army, 96, 150, 154
Fürstenberg, Maximilian Egon, member of the Prussian, and President of the Austrian, House of Peers, 189

GALLWITZ, von, General, G.O.C. 12th Army; later G.O.C. the Gallwitz Army Group, 52, 61, 64-70, 72, 73, 77, 99

George, Prince of Bavaria, 174, 226
Gontard, Lt.-General, 149
Gossler, von, General, head of the Joint Administration for Lithuania and the Baltic Lands, 226
Grey, Sir Edward, 59
Gronau, von, G.O.C. XXXXI. Reserve Corps, 139
Gröner, General, Director-General of Field Railways; C.G.S. to Kiev Army Group; subsequently first Q.M.G., 102, 108, 111, 120, 140, 212, 245
Grünert, General, Q.M.G. 8th Army, 18

HARBOU, von, General, Military Governor of Lithuania, 1918, 225
Helfferich, Dr Karl, Secretary of State for the Interior, 130, 132, 155, 168, 199, 235
Hell, Colonel, Chief of Staff to the XX. A.C., 108, 167, 236
Henry, Prince of Prussia, Admiral, 89, 167
Hertling, Imperial Chancellor, 114, 183, 202, 240
Hey, Major, Intelligence Officer, 226
Heye, Colonel, Chief of Staff to the Landwehr Corps; subsequently Chief of Staff to the Army Group in the West; later on the Great General Staff, 236
Hindenburg, von, Field-Marshal, 17, 20, 40, 42, 45, 48, 49, 61, 63, 65, 71, 77, 81, 82, 99, 101, 109, 133, 135, 138, 142, 144, 146, 148, 156, 168, 169, 202, 213, 230, 245, 252
Hindenburg, von, Major, son of the Field-Marshal, 100
Hintze, von, Admiral, Secretary of State for Foreign Affairs, 29, 223, 231, 233, 239, 240, 242
Hohenlohe-Langenburg, Prince Ernst zu, head of the Red Cross, and then German Ambassador in Constantinople, 56, 63
Holstein, von, counsellor in Foreign Office, 259

ISENBURG, Alfred, Prinz zu I. und Budingen, Lt.-Colonel, 169
Isvolski, A.P., Russian Foreign Minister, 1906-1910; then Ambassador in Paris, 94

INDEX 269

JOFFE, Commissary of the People, Chairman of the Russian Armistice Delegation in Berlin, 229, 252
Joffre, French C.-in-C., 69
Johann Albrecht, Duke of Mecklenburg, 195

KAMENEFF (Rosenfeld), member of the Soviet Delegation of Brest-Litovsk, 25
Kapp, Dr, Director of Agriculture for E. Prussia, 53, 54, 100, 120, 124, 128, 131, 132, 136, 166
Karl, Archduke, Emperor of Austria, 1916-1918, 140, 146, 148, 156, 162, 189, 193, 197, 198, 237
Karol, Crown Prince of Rumania, 237
Keller, Lt.-Colonel, on the Staff of Eastern Front; subsequently Chief of Staff to Linsingen's Army Group, 108, 146, 212
Kerenski, President of Russian Provisional Government, 181, 197
Kitchener, Viscount, 262
Kluck, G.O.C. 1st Army, 56
Knobelsdorff, General, Chief of Staff to the Crown Prince, 101, 108
Korniloff, Russian General, 197
Kövess, von, Austrian Field-Marshal, 193
Krasnoff, Peter, General, Hetman of the Don Cossacks, 217
Kress, von, Colonel, 213
Kühlmann, Dr Richard von, Secretary for Foreign Affairs, 24, 25, 207, 221, 223, 225, 231, 236, 261
Kundt, Hans, Colonel, 34

LAMBRINO, Zizi, wife of Prince Karol of Rumania, 237
Lauenstein, von, General, G.O.C. XXXIX. Reserve Corps, 95, 259
Ledebour, member of Reichstag, 200
Lenin, Ulianoff, President of the Council of People's Commissaries, 252
Lentze, von, Prussian Minister of Finance, 186

Leopold, Prince of Bavaria, Field-Marshal, C.-in-C. on Eastern Front, 71, 137, 146, 148, 150, 154, 155, 174, 182, 189-192, 197-198, 202, 233
Lewaldt, Under-Secretary in Ministry of Interior, 132
Lichnowsky, Prince, German Ambassador in London, 212
Liebknecht, Karl, member of the Reichstag, 250, 254
Lindenau, von, Chief of Section on the General Staff, 11
Lindequist, Secretary of State, 211
Linsingen, G.O.C. Army Group, 64, 105, 123, 125, 134, 137, 138, 147, 149
Litzmann, General, G.O.C. XXXX. Reserve Corps, 70, 75, 149
Lloyd George, 223
Lossberg, Chief of Staff to Duke Albrecht of Wurtemberg's Army Group, 245
Ludendorff, Erich, 17, 18, 19, 20, 24, 26, 27, 40, 41, 46, 47, 49, 60-63, 74-76, 82, 87, 90, 94, 101, 105, 108, 121, 131, 135, 136, 138, 142-148, 151, 154, 156, 158-164, 166-177, 185, 186, 190, 191, 194-196, 198, 202, 208, 213, 220, 222, 225, 230, 231, 233, 239, 242, 244, 245, 247
Ludwig III., King of Bavaria, 154, 183, 192
Lukoff, Chief of Staff of the Bulgarian Army, 240
Lyncker, Freiherr von, Chief of the Military Cabinet, 81, 121, 133, 146, 149, 155, 197, 226

MACKENSEN, Field-Marshal, G.O.C. XVII. A.C.; later G.O.C. 9th and 11th Armies, 66-72, 76, 80, 81, 147, 148, 160, 192, 194
Madelung, Secretary in the Eastern Dept. of the Foreign Office, 240
Malinoff, Bulgarian Prime Minister, 240
Maltzahn, von, Provincial Councillor, 231
Maltzahn, von, counsellor in the Foreign Office, 185
Mendelssohn, banking-house of, 252
Mengelbier, Lt.-Colonel, Chief of Staff of XXXX. A.C., 108

Metternich, Count Paul von Wolff, M., Ambassador in Constantinople, 52
Michaelis, Dr, Imperial Chancellor, 199
Michalkiewicz, Polish Commissioner in Vilna, 222
Mirbach, Count, German Ambassador to Russia, murdered in Moscow, 1918, 224
Mirko, Crown Prince of Montenegro, 105
Moltke, Count Helmuth von, M., Colonel-General C.G.S., 7, 264
Morgen von, G.O.C. I. Reserve Corps, 51, 94
Mühlmann, von, General, 40
Müller, von, Admiral, Chief of Naval Cabinet, 83
Mumm von Schwartzenstein, Freiherr, of the Diplomatic Service, 52, 209

Napoleon I., Emperor of the French, 53
Nicolai Nicolaievich, Grand Duke, C.-in-C. Russian Army, 49, 58, 80, 91, 175
Nicolai, Lt.-Colonel, head of Section on the Great General Staff, 173, 177, 198, 245
Nicolaus (Nikita), King of Montenegro, 1894-1917, 97, 100, 105
Nicholas II., Emperor of Russia, 1894-1917, 58, 70, 80, 84, 145, 173, 259

Oskar, Prince of Prussia, 108

Pétain, Marshal of France, 180
Peter I. of Serbia, etc., 96, 97
Petlura, Republican leader in the Ukraine, 252
Pflanzer-Baltin, Austrian General, 138
Plessen, von, Colonel-General, Adj.-General to the Kaiser and Commandant of Imperial Headquarters, 121, 155
Poincaré, 58
Pollio, Chief of Italian General Staff before the war, 260
Prittwitz und Gaffron, von, G.O.C. 8th Army at commencement of war, 7, 16, 17, 37, 39, 40

Radek (Sobelsohn), member of the Third International, and of the Peace Delegation of Brest-Litovsk, 252
Radowitz, von, Under-Secretary of State in the Imperial Chancery, 233
Reischach, Hugo, Freiherr von, Marshal of the Court, 88
Rennenkampf, G.O.C. Russian Army of the Niemen, 18, 42
Richthofen, member of Reichstag, 172, 174, 177, 233
Richthofen, Freiherr von, Rittmeister, airman, 214
Riemann, G.O.C. VI. A.C., 174
Rohrbach, Dr, author, 217
Rosenberg, Representative of the German Foreign Office at Brest-Litovsk, 204

Samsonoff, G.O.C. Russian Army of the Niemen, 18, 19
Scheidemann, Philipp, Secretary of State; People's Commissioner; Chancellor of the Empire, 224, 248
Schlieffen, Count, Field-Marshal, Chief of Great General Staff, 12, 263, 264, 265
Scholtz, von, G.O.C. XX. A.C., 68
Schubert, von, G.O.C. 8th Army, 42
Schubert, Major, Military Attaché in Moscow, 229
Seekt, von, Colonel, Chief of Staff to the 11th Army; later Commander of the Archduke Karl's Army Group, 108, 138, 140, 147, 148, 151, 156, 167, 193
Seydewitz, Saxon Minister, 222
Skoropadski, Hetman of the Ukraine, 215, 218
Solf, Secretary for the Colonies; Secretary of State for Foreign Affairs, 1918, 52, 130, 132, 231, 242
Stein, von, General, War Minister, 180
Stresemann, Dr Gustav, 223, 240
Stumm, W., von, Under-Secretary in the Foreign Office, 185
Suchomlinoff, General, Russian Minister, 91

INDEX

TAPPEN, General, head of the Operating Section on the General Staff, 63, 108, 118

Tirpitz, von, Grand-Admiral, 23, 73, 107, 110, 112-115, 136, 155, 166

Treutler, Diplomatic Service, 83

Trotha, von, Captain, Senior Adjutant on Eastern Front, 174

Trotzky (Braunstein) Leo, President of the Russian Peace Delegation at Brest-Litovsk, People's Commissary for Foreign Affairs, C.-in-C. Bolshevik Army, 24, 25, 206, 207

VALENTINI, head of Civil Cabinet, 83

Venizelos, Greek Prime Minister, 90, 93, 95

WAHNSCHAFFE, Under-Secretary of State in the Imperial Chancery, 89

Waldersee, Count, Chief of Staff 8th Army; later on the Ober-Ost Administration, 17, 37, 38, 40, 203, 212, 226, 227

Wangenheim, Freiherr von, Ambassador in Constantinople, 63

Wetzel, Lt.-Colonel, head of Section on the Great General Staff, 236

Wilhelm II., German Emperor, and King of Prussia, 21, 24, 50, 51, 58, 61, 65, 67, 69, 71, 75-77, 83, 92, 97, 101, 107, 110, 112, 114, 120, 121, 130, 132, 135-138, 141-146, 149, 168, 177, 189, 196, 200, 202, 212, 216, 223, 257

Wilhelm, Crown Prince of Prussia, 81, 101, 108

Wilson, Woodrow, President of the United States of America, 168, 169, 178, 242, 244

Witting, President of Council of Bank of Germany, 167, 181, 183, 212, 223

Woyrsch, von, G.O.C. Woyrsch Army Group, 42, 45, 64, 67, 68, 71, 124, 125, 132, 153, 153

Wrisberg, von, Colonel, Principal Secretary in the War Office, 198

Wussow, von, Major, General, G.O.C. 14th Infantry Brigade, 40

YORK VON WARTENBURG, Count, head of Dept. in the Great General Staff, 11

ZAIMIS, Greek Prime Minister, 95

Zimmermann, Secretary of State for Foreign Affairs, 93, 110, 168, 172, 183

Zita, Empress of Austria, 84, 197, 237

www.ingramcontent.com/pod-product-compliance
Ingram Content Group UK Ltd.
Pitfield, Milton Keynes, MK11 3LW, UK
UKHW021325180426
11947UKWH00017B/1435